CICERO

CLASSICAL LIFE AND LETTERS

General Editor: HUGH LLOYD-JONES

Regius Professor of Greek in the University of Oxford

CICERO

D. R. Shackleton Bailey

CHARLES SCRIBNER'S SONS
NEW YORK

A-9.71 (I)

Printed in Great Britain
Library of Congress Catalog Card Number 78–176156

SBN 684–12683–4

123160

AMBABVS

Acknowledgments

I have to thank the Horace H. Rackham School of Graduate Studies in the University of Michigan for financial help in connexion with this book. Acknowledgments are also due to the Syndics of the Cambridge University Press for their permission to make use of the translation published in my edition of Cicero's Letters to Atticus (1965–1971), to Mr Patrick Leason for drawing the map of Italy on page 6 and to the Mansell Collection for permission to reproduce the bust of Cicero as frontispiece.

D.R.S.B.

Ann Arbor
June 1971

Contents

Introduction

AT two crises in the drama of the dying Roman Republic the leading part fell to Cicero. But the immortality for which he always hungered is due to what he wrote rather than to what he did, and largely to the sheer bulk and variety of his writings. He was not one of literature's creative giants. His poetry (not much survives, but enough) was mediocre; and of his prose perhaps the little tract 'On Old Age' stands alone as first and foremost an artistic success. Not that artistic merits are lacking in his output as a whole; but they subserve some practical purpose, and are not of so high an order as to transcend that purpose.

In his own times his speeches were admired (though not by every-body) as supreme examples of the art of eloquence. Moderns, for whom eloquence is hardly an art any longer, may be poor judges, but they do and must defy the judgment of Quintilian. Between Cicero and Demosthenes the gulf is too apparent. Equal in technique, superior in variety, breadth of outlook, humour, Cicero lacks voltage. His rhetoric (the 'Philippics' may count as a partial exception) is wanting in the disciplined energy that comes from deep commitment to a clearly apprehended cause. It aims at the emotions through the ear rather than the mind. None the less, the fifty-eight surviving speeches (some incomplete) are a valuable legacy. Most, whether forensic, political, or both, interest by content, with their wide range of Roman types and situations. Also, of course, they present aspects of the speaker, or rather the writer. For a Ciceronian speech, as we have it, was always edited, sometimes years after delivery; a few were never delivered at all. So there is a mingling, in varying proportions, of the *pièce d'occasion* for Senate or jury and the pamphlet aimed at the contemporary public and posterity.

In middle age Cicero began to produce other kinds of literary prose —treatises on rhetoric, politics, and finally philosophy. These mostly took the form of imaginary conversations, sometimes with the characters taken from history (as Cato the Censor, Scipio Africanus the Younger, and Laelius in the essay on old age), sometimes between the author and his brother or friends. In contrast to Plato's earlier dialogues the dramatic scaffolding is very slight, but even so it is a serviceable device. The reader gets a ration of entertainment with his edification. The writer stands excused for 'conversational' vagueness and inconsequence, and can indulge in self-applause by making one speaker congratulate another.

In his book 'On the Orator,' the most important of his works on rhetoric, Cicero wrote as a practical expert who was also a man of liberal culture with a soul above text-books. The result is at best a qualified success. High-flown disquisition fails to amalgamate with chunks of technical detail into an aesthetically satisfying whole. The primary thesis, that the orator's art ideally embraces the whole range of knowledge, is effectively refuted in the name of common sense and practical experience by one of the characters, who is arbitrarily deprived of the honours of the argument. Even in his own subject Cicero tends to prefer second-hand doctrine to the results of self-examination. Take his treatment of prose rhythm. He stresses its importance and expounds the rules (in another treatise, 'The Orator'), apparently on the basis of Greek manuals. His own practice has been brought to light by modern research. It must have been at least partly unconscious.

In the field of political theory two works, 'On the Republic' and 'The Laws,' have come down, both incomplete. Some large claims have been made for the former, as a theoretical anticipation of the Principate which Caesar Augustus was to establish in the next generation on the ruins of the republican constitution; but they hold no water. Cicero was no political genius, either abstract or pragmatic. Still less does he (or any other Roman, for that matter) rank as an original thinker on ethics or metaphysics. Early and late in life he was fascinated by Greek philosophy, as were other contemporary Romans; it could be both an absorbing intellectual pursuit and the nearest available thing to a religion. Cut off from his former activities under Caesar's Dictatorship, Cicero hit upon the idea of presenting the principal points in the current systems in his elegant, readable Latin. Hence a rapid flow of tracts, some predominantly technical, others (like the 'Tusculan Disputations' and the treatise 'On Duties') more in the way of homily and moral edification. But Cicero was not a practical moralist, whose life lay behind his maxims. His ideas and experience were never in easy communication; and in the speculative sphere his ideas were almost entirely borrowed. Through these hasty compositions Greek thought, especially of the two and a half centuries after Aristotle, filtered down to mould the minds of Christian Fathers and eighteenth-century

philosophers—a stupendous triumph of popularization, which has had
its day.

There remain the Letters. Over nine hundred survive (many more
seem to have been extant in antiquity), of which about one tenth were
not written by Cicero. Of those that were, about half are addressed to
his close friend and family connexion, Pomponius Atticus. Twenty-
seven, some very long, are to his brother, Quintus Cicero. The rest are
to various friends or acquaintances, some highly formal, others the
opposite; but to none of these people could he write as intimately as to
Atticus and Quintus. All were published after Cicero's death in a
number of separate collections. The times and circumstances of
publication are uncertain, but it is generally thought that, except for the
Atticus correspondence (which may not have appeared until half-way
through the first century A.D.) Cicero's freedman, secretary, and biographer Tiro, who survived him some forty years, was responsible.
There is very little sign of editing. Once or twice a passage seems to
have been deliberately omitted, but of tamperings or interpolations no
trace.

Cicero's prestige has soared at different periods for different
reasons. In the time of Quintilian and the younger Pliny he was
idolized as the master-orator. In the Middle Ages the more liberal clergy
admired him as a moral instructor, and his *rhetorica* were the basis of
one of the seven recognized 'Arts'. Renaissance humanists saw in the
philosophica an engine of liberation from the trammels of scholasticism;
but to many of them, after Petrarch's rediscovery of some of the speeches
in 1333, Cicero's prime importance was stylistic. At a time when the
writing of classical Latin ranked high among intellectual priorities,
Cicero became the standard; inevitably, because no other classical author
offered such abundance of material in various *genres*, and because the
absence of obtrusive individuality in his style, along with its positive
virtues, commended it to imitators. In the fifteenth and early sixteenth
centuries 'Ciceronianism' became an intellectual disease. In the
eighteenth his reputation benefited from the prevailing taste for noble
commonplace, and (in its latter half) from his status as a republican
martyr.

As rhetorician, stylist, moralist, and freedom-fighter Cicero's appeal
has dwindled, even to classical specialists. His personality remains of
unique interest, because it is accessible. No other Greek or Roman has
projected himself into posterity like Cicero in his extant correspondence. Socrates and Horace have left sharper images; but how much of

our Socrates is Plato's artifact, and how much of our Horace is Horace's? No similar suspicion can arise with Cicero, because the letters that reveal him were never meant to become public property— his state of mind if anyone had told him that this would one day happen hardly bears imagination. Nothing comparable has survived out of the classical world: not the 'literary' letters of Plato, Seneca, and Pliny; not Fronto's correspondence with imperial pupils or patrons, the prosings of a hypochondriac pedagogue in a dull epoch; not the flotsam of papyrus finds. In Cicero's letters we see a Roman Consular, on any reasonable estimate one of the most remarkable men of his eventful time, without his toga.

Admittedly it is not a complete picture. There was a great deal in Cicero's life which his letters do *not* reveal. Nearly all of them belong to its last twenty years—years mainly of disappointment and frustration; the success-story of his youth and early middle age can only be reconstructed in outline. Nor was Cicero always frank even with Atticus, or with himself. Moreover, the discursive letter, in the manner (or rather contrasting manners) of Cowper or Byron, flowing or jumping from topic to topic, particular or general according to mood or fancy, was not an ancient phenomenon. Thus the light thrown on his personal history, as on that of his times, is spasmodic; and it comes at an angle— the often-quoted remark in Cornelius Nepos' life of Atticus that nobody who reads Cicero's letters to his subject will much need a consecutive history of the period is a foolish exaggeration. Their evidence is to be evaluated, as well as exploited, in constant mindfulness of its limitations.

Secondary authorities are comparatively meagre and unreliable. The most important are Plutarch's largely anecdotal 'Life' in the second century A.D. and Cassius Dio's Roman History (with a strong anti-Ciceronian bias) in the third. Plutarch twice refers to Tiro's work, but as a rule it is impossible to trace particular statements in either to their sources. Even in Cicero's case, the materials do not allow of a full and balanced biography, but there is enough to show the manner of man he was. The design of this book is to let him do that, as far as possible, for himself.

CHAPTER ONE

Arpinum

'Well, I shall go to Arpinum, "my native hills, the cradle of my being".'[1]
Cicero to Atticus

THE town still called Arpino is about seventy miles as the crow flies to
the east of Rome on a hill top in central Italy. Two thousand years ago
it was an ancient place, once a stronghold of those fighting Volscians
whose clashes with the embryonic Roman war machine claim many of
the less historical pages of Livy's History. But for almost a century
before Cicero's birth in 106 B.C. its inhabitants had been fully privileged
citizens of Rome. As Cicero remarks in his 'Laws,' a member of such a
community was a man of two 'fatherlands', with the typically Italian
affection for his native district but with a greater and prouder loyalty to
the imperial city, prizing her history and traditions all the more because
he himself to the Roman *pur sang* was still something of a foreigner.
The Arpinates had a special reason to be proud. In their town was born,
half a century before Cicero, the great general Gaius Marius, seven
times Consul, saviour of Rome from two mammoth barbarian inva-
sions; a crowning mercy which his political ineptitude and ferocity
never cancelled.

The family of Tullius Cicero was very old, and also well-to-do;
though talk (not Cicero's) of a royal or semi-royal ancestor, Attius or
Attus Tullius the Volscian, can be discounted. The clan name Tullius
crops up widely at this period, and its bearers are no more relatable to
one another than so many Robinsons. The family name Cicero went
back as far as the orator's grandfather, perhaps farther. Like many
Roman family names it sounds undignified—*cicer* is Latin for 'chick-
pea.' According to one story the first Cicero got it from a wart on his
nose. But there are other possible etymologies, and the name is
attested in a different family at a very much earlier period.

The individual name Marcus was handed down in the common
Roman fashion from father to son, so that the full name Marcus

[1] The quotation may come from Ennius.

Tullius Cicero runs to our knowledge through four generations, beginning with the orator's grandfather and ending with his son. The grandfather was alive when this grandson was born, but probably died in the course of the next few years. He was a burgher of the old school, a staunch conservative in politics and culture. One quoted saying of his about Greek-speaking Romans no doubt passed into family currency: 'Romans are like Syrian slaves—the better the Greek, the bigger the scoundrel.' The old gentleman was not talking at large. He had married into another local family, the Gratidii, but his brother-in-law, Marcus Gratidius, moved in a wider orbit, on close personal terms with the great orator Marcus Antonius (grandfather to Mark Antony); and Gratidius was an amateur of Greek literature. He was also, to speak anachronistically, a man of the left, married to a sister of Gaius Marius; their son (adopted by an uncle into the Marian family) had a notable career on the 'popular' side of politics, and was brutally executed when Sulla came back to power (Cicero was fourteen at the time). Gratidius and Cicero's grandfather, not surprisingly, were at odds in municipal politics. Information is scrappy, but it shows the family into which Cicero was born reflecting the political and cultural tensions of the time.

Marcus Cicero and Gratidia had two sons, Marcus and Lucius. Their education was apparently not affected by the parental equation of good Greek with bad morals. Cicero says of his father that he spent most of his life in literary pursuits, and describes his uncle Lucius as a 'very highly cultivated person.' When (in 102, perhaps after the old man's death) Gratidius went on his friend Antonius' staff to Cilicia, the province in Asia Minor which Cicero was one day to rule, Lucius Cicero went too. Gratidius died while abroad, and Lucius seems to have died not very long after his return. He left a son named after him and, probably, a daughter.

The orator to be was born on his grandfather's country estate, or farm, on 3 January 106. Not much (probably about two years) later his brother Quintus was born in the same place. The farm, or villa, lay in a broad valley several miles from the town. Its exact location is uncertain; perhaps the site is now occupied by a paper factory. It was a place of streams, where the river Fibrenus formed a delta, with arms running into another and larger river, the Liris. But modern accretions have changed and obscured the terrain. Only the background of hills and mountains, some high enough to carry traces of snow into mid-May, must still be much as Cicero saw it. It is a plausible conjecture that some ancient granite and marble columns in the crypt of the eleventh-century monastery church of San Domenico (Isola di Liri) may have been taken from the remains of his home.

How long the farm remained the family headquarters we do not know. In the first ten years or so of his life young Marcus Cicero may never have left it, except perhaps for visits to a town house in Arpinum. His father had poor health and bookish tastes. After coming into the property he rebuilt the country house on a more handsome scale. But his wife Helvia was of good family with connexions in Rome, and other threads may have been drawing him toward the capital—the alliance with the Marii, the connexion with Marcus Antonius, and resulting acquaintance with other Roman notables. Then there was his sons' education to be considered; and perhaps the head of the family himself hankered for sophistication and variety. They moved into a house in the select quarter of Carinae, near the modern church of S. Pietro in Vincoli—'smart Carinae,' as Virgil calls it in the Aeneid. No doubt the three days' journey to and from Arpinum was frequently made, and Cicero senior later came again to spend most of his time there. For his children Arpinum was henceforward a home for holidays.

Cicero never lost his affection for the place, which he kept and visited throughout his life. Affairs and study left him little time for the traditional country occupations, but his description of the skills and pleasures of agriculture in his little book 'On Old Age' seems to reflect a personal sympathy. For example, this on vine-growing (old Cato the Censor is supposed to be talking):

And then, need I say, there are the vines, their beginning, planting, and growth. If you care to know my own principal recreation and pleasure as an old man, here it is—inexhaustible. There is the vital force of everything born of the soil, that makes a tiny fig-seed, or a grape-stone, or the most minute germ of fruit or tree, procreate mighty trunks and branches. Think of the mallet-shoots, sprouts, twigs, quicksets, layers—a wonder and delight to any man. The vine being by nature prone to fall, it droops earthward unless it is propped up; but to raise itself it clutches at anything that offers with its tendrils, like human hands. Then the farmer's skill will curb the creeping, twisting, proliferating growth with the pruning-knife, for he must not let the twigs run to wood, issuing abroad in rank profusion. Well then, in early spring buds appear at the joints of the remaining branches; and out of the buds grape-clusters come to view, fostered by the moisture of the earth and the heat of the sun. At first the grapes taste very sour, but they mellow with maturity. Foliage clothes them, to fend off the sun's scorching rays without excluding gentle warmth. Is there anything more joyous to taste or more beautiful to look upon than a bunch of grapes?

The Cicero who defended order and tradition, respected domestic and other proprieties, hated mob violence and aristocratic licence; the bourgeois, provincial, chauvinistic Cicero sometimes visible in the Roman Consular and Hellenist, was the child of Arpinum. In the life-long student and prolific writer can be seen the same child, fascinated by the papyrus rolls in his father's library.

A happy child? Cicero throws no direct light on the question. Negative evidence prompts certain doubts. He never refers to his mother; our only clue there is a slight reminiscence in a letter of Quintus to Tiro, suggesting a strict, parsimonious housewife. As for his father, we may leave aside what seems to be a remarkably curt announcement of his death in a letter of 68 as not certainly significant. But the references scattered among Cicero's writings are suspiciously lacking in warmth and colour. For a man who used words lavishly, 'an excellent father, a very wise man' is not much of a tribute (the writer felt insulted when he himself was referred to as 'an excellent Consul'); and it is exceptional. One would have expected to find a grateful allusion to the paternal stimulus which, according to Plutarch, Cicero received in his early days as a pleader; there is none, not even in the obvious place for it, the account of his oratorical career in the 'Brutus', though he does mention the 'friends and doctors' who advised him to give up practice in 79. One thinks of the unforgettable lines in which that other great Roman self-portrayer, Horace, acknowledges *his* debt to his father. The reticence is the more notable because of Cicero senior's incidentally attested interest in literature and in his sons' education.

If it were legitimate in such a case to argue from effects to causes, certain of Cicero's basic characteristics might be associated with an early emotional lack. There was something fluid in the core of his personality. His political career was notoriously erratic. His relations with contemporaries tended to be complex and unstable. Men he publicly vilified as monsters turn into political allies or personal friends, and vice versa—Pompey, Caesar, Cato, Hortensius are only the most conspicuous illustrations of changefulness and ambivalence on Cicero's part. Nor was he beyond cultivating friendship with people whom he disliked and scorned. His family history tells the same story—divorce after thirty years of marriage, estrangements from his brother and nephew, discontent with his son. Tullia, his daughter, and Atticus, his almost life-long friend, were fixed stars among planets, though even the relationship with Atticus had its ups and downs. His judgments were as variable as his feelings, and his principles, though far from being a mere cover for self-seeking, were apt to give under strain. His level of sincerity, sentimental or intellectual, was often shallow, even when he was not consciously playing a part. As his professed philosophy (Romans of culture usually favoured one or other among the current Greek systems) he chose the Academic, which discountenanced dogma and condoned inconstancy of opinion—though he sometimes leaned toward the rigorous positivities of the Stoics. All allowances made for the exigencies of public life and the professional flexibility of an advocate, there remains in him an elusive, ambiguous quality to baffle historians and biographers. Cicero the upright patriot (with human weaknesses) and Cicero the time-serving humbug are familiar figures. Neither convinces.

A recent biographer of Benjamin Disraeli associates his subject's extraordinary determination to climb to the top with a shortage of maternal affection in early life.[1] The complement of Cicero's inner insecurity, whatever its origins, was a dynamic impulse to be first. From a boy, as he wrote to his brother, he took his watchword from Homer's Achilles, 'Far to excel, out-topping all the rest!' Like Disraeli, Cicero needed such an emotional thrust to make his way among social superiors in a highly caste-conscious community. His spectacularly successful advance is easily related to the egotism that pervades every category of his writings. Within the conditions of nineteenth-century English politics Disraeli was an old man before he reached the top of the greasy pole. Cicero, to his misfortune, had arrived at forty-three.

[1] Robert Blake, 'Disraeli', pages 16 ff.

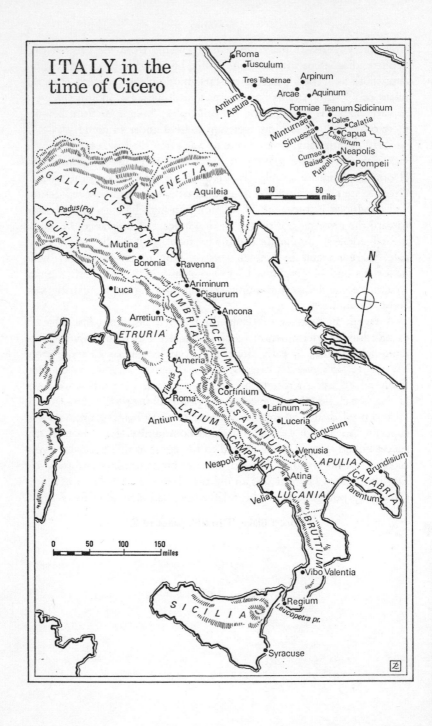

ITALY in the time of Cicero

Roma
Tusculum
Tres Tabernae
Arpinum
Antium
Arcae
Aquinum
Astura
Formiae
Teanum Sidicinum
Minturnae
Cales
Calatia
Sinuessa
Casilinum
Capua
Cumae
Neapolis
Baiae
Pompeii
Puteoli

0   10   50
miles

GALLIA CISALPINA
VENETIA
LIGURIA
Padus (Po)
Aquileia
Mutina
Bononia
Ravenna
Luca
Ariminum
Pisaurum
UMBRIA
Ancona
Arretium
ETRURIA
PICENUM
Ameria
Tiberis
Corfinium
Roma
LATIUM
Larinum
Antium
SAMNIUM
Luceria
Canusium
CAMPANIA
Venusia
Neapolis
APULIA
Brundisium
Atina
CALABRIA
Velia
LUCANIA
Tarentum
BRUTTIUM

0   50   100   150
miles

N

Vibo Valentia
Regium
Leucopetra pr.
SICILIA
Syracuse

CHAPTER TWO

Emergence

IN Rome Cicero senior already had, or soon acquired, a distinguished acquaintance, including several members of the aristocracy connected by marriage with the Marii. The most eminent was Lucius Licinius Crassus, statesman, orator (even more celebrated than Marcus Antonius), and man of culture. Crassus' daughter married Gaius Marius' son, and he was also a close friend of the noted jurist Aculeo, who had married a sister of Helvia's. The great man took a benevolent interest in the education of Aculeo's two sons and of their cousins the two young Ciceros, even to prescribing their teachers and curriculum. He died when Marcus Cicero was fifteen.

Cicero was a brilliant schoolboy to the admiration (says Plutarch) of his fellows and the disgruntlement of their aristocratic parents. He brought an excellent memory to the traditional tasks of learning by heart the antique legal code of the Twelve Tables (not much longer to be inflicted on Roman youth) and the primitive verses of Livius Andronicus' Latin translation of the Odyssey. But Roman education offered more attractive pabulum. Latin poetry, chiefly epic and dramatic, had travelled a long way since Livius, though still leaning heavily on Greek sources; Cicero became personally acquainted with its contemporary grand old man, the playwright Accius. He always professed a patriotic admiration for this early Roman literature, and much of the little that remains of it has survived through quotations in Cicero's works. Under Greek instructors he came to know the great Greek poets, especially Homer and Euripides, and got his first lessons in the art of speaking from Greek rhetoricians, according to the practice of the time. As a boy and young man he produced poetry of his own which had a considerable though temporary vogue. The specimens that survive, mainly by way of self-quotation, show technical ability, nothing more.

The great friendship of Cicero's life began at this period. Titus Pomponius, later called Atticus, was at least three years older, an important difference at that time of life; the relationship will have started with Pomponius in the role of guide and mentor, and so, even in Cicero's grandest days, it was to continue.[1] Like Cicero, Pomponius was the son of a 'Knight' (i.e., the possessor of wealth above a certain level who was not a member of the Senate), though his family had been Roman from time immemorial. Like Cicero, he loved books and things Greek. No doubt many other contacts of more or less importance in Cicero's career began in the class-room.

Childhood officially ended for a Roman when his father decided to give him the 'manly toga,' white instead of the purple-bordered toga worn by boys. This probably happened to Cicero at the usual age, sixteen. Soon afterwards his father introduced him to another friendly nobleman, Crassus' father-in-law Quintus Mucius Scaevola the Augur, an eminent legal expert now eighty years old. Cicero, and Pomponius too, studied law with him, listening to his answers to consultants, and retained a vivid memory of the old gentleman's sense of humour and his anecdotes of the younger Africanus and his circle—Scaevola's wife (also known to Cicero) was the daughter of Scipio Africanus' bosom friend Laelius Sapiens. When the Augur died, about 87 B.C., Cicero attached himself to a younger member of the same family, Scaevola the Pontifex Maximus (head of the state religion), likewise a great jurist. Contact with the 'grammarian' Aelius Stilo, the most learned man of his period, is also recorded. Cicero's interest in Greek philosophy had already begun; two of the most eminent Greek professionals of the day were his teachers. At the same time he was listening almost every day to leading public speakers, in court or at political meetings.

It was as a speaker that Cicero was determined to make his mark. Romans of any standing set vast store by *dignitas*, their prestige or 'public image,' and the highest prestige was traditionally won by services in offices of state—magistracies, or, as they were often significantly called 'honours.' These went by popular election, though the voting scales were variously weighted in favour of birth and property. They were held in a sequence (the 'course of honours') —Quaestor (qualifying for life membership of the Roman Senate), Aedile (or Tribune), Praetor, Consul—and the minimum ages for each and intervals

---

[1] For a fuller account of Atticus' personality and relations with Cicero I may refer to the Introduction to my edition of Cicero's letters to him.

between them were laid down by law. Cicero, for instance, who held each office in 'his year' (i.e., at the earliest age legally permissible), became Quaestor at thirty, Aedile at thirty-six, Praetor at thirty-nine, and Consul at forty-two. Immediately after a year as Praetor or Consul it was usual to go abroad as governor of a province, though here Cicero was an exception.

This conception of 'dignity' as deriving from office went along with a massive respect for the hereditary principle. The Consulship, highest magistracy of all, not only reflected supreme 'dignity' on the Consulars who had held it, but made their lineal descendants 'noble' for all time. Year after year the two Consuls were generally elected from among such families, many of them with a roll of consular forebears stretching back for three or four centuries to the beginnings of the republican constitution. The lower magistracies, each in its own degree, also conferred 'dignity' (though not 'nobility' as generally understood) upon the families which had held them, and thereby gave advantage in the race for office. In Cicero's time such Consuls as were not 'noble' nearly always came from 'praetorian' stock. One result of Sulla's restitution of power to the Senate, the traditional governing body in the Roman state, in 82–79 was that the Consulship became even more of an aristocratic preserve than at earlier periods.

Still, even a 'new man', whose forebears had never sat in the Senate, might reasonably hope to get as far as the Praetorship, provided he had money, connexions, and ability. Even noblemen did not climb the ladder without effort—there were not enough offices to go round. The 'new man' naturally had to work harder to establish himself as a political prospect and collect votes. He might do it by making a name for himself as a soldier, like Marius. That was no good for Cicero. His only experience of military life, until he found himself in command of an army in his middle fifties, was as a recruit of seventeen during the war between Rome and her revolted Italian allies. Though brief, it was apparently enough to give him a lasting distaste for active service. Almost the only alternative way of attracting favourable notice was by public speaking, which had long been a major element in Roman political life and in the hands of masters like Crassus and Antonius had become a highly sophisticated art—as formerly in Athens. One started as an advocate in the courts. Successful advocates established a claim on their clients' gratitude (they could not legally take money); and the accumulation of such debts, of *gratia*, was the indispensable preliminary to victory at the polls. Once launched on the 'course of honours' one's influence and *réclame* would largely depend on ability to give an effective oratorical performance at public meetings and in the Senate.

Cicero made a late start. The end of the Italian War was followed by a series of internal convulsions. Dismissed from his command for political reasons in 88, Sulla marched on Rome, killed his leading opponents or drove them into exile, then left for the East to cope with the formidable King of Pontus. In his absence, Gaius Marius, who had managed to escape, turned the tables; after a violent struggle he and his ally the Consul Cinna became masters of Rome and Italy. Several highly placed friends of the Cicero family, including Marcus Antonius, perished in the resulting blood-bath; Scaevola the Pontifex got off for the time with a serious wound. After Marius' death early in 86 things settled down for three years under the régime of the 'popular' leaders Cinna and Carbo. Cicero was now old enough to make his public début—Lucius Crassus had shot into prominence at twenty-one with a sensational political prosecution. The moment might have seemed favourable, for the leading orators of the nineties had mostly disappeared and new reputations were in the making, notably that of Quintus Hortensius. Yet Cicero held back; training in private, pursuing philosophy, composing verses. He disliked and despised the régime, which, with Sulla still to reckon with, had no security of tenure. Clearly it would be unwise to meddle in politics, and in the forensic field he could not hope in such circumstances to make his name with a political *cause célèbre*, as Crassus had done and as he himself was later to do. Best then to wait for Sulla.

Sulla and his army came back for the final round in 83. Cicero wished him well, but took no part in the eighteen months of fighting up and down the peninsular. This new conflict too took toll of mentors, friends, connexions. Scaevola was murdered in a new 'popular' terror. Gaius Marius the Younger headed the Dictator Sulla's first published list of victims, and Marius Gratidianus met a specially unpleasant end by Sulla's orders; his executioner, Catiline, was one day to play an important part in Cicero's career. Yet Sulla's new constitution was felt as a return to traditional order and 'dignity;' a Republic was restored in which Cicero's talents could thrive.

He began, naturally, with some court cases of minor importance. One of them is known because Cicero's speech for the defence has survived; it is an affair of tangled legal technicalities, but includes a phrase or two of topical relevance. 'No decent man wants to kill a fellow-countryman, even if he can do it legally:' in the first half of the year 81, as Cicero spoke, Sulla's massacres by advertisement, the Proscriptions, were in full swing. Towards the end of it, a rich burgher of Ameria in Umbria was murdered in the streets of Rome on his way back from a dinner-party. Part of the profit went to two of his relatives, but most of it to a young but influential freedman of the Dictator, who managed to get the victim's name posthumously into one of the fatal lists and so to buy up his confiscated estate for a song. The affair caused a scandal in Ameria, and the villains decided that the son and rightful heir, Sextus Roscius by name, had better be eliminated. So they had him charged with the murder. But Roscius had friends or patrons among the Roman nobility, many of whom were sick of bloodshed and resentful of profiteering by the Dictator's hangers-on. Roscius' case gave an excellent opportunity for a public protest, if somebody could be found to take the risk. If it were done by a man of rank, Sulla might feel his authority challenged; a young man, little known and of comparatively humble position, would be better for the job. At the request of Roscius' aristocratic protectors, who appeared in court to support him, Cicero spoke for the defence. The speech is one of his best, in spite of its juvenile exuberance, for which he later apologized, and its aura of the rhetorical classroom. His full-blooded indictment of Chrysogonus (the powerful freedman) and of the system of legalized robbery and murder into which Sulla's political reprisals had degenerated must have electrified the court—Sulla himself is deftly exonerated, as too busy with great matters to know what was going on. Roscius was acquitted, and Cicero's name was made. The first important episode of his career had shown courage; but courage in a clear cause, with powerful backing and personal glory to gain.

Sulla seems to have shown no offence, and Cicero's services in court were now in brisk demand. At twenty-six he was fairly launched on a tide of success. Then, probably after Sulla's abdication of his Dictatorship early in 79, there was an interruption. Cicero explains in his 'Brutus:'

At that time I was very thin and physically weak, with a long, slender neck—a bodily habit and appearance that is generally associated with critical danger to health, if accompanied by hard work and severe strain on the lungs. Those who cared for me were all the more concerned because I always used to speak at full pitch, never relaxing and straining my voice and my whole body to the limit. When my friends and doctors urged me to give up practice at the bar, I felt that I ought to run any risk rather than turn away from the prospect of

becoming a famous orator. However, I reflected that by relaxing and modera-
ting my vocal effort and changing my style of speaking I might avoid the
danger to health and speak with more restraint. That was the reason, to
change my habit of speaking, that I went to Asia. So after two years of
practice, when my name was already known in the courts, I left Rome.

Plutarch's version, that Cicero retired in fear of Sulla, is clearly
wrong, but Cicero's own account may simplify. One suspects that
something in the nature of a physical or nervous breakdown was
involved.[1] However reluctant he must have been to interrupt his career,
the opportunity to see the Greek world, especially Athens, will have
sweetened the medicine. Seven years previously Athens had fallen to
Sulla's troops after a long, destructive siege. But besides beauty and
memories, the city was still an intellectual headquarters where young
Romans of rank went to study philosophy and rhetoric, especially the
former, under leading teachers, some of whom were independent
thinkers. Cicero spent six months there in congenial work and no less
congenial company—his brother, his cousin Lucius, and his old friend
Pomponius, who had made his home in the city some years previously.
He also took at least one trip to the Peloponnese, visiting Sparta and
the ruins of Corinth. Then, still with Quintus, on to Greek-speaking
Asia Minor, where celebrated rhetorical professionals were to be found.
Finally to Rhodes, home of Posidonius, the greatest savant of his
period, and of Apollonius Molon, another famous teacher of rhetoric,
under whom Cicero had already sat in Rome. We have his word for it
that the primary purpose of the tour had been answered when after
two years he came home 'not only a more practised speaker, but one
might say a new one.' He had learned to economize his voice, his lungs
were stronger, he had put on weight. For the rest of his life his health
was adequate, with no serious illnesses.

[1] As in Disraeli's case (to pursue a parallel which may be thought fanciful). He
left for *his* two years' tour of the Near East at about the same age as Cicero, with
similarly happy results for his health.

CHAPTER THREE

Up the Ladder

'Every day as you go down to the Forum you should say to yourself: "I am a new man. I am a candidate for the Consulship. This is Rome".'

Quintus Cicero (if not a forger) to his brother in 64

PLUTARCH says that Cicero held back from advocacy and office-seeking after his return in 77, partly in deference to a Delphic oracle, and that people called him 'Greek' and 'scholar;' but that the promptings of his father and friends, working on a naturally ambitious temperament, relaunched him. 'Greek' and 'scholar' sound authentic; he may have acquired some mannerisms abroad—unless this item really belongs to an earlier period. As a whole the story can hardly be taken seriously, even though Cicero himself may have started it later on by wishing or half wishing he had stayed in his library; in such a mood as when he wrote to Atticus in 67:

... Mind you don't hand over your books to anybody. Keep them for me, as you say you will. I am consumed with enthusiasm for them, as with disgust for all things else. ...

But his account in the 'Brutus' shows that his tour abroad was largely devoted to preparation for a new start as a speaker. And from the words in his defence of Roscius, 'I have not yet entered politics,' it may be gathered that he had every intention of entering them in due course, as successful speakers normally did.

He was now twenty-nine, and could begin canvassing for the Quaestorship, to which he was elected the following year (76). The thirteen years after his return were in effect one long canvass—for the Consulship. *Gratia* was to be accumulated not only by services rendered in and out of the law-courts but by private affability. With his wit, already famous, and the social tact and charm conspicuous in his letters, Cicero had no difficulty in making himself agreeable. He made a point of memorizing names and personal particulars. A man with a vote was a valuable acquaintance; property and position made him especially valuable. On any road in Italy Cicero could point out the houses and lands of his 'friends.' We know very little about all this activity in detail; hardly more than the stages of his progress along the 'course of honours' and some of the cases he pleaded.

Quaestor in 75, he served for a year in Western Sicily under a good governor, who became a highly respected friend. The work was financial and administrative, such as purchase of grain to relieve a shortage in Rome. Sicily, earliest of Roman provinces, with its ancient Greek civilization rich in art and literature, suited Cicero, and he made many friends there. In one of his philosophical writings thirty years later we get an interesting glimpse of him off duty, discovering the grave of the mathematician Archimedes (of the famous Principle) in Syracuse:

I managed to find the tomb when I was Quaestor, covered all over with thorn-bushes. The Syracusans had no knowledge of it, told me there was no such thing. But I possessed a copy of some verses which I had been informed were engraved on the monument, and according to these there was a ball and a cylinder on the top of the tomb. Near Agrigentum Gate there is a great quantity of graves, so I let my eyes roam all over the area; and there I noticed a little pillar just showing above the bushes, surmounted by a carving of a ball and a cylinder. I said to my Syracusan companions (important people in the town) that I thought this was what I was looking for. A multitude of men with sickles was put in to clear away the undergrowth, and when a path was open we went up to the base of the pillar, where the epitaph was still to be seen, though the latter half of each verse had been obliterated by weather. So one of the most famous of cities, formerly too one of the most devoted to the things of the mind, would never have known where to find the memorial of the cleverest of all her citizens, if a man from Arpinum had not supplied the information.

On getting back to Italy Cicero was asked by an acquaintance where he had been all this while. The question deflated him, for he had flattered himself that his record in Sicily had been rather distinguished. Evidently a province was no place for him to shine. Provincial governorships were generally regarded as one of the chief prizes of an official career, and the better ones were eagerly sought and held as long as possible. They meant practically unlimited power within the area and handsome opportunities for self-enrichment, even if the governor happened to be more scrupulous than most. But power and money were not Cicero's lodestars; he came to the Senate, as Disraeli to the House of Commons, 'for fame;' and fame, except for soldiers, was a metropolitan commodity. So when nearly twenty-five years later he found himself Proconsul he wrote home to a rising young politician:

. . . Rome! Stick to Rome, my dear fellow, and live in the limelight! Residence abroad of any sort, as I have thought from my youth upwards, is squalid obscurity for those whose efforts can win lustre in the capital.

Cicero was Aedile in 69 and Praetor in 66, scoring impressively in the voting at both elections, but doing nothing very remarkable in office. He must not be imagined as a man with a mission to society. A Roman politician did not require a platform. Parties in the modern sense did not exist, and nobody was under the necessity of professing a political cause or principle. Since Rome at this time possessed only the embryo of a civil service, the conduct of public business devolved on the elected magistrates, those actually holding office and their predecessors, who made up the Senate; except that a great deal was handled by way of private relationships, of patron and client, existing between Romans of rank on the one hand and individuals, corporations, and regions in and out of Italy on the other. The system had not been built to run an empire, and was breaking down in all directions. But it meant that the only title a legally qualified candidate for public office need offer was his willingness to serve. The electors, when not actually bribed, usually cast their votes on personal grounds of one sort or another. A candidate's attitude to particular issues or his general political colour (if any) was important only at special crises.

No more time then need be wasted in looking for evidence of political ideas in the records of Cicero's ascent. Even later, when he had more leisure and greater personal motive to ruminate on the troubles of the Republic, he never analysed them in depth or proposed a workable cure. Nor to our knowledge did any of his contemporaries, with the possible exception of Caesar. Half a century of unrest, resulting in the horrors of the eighties, gave food for thought, but Roman stomachs could not digest it. Rome's unparalleled history seemed to guarantee the essential, god-given rightness of her social and political institutions; and the moral and material benefits of being a Roman citizen, even of low degree, were such that the urge to find an alternative was lacking. With the expansion of the empire the machinery of government had become hopelessly inadequate; wars were mismanaged, provinces oppressed and exploited, corruption was rampant in polling-booth and court-room. High politics were normally an affair of shifting personal alliances, grouping and regrouping against a background of private interests, overlapping, colliding, interlocking.[1] Yet most Romans found their account in it all. Even the poor had their 'bread and circuses' —free (or at least subsidized) corn and free shows. For the well-to-do there were endless opportunities to get richer; the excitement and rewards of the 'course of honours' (short, at any rate, of the Consulship) lay open to the ambitious and able. Personal liberties were wide, direct taxation non-existent; many of the old social conventions had lost their grip, and a man could do what he liked with his own. The Senate had often been challenged on particular points; a tradition of 'popular' politics had grown up, whereby the assemblies of the people (theoretically supreme) were brought into legislative action to carry particular measures against the Senate's will, measures which often really or supposedly favoured the man in the street. During the seventies and sixties the authority of the Senate as re-established by Sulla was steadily undermined. Safeguards disappeared, and a series of foreign and domestic embarrassments weakened senatorial standing and morale. But no far-reaching scheme of reform, no alternative system, was in men's minds; certainly not in Cicero's, with his lack of intellectual ruthlessness and his more than Roman reverence for the past, later to be reinforced by his own spectacular success—a system which had worked so well in his case could not be basically bad. For him the trouble (and here too his views were quite typical) lay with the decline in moral standards from the good old days, only three or four generations ago, when (as he says in a speech he made as Aedile) you might look for a rascal and never find one.

To be sure, the middle-aged or elderly Consular has to be distinguished from the *arriviste* of thirty-six whose denunciations of senatorial shortcomings are on record in the 'Verrines.' Gaius Verres, for three years governor of Sicily, had bled its people white, and they appealed to Cicero in virtue of his recent connexion with the province to undertake a prosecution. Although it was his life-long practice, never broken before and very seldom after, to appear only for the defence, he agreed. Verres, the son of a Senator but not a nobleman, had important aristocratic friends, including his defending counsel, Cicero's forensic rival Quintus Hortensius. But the evidence which Cicero and his cousin Lucius were able to gather in a seven-weeks' tour of the island was so overwhelming that Verres exercised a Roman's

---

[1] This is less true (though not wholly untrue) of the fifties, after Pompey's prepotence had created an exceptional situation, than of the years of Cicero's rise in the seventies and sixties.

privilege of retiring into exile in the middle of the trial. Cicero clinched his victory by publishing the series of speeches which, in theory at least, he would have delivered in court if Verres had stayed the course.

The year of the trial, 70, was a bad one for Sulla's constitution. The Consuls, Pompey and Crassus, had been elected with armies at their backs, the former in blatant defiance of legal requirements as to age and previous office. Though former adherents of Sulla and personally at loggerheads with each other, they collaborated in undoing Sulla's work. When Verres came to trial, a law was in prospect to deprive Senators of their exclusive right to man the juries in the standing criminal courts, which Sulla had restored to them. Probably the law had passed before the 'Verrines' were published; so that in presenting himself as the spokesman of a Roman People at the end of its patience with malfeasant senatorial governors and the senatorial courts which acquitted them Cicero was not so much swimming with the tide as spurring on a horse that had already passed the winning-post. As a Senator addressing Senators he professes respect and good will to the Order, but in key passages his tone is minatory and militant. Sulla and his institutions are criticized; so are aristocratic contemporaries:

> Is it not enough to stir any man's indignation to see how you[1] and our other grandees admit this worthless scoundrel to your friendship in preference to the honest merit of any one of *us?* You and your peers find the activity of new men distasteful, you despise their sober habits and sense of decency, you would like to see their ability and energy permanently kept under. But you love Verres! . . . He is so popular with your butlers and footmen, such a favourite with your freedmen and slaves—of both sexes! When *he* arrives he is ushered in out of turn, admitted all on his own, while the doors are closed to other callers, very worthy people often enough. It may be inferred that you make your favourites out of people whose survival in the community depends on your protection.

Cicero's attitude to the Roman aristocracy was inevitably equivocal. 'You know I have always been devoted to the nobility,' he says in his 'Academic Questions.' He was joking, but in fact nobody so traditionally-minded could fail in the respect for birth which underlay Rome's political and social structure. At the same time he had to resent aristocratic exclusiveness as a bar to his progress and a constant social irritant. Even at a much later period a nobleman's sneer touched him on

[1] Hortensius.

the raw. In 50 he wrote to Appius Claudius, in whose family the Consulship had passed from father to son with hardly a break ever since the Sabine chieftain Attus Clausus migrated to Rome five years after the foundation of the Republic:

> . . . Pausanias also told me of the following remark of yours: 'Well, of course! Appius went to meet Lentulus,[1] Lentulus went to meet Appius; but Cicero go to meet Appius—oh dear no!' These absurdities from *you* . . ! Do you suppose that any Appiosity or Lentulity counts for more with me than the ornaments of merit? Even before I gained the distinctions which the world holds so high, I was never dazzled by aristocratic names; it was the men who bequeathed them to you that I admired. But after I won and filled positions of the highest authority in such a fashion as to let me feel no need for further rank or fame, I hoped I had become the equal (never the superior) of you and your peers. And I may add that I have never observed a different way of thinking in Gnaeus Pompeius or Publius Lentulus, one of whom I hold to be the greatest man that ever lived, the other greater than myself. If *you* think otherwise, you might do worse than pay rather particular attention to what Athenodorus,[2] son of Sandon, has to say on these points—in order to understand the true meaning of *noblesse*. . . .

His letters show how hard Cicero found it to be intimate with a nobleman. One reason why he got along easily with Pompey may have been that Pompey's nobility was of very recent vintage.

The years of Cicero's rise were those of Pompey's also. They were born in the same year. Shortly before Cicero spoke for Sextus Roscius Pompey had established his military reputation by a whirlwind campaign against the Marians in North Africa. His unconventional career represented a dangerous challenge to the oligarchic system, and the senatorial leaders, the 'Optimates', had reason to resent his bullying. Against their opposition he received in 67 by popular suffrage a special command with vast powers to deal with the intolerable menace of piracy, and in the following year a similar bill placed him in charge of the eastern provinces, where Rome was again at grips with her old enemy, King Mithridates of Pontus, and his ally the King of Armenia. Cicero, Praetor at the time, supported it. But his speech on that occasion is in notable contrast with the 'Verrines.' The Optimate chiefs, including Hortensius (so roughly handled in the 'Verrines') and Lucullus, the general whom Pompey was to supersede, are treated with respect bordering on the sycophantic. Likewise, in a (lost) speech the next year

---

[1] Another aristocrat.
[2] A contemporary philosopher.

on behalf of a 'popular' Tribune,[1] the ancient commentator Asconius praises the skill with which Cicero avoided offence to the 'dignity' of his Optimate opponents. In 70 he had apparently envisaged himself as reaching his goal in their despite. But times could change, and so could Cicero.

[1] Gaius Cornelius.

CHAPTER FOUR

Domesticities

'So verfluch' ich die Liebe.'
Wagner, 'Das Rheingold'

A CORRESPONDENT of Cicero's (it was in the year 45) used in one of his letters a word[1] not ordinarily admitted into polite Latin conversation. The Stoics disapproved of such conventions, and in reply Cicero amused himself by setting out their arguments on the theme that 'the philosopher will call a spade a spade'—though not himself endorsing them. In protecting its sensitivity in this respect Roman society went to lengths which seemed morbid even to Cicero's Victorian editors. Tabu applied not only to words like the one in question (in his own letter Cicero avoids using it), but to innocuous words, or combinations of words, which happened to resemble them phonetically.

These restrictions, however, only operated in certain social contexts. The Roman literary convention, like the Greek, allowed writers who wanted it virtually unlimited freedom. Both of the two great Latin poets of Cicero's time wrote about love. For Lucretius, as an exponent of Epicurus' doctrines 'On the Nature of Things,' the subject was scientific material, but his treatment is anything but tepidly academic. The phenomenon of love (i.e., 'being in love,' as opposed to casual sex experience) is etched with a puritanical ferocity that has suggested comparison with Swift, and condemned as both noxious and unnecessary to the satisfaction of biological demands. Catullus (whose affair with 'Lesbia' might have served Lucretius as an object-lesson) is sometimes prodigiously obscene. Even eminent and respectable persons, including Cicero, composed metrical improprieties to entertain themselves and their friends. In his published speeches the erotic aberrations (real or alleged) of his enemies are considered fair game.

But apart from the odd 'unconsular'[2] joke, what we have of Cicero's

---

[1] *mentula.*
[2] So to Atticus in 60, after retailing a *risqué* hit at Clodius and his sister (wife of the Consul of the year): 'Not a very consular sort of joke, you may think. I admit it, but I can't abide that consular female.'

correspondence is 'clean'—it is said to have been otherwise with his lost letters to a septuagenarian lady called Caerellia. Scandalous gossip about his private life, for example his relations with his daughter, is found in late and hostile sources. The jury will disregard it. The breakdown of his first marriage after thirty years and the near-comic episode of his second are matters of record, but reliable detail is lacking. For the rest, a surface of Arpinate decorum is dented only faintly by a very few shy, authentic indications.

Another of his letters to Papirius Paetus (the correspondent already mentioned), a rich, elderly resident of Naples with Epicurean leanings whose friendship, or friendly acquaintance, with Cicero went back to the sixties if not further, describes a dinner-party in Rome at which a notorious actress was among those present. Would his old friend be shocked to hear of a pillar of society in such company? Well, he had had no idea the lady would be there. Anyhow, a famous Greek philosopher had been known to laugh off a liaison with an even more famous courtesan. 'But as for me, even when I was a young man nothing of that sort ever meant anything, much less now that I am an old one.' The wording is noticeable. Not only had Cicero (so he says) never sown any wild oats of this particular colour; he had never wanted to sow them.

Regarding Pompey in 49 he wrote to Atticus: 'In short, just as *en choses d'amour*[1] anything uncleanly, uncouthly, unbecomingly done alienates, so the unsightliness of his flight and discourtesy turns me from my affection.' Possibly a literary quotation is embedded here. Even so, the comparison, with its hint of aesthetic fastidiousness in matters of sex, is suggestive. We have it on contemporary authority[2] that Cicero was a good-looking man, and his care about his personal appearance was reflected in accusations of foppishness and effeminacy.

A specimen of his erotic verses *à la mode* happens to be on record; it concerns Tiro.[3] Taken at face value it would amount to proof of a homosexual relationship between the writer and his favourite secretary, but it would be naïve to go so far. The thing may well have been simply what Pliny the Younger, our informant, calls it, a 'naughty jest.' As such it would not mean much, given the general tolerance of

---

[1] He uses a Greek expression, 'in erotica.'

[2] Asinius Pollio, whose statement is borne out by half a dozen surviving portrait busts, all copies deriving (probably) from a single contemporary original, done in Cicero's late middle age.

[3] Contrary to what is usually assumed, there is no good reason to question Cicero's authorship.

ancient sentiment on this topic—which Cicero seems on the whole to have shared.

Finally, and perhaps most significant, there is the treatment of love in Cicero's 'Tusculan Disputations,' written nearly at the end of his life. In this work, at any rate in the relevant part of it, he almost certainly followed a Stoic source, and on love the Stoic position was surprisingly liberal: 'They say that the Sage will fall in love, and define love itself as an "impulse towards making friends which appears as a consequence of beauty".' But Cicero does not agree; like Lucretius, he is against it. For him Eros is the parent of irresponsibility and misconduct; intense amatory desire and enjoyment are alike disgraceful. Moreover, the passion of love does not exist apart from lust—on this point too Cicero opposes his 'divine' Plato as well as the Stoics, and explicitly sides with his butt and bugbear Epicurus. This exceptional alignment cannot but imply a strong personal bias.

Do these items, taken along with an undeniable instability in matters of personal sentiment, an ever-driving hunger for prominence, and the lack of deep and enduring emotional attachments, his daughter excepted,[1] justify further inference? Perhaps none more specific than this: the God whom Cicero abuses in the 'Tusculans' was never his friend.

Exactly when he married Terentia is uncertain; probably not long before his eastern tour. There is no record of her age or looks, but she was certainly rich and well-connected, though we hear of only one relative—a cousin or half-sister, a member of the patrician house of the Fabii and a Vestal Virgin, who was brought to trial (but acquitted) in 73 on a charge of 'incest' with none other than Catiline. Clearly a good match for a man with his way to make. Was it anything more? Plutarch describes Terentia as difficult, dominating, and ambitious, quoting a remark of her husband's that she was more inclined to take a share in his political concerns than to let *him* have any say in his own household. The affectionate, if egoistic, letters he wrote to her *de profundis* during his exile in 58 are not necessarily representative of their normal relations. But at least in that time of trouble she showed staunchness and stamina.

There were two children. First a girl, Tullia (Cicero often calls her Tulliola, 'little Tullia'), born soon after the marriage; in 67 she was old

---

[1] That is not to deny that Cicero was fond in different ways and degrees of other members of his family (including Atticus) and household, though time brought estrangements. But his feeling for Tullia seems to have been at an altogether more radical level. In reading his less familiar correspondence one soon learns to discount expressions of affection to or about outsiders.

enough, by Roman convention, to be promised in marriage to a young nobleman, Gaius Piso Frugi—the wedding took place, probably, in 63. A boy, another Marcus Tullius Cicero, followed in 65. Cicero liked young children and made an affectionate father; an affectionate uncle also, for at a date again not exactly to be fixed (the year 70 is as likely as any) another family event took place, which must have given him great satisfaction. His friendship with Pomponius had flourished since their schooldays, though they saw one another only during Cicero's six months in Athens in 79 and Pomponius' fairly frequent visits to Rome. Now Quintus Cicero married Pomponia, sister of Pomponius, or Atticus ('the Athenian'), as he may already have begun to be called. Marcus Cicero had made the match. It lasted about twenty-five years, thanks perhaps to Quintus' lengthy absences abroad, but there was trouble almost from the first. Pomponia was older than her husband by several years and temperamentally the opposite of tactful, easy-going Atticus, taking rather after their 'extremely difficult' uncle Caecilius. And peevishness was Quintus' leading characteristic. Their discords were a recurrent motif in the correspondence between their brothers, right from Cicero's first extant letter to Atticus in November 68:

... You write to me of your sister. She will tell you herself how anxious I have been that my brother Quintus should feel toward her as a husband ought. Thinking that he was rather out of temper, I sent him a letter designed to mollify him as a brother, advise him as my junior, and scold him as a man on the wrong tack; and from what he has since written to me on a number of occasions I feel confident that all is as it should be and as we should wish. ...

A little later:

... My brother Quintus seems to feel toward Pomponia as we wish, and is now with her on the estates at Arpinum. He has with him one Decimus Turranius, a scholarly person. ...

May 67:

... As to my brother, I feel sure things are as I have always wished and worked for. There are many signs, not the least that your sister is expecting a baby. ...

This baby, Quintus' only child, was a boy, named after his father. Meanwhile Quintus too had gone into politics. Perhaps Marcus Cicero's encouragement and support was partly a reward for Quintus' amenability in his choice of a wife. He would scarcely have got far on his own. Though trained for public speaking, he deliberately avoided it. Cicero in his 'Orator' suggests two reasons: it might have been from 'modesty, and a sort of gentlemanly shyness,' as Isocrates said of himself; or perhaps Quintus (to quote a joke of Cicero's own) thought one orator enough in a family, or even (almost) in a whole community. That was to say, Quintus had not cared to invite comparisons. The date of his Quaestorship is not recorded, but he was elected Aedile and Praetor during his brother's Praetorship (66) and Consulship (63). If Cicero's position in the fifties had remained what it used to be, he might even have tried to propel Quintus into the Consulship.

Two other family events may have tended to draw them closer. Young Lucius Cicero, their cousin, who had been their companion in Athens and Marcus' assistant in the Verres case, died in 68. Cicero to Atticus:

> Knowing me as well as you do, you can appreciate better than most how deeply my cousin Lucius' death grieved me, and what a loss it means to me both in public life and private. All the pleasure that one human being's charm and good nature can give another I had from him. So I do not doubt that you too are sorry; for you will feel for my distress, and you yourself have lost a family connexion and a friend, one who possessed every good quality and disposition to serve others, and who loved you both of his own accord and from hearing me speak of you. . . .

Cicero remembered Lucius warmly to the end of his life, when he gave him a role in one of his dialogues: 'our cousin by blood, but our brother by affection.'

The second letter in the series to Atticus contains a briefer notice: 'We lost our father on 23 November.'[1] The event was of considerable importance to Cicero financially. He inherited the ancestral property at Arpinum and the house in Carinae, though the latter was subsequently made over to Quintus. Shortly before he had bought a country house which had once belonged to Sulla at Tusculum, close to the modern Frascati in the hills about 13 miles from Rome. Many eminent Romans had places there. The next thing was to fit it up with a library and *objets d'art*, and the early letters to Atticus are full of the subject. Some statues in Megarian marble cost 20,400 sesterces (roughly = £650). Many wealthy Romans, like Appius Claudius or Verres, were passionate art collectors. Cicero was not. The Arpinate in him deprecated what he

---

[1] The text has been suspected, not without reason, but I think it is sound.

considered undue expense of time and money on such things. This was not just a public pose, conformable to the warning in his book 'On the Orator' not to flaunt Greek culture before a Roman audience. Witness the following from a letter to a connoisseur friend, Fabius Gallus,[1] who had exceeded a commission:

... But everything would be straightforward, my dear Gallus, if you had bought what I wanted and within the price I had wished to pay.... Not being acquainted with my regular practice, you have taken these three or four pieces at a price I should consider excessive for all the statuary in the world. You compare these Bacchantes with Metellus' Muses. Where's the likeness? To begin with, I should never have reckoned the Muses themselves worth such a sum—and all nine would have approved my judgment! Still, they would have made a suitable acquisition for a library, and one appropriate to my interests. But where am I going to put *Bacchantes?* Pretty little things, you may say. My dear fellow, I know them well, I've seen them often. I should have given you a specific commission about statues which I know if I had cared for them. My habit is to buy pieces which I can use to decorate a place in my palaestra,[2] in imitation of lecture-halls. But a statue of Mars! What can I, as an advocate of peace, do with that? I'm glad there was none of Saturn—I should have thought those two between them had brought me debt! I had sooner have had one of Mercury[3]—we might fare better in our transactions with Avianius![4]

As for that table-rest[5] which you had earmarked for yourself, if you like it you shall have it; but if you have altered your mind, I'll keep it of course. For the sum you have spent I should really have much preferred to buy a lodge at Tarracina, so as not to be continually imposing on hospitality. To be sure I realize that my freedman is to blame (I had given him quite definite commissions), and Junius too—I think you know him, Avianius' friend. I am making some new sitting-rooms in the little gallery of my house at Tusculum, and I wanted some pictures for their decoration—indeed, if anything in this way appeals to me, it is painting. However, if I have to keep these things of yours, please let me know where they are, and when they are sent for, and by what

[1] Usually (but wrongly) called Fadius. The date of the letter is not agreed. Some say 62 or 61, others 55. But the words 'advocate of peace' and other indications make it pretty certain that it belongs to 46 or 45, like the other three letters to Gallus in the collection.

[2] A space surrounded by colonnades. The word and the thing came from Greece (literally = 'wrestling-school'). Cicero probably refers to the *palaestra* in his town house on the Palatine.

[3] God of gain and good luck. In astrology Mars and Saturn generally bring the opposite.

[4] Seller of the statues, perhaps the sculptor Avianius Evander.

[5] A table-leg, probably in the form of a sculptured figure. A table might have one or more.

mode of transport. If Damasippus[1] changes his mind, I shall find some Damasippus *manqué*, even if it means taking a loss. . . .

Cicero delighted in his convenient refuge at Tusculum and kept it to the end of his life, as also another house he had acquired at Formiae on the Bay of Gaeta about 80 miles down the coast south of Rome. Then as now the town stretched along a narrow strip of coast backed by mountains, steep and austere in contrast to the lush vegetation of the coastal mountains further south. Near the western end of the modern town relics of a Roman villa have been plausibly identified as Cicero's Formianum; but the imposing monument traditionally called his tomb, standing near the place of his death in 43 B.C., probably had nothing to do with him. Formiae was a lively place, and Cicero humorously complained that its inhabitants turned his house into a sort of town hall, but it remained one of his favourite resorts.

Collecting 'my little villas, the pearls of Italy,' was to become something of a passion with him. Some years later we find him in possession of a house (which he later sold) in the sleepy little coast town of Antium (Anzio) and another at Pompeii, one of three that he later came to own on the Bay of Naples. He spent comparatively little time there because of the distance from Rome, but scenically it was perhaps the best of all. The eighteenth-century excavators gave his name to a villa in the Street of Tombs on high ground just outside Hercules Gate at the north-western end of the town. Either this or the splendid 'Villa of Diomedes' next door does in fact suit what Cicero tells us of the site. But the modern tourist has to do some illicit scrambling to see the view of the Bay which enraptured Otto Eduard Schmidt at the end of the nineteenth century before industrial development had invaded the shore.

[1] A well-known art-fancier, who bankrupted himself collecting. He reappears in Horace's Satires.

CHAPTER FIVE

Consul

'That consular office . . . which Curio once used to call an apotheosis . . .
Cicero to Atticus

Two letters from Cicero to Atticus in July 65, a year before his consular elections, breathe the cheerful excitement with which he approached the climax of his political career:

The position as regards my candidature, in which I know you are deeply interested, is as follows, so far as can be seen up to date: Only Publius Galba is canvassing, and he is getting for answer a plain, unvarnished, good old Roman 'No.' It's generally thought that this premature canvass of his has rather helped my prospects, for people are commonly refusing him on the ground that they are obligated to me. So I hope to draw some advantage when the word goes round that a great many friends of mine are coming to light. I was thinking of starting *my* canvass just when Cincius[1] says your boy[2] will leave with this letter, i.e. 17 July, at the tribunician elections in the Campus. As apparently certain rivals I have Galba, Antonius, and Quintus Cornificius. When you read this last I fancy you will either laugh or cry. Now get ready to slap your forehead: some folk think Caesonius[3] may stand too! As for Aquilius, I don't expect he will. He has both said he won't and entered a plea of ill health and alleged his monarchy over the law courts in excuse.[4] If Catiline's jury finds the sun isn't up at midday,[5] he will certainly be a candidate. I don't think you will be waiting for me to write about Aufidius and Palicanus.

[1] A confidential agent of Atticus.
[2] i.e., slave.
[3] He and Cornificius were respectable enough, but not consular timber.
[4] The wording is facetious and ironic. Aquilius was an eminent jurist (hence 'entered a plea'), whereas 'monarchy over the law courts' was a phrase which might apply to great advocates, like Hortensius or Cicero himself. Moreover, nobody had to offer excuses for *not* standing for the Consulship—at least not Aquilius, who would have stood a poor chance anyway.
[5] i.e., acquit him, though his guilt was clear as noon. Catiline was facing a charge of extortion in Africa, where he had been governor. See Cicero's second letter.

Of the present candidates[1] Caesar[2] is regarded as a certainty. The other
place is thought to lie between Thermus and Silanus. They are so poorly off
for friends and reputation that it doesn't seem to me an absolute impossibility
to put Turius in their light, but I am alone in thinking so. From my point of
view the best result would seem to be for Thermus to get in with Caesar,
since he looks like being as strong a candidate as any of the present lot if he is
left over to my year. . . . For my part I shall spare no pains in faithfully
fulfilling the whole duty of a candidate. I shall run down to join Piso's staff[3]
in September, in the dead period after the courts have closed, returning in
January. When I have made out the attitude of the nobles I shall write to you.
I hope the rest is plain sailing, at any rate as far as these local competitors are
concerned. *You* must answer for the other phalanx, since you are not so far
away, I mean our friend Pompey's. Tell him I shall not be offended if he does
not turn up for my election![4]

Well, that's how it all stands. But I have something to tell you for which I
very much hope you will forgive me. Your uncle Caecilius, having been
defrauded by Publius Varius of a large sum of money has taken proceedings
against Varius' cousin, Caninius Satyrus, for articles alleged to have been
fraudulently conveyed to him by Satyrus. The other creditors are joined with
him. . . . Now for the point. Caecilius asked me to appear against Satyrus. Well,
hardly a day goes by without this Satyrus calling on me. Lucius Domitius[5]
comes first in his attentions, I next. He made himself most useful both to me
and to my brother Quintus when we were candidates. I was naturally most
embarrassed in view of my friendship not only with Satyrus but with
Domitius, on whom my hopes of success depend beyond any other man. I
explained all this to Caecilius, making it clear at the same time that had the
dispute been solely between himself and Satyrus I should have met his wishes.
As it was, seeing that the whole group of creditors was involved, men
moreover of the highest station who would easily maintain their common
cause without help from anyone Caecilius might bring in on his own account,
I suggested that it would be reasonable for him to make allowance for my
obligations and my present position. I had the impression that he took this
less kindly than I should have wished or than is usual among gentlemen,
and from that time he entirely dropped our friendly contacts, which had
begun only a few days previously.

[1] For the Consulship of 64.
[2] Lucius Caesar, a distant relative of the future Dictator. He was duly elected.
[3] Gaius Piso (Consul in 67) was governor of Gaul on both sides of the Alps.
A post on his staff (as *legatus*) might be nominal, leaving Cicero free to do his
canvassing. Cisalpine Gaul south of the Po had been granted Roman citizenship
in 89 and was an important electoral factor.
[4] The last thing Cicero wanted was interference by Pompey, who might put up
a candidate of his own, as he did in 61 and 62.
[5] Lucius Domitius Ahenobarbus, Consul in 54. He was now only about
thirty-three, but birth, wealth, and connexions made him influential.

May I ask you to forgive me over this, and to believe that it was good feeling that prevented me from appearing against a friend in great trouble, who had given me every support and service in his power, in a matter most gravely affecting his good name? If, however, you like to take a less charitable view, you may assume that the exigencies of my candidature were the stumbling-block. *I* consider that even if it were so I might be pardoned, 'since for no hide of bull nor slaughtered beast. . . .'[1] You know the game I am playing and how vital I think it not only to keep old friends but to gain new ones. I hope you now see my point of view in the matter—I am certainly anxious that you should.

I'm quite delighted with your Hermathena.[2] It's so judiciously placed that the whole hall is like an offering at its feet. Many thanks.

The second letter followed at a short interval:

I have the honour to inform you that I have become the father of a little son . . . Terentia is well. It's a long time since I had a line from you. I have already written to you in detail about my prospects. At the moment I am proposing to defend my fellow-candidate Catiline.[3] We have the jury we want, with full co-operation from the prosecution.[4] If he is acquitted I hope he will be more inclined to work with me in the campaign. But should it go otherwise, I shall bear it philosophically.

I need you home pretty soon. There is a decidedly strong belief abroad that your noble friends are going to oppose my election. Clearly you will be invaluable to me in gaining them over. So mind you are in Rome by the beginning of January as you arranged.

In the event there were seven candidates in all, with Cicero as the only 'new man'; the other six came of senatorial families, four of them noble. No 'new man' had been elected Consul since the year 95, yet Cicero could feel sanguine. His competitors were bad characters or nonentities. He had behind him his personal popularity, his *gratia* built up through the years, especially among the rich business men of his own 'equestrian' order whose interests he had served in the courts. Of the two jokers in his electoral pack, Pompey did not put up a candidate of his own, as Cicero at this stage was afraid he might. In the flood tide of

[1] From the Iliad: 'Since for no beast for sacrifice or ox-hide were the twain striving, such as make prizes in a foot-race, but they ran for the life of godlike Hector.'
[2] A square pedestal (herm) surmounted by a head of Athena. Atticus had obtained one for Cicero's house at Tusculum.
[3] See page 27, note 5. For some reason Cicero changed his mind, and did not appear in the case.
[4] i.e., the prosecutor (Cicero's future arch-enemy, Publius Clodius) was hand in glove with the defence. Catiline was in fact acquitted.

eastern victories he was perhaps too busy to play Roman politics. As for the nobility, the manuscripts of the correspondence contain a tract in the form of a letter of advice from Quintus Cicero to his brother on how to conduct his campaign. If he received it, Marcus Cicero must have felt like a grandmother instructed in the art of sucking eggs (or, as he would have put it, like Minerva edified by the Pig). It may in fact be supposititious, but if so the writer had taken trouble with his details and much of it is *ben trovato,* as this to the point in question:

> Another thing that seems likely to be of much assistance to a new man is the good will of the nobles, especially the Consulars. . . . All of them must be diligently canvassed. They must be approached through third parties and persuaded that our political sentiments have always been pro-Optimate. If we should appear to have said anything in the 'popular' way, they must be told we did it to put Gnaeus Pompeius on our side, so as to have this power-full figure friendly to our candidacy, or at any rate not hostile.

If this is what the Optimates were told, they were told something like the truth, so far as recent history was concerned. Cicero's support for Pompey's eastern command in 66 and his defence of the Tribune Cornelius in 65[1] had brought him up against the senatorial leaders, but in both speeches he had taken care not to affront them.

Atticus received these letters in Epirus on the Adriatic coast opposite the island of Corcyra (Corfu), where he had bought a large estate in 68. The strengthening of his ties with Cicero through Quintus' marriage may have been one reason for his leaving Athens and moving nearer Italy. Soon after Cicero's summons he returned to Rome, to stay for three years. Cicero's appeals for his help in the campaign were doubtless not made in vain. As regards Pompey indeed, he was not serious—Atticus could do little or nothing in that quarter, and the geographical point ('since you are not so far away') can only be taken as a joke. But Atticus' connexions with the nobility were a very different matter, for they were extensive and solid. In particular, Hortensius and Manlius Torquatus (Consul in 65) were old and intimate friends. Atticus was a political animal, so Cicero later told him, and took a keen interest in the political scene, though nearly always from the wings; and he possessed the qualities of an ideal intermediary. His Optimate friends found themselves in a dilemma. Cicero's origins, personality, and record did not endear him to their class, but he was their only chance to keep out

[1] See page 19.

Catiline; and Catiline, though a nobleman with a luridly Sullan past, was rightly regarded as a menace to established order.[1] Result: an overwhelming victory for the 'new man.' The other successful candidate, Gaius Antonius, was a sad rogue, but lacked the energy that made Catiline dangerous. The old relations between his father the orator and the Cicero family will not have been forgotten.

The year of Cicero's Consulship (63) is, lamentably, a blank in the correspondence. He and Atticus were both in Rome, and the letters 'to friends' do not start until 62. Politically it was a tense and lively period. Rome lay in Pompey's shadow; all the more reason to make one's play before Pompey and his legions came home. At the very outset Cicero had to take a stand on a bill of traditionally 'popular' type to distribute land, owned or to be purchased by the state, among the poor. This particular proposal, however, reached beyond its ostensible purpose because of the enormous powers it vested in a commission to be appointed to implement it. Its real backers, working through a member of the Board of Tribunes, were the two 'popular' leaders: Pompey's former colleague and personal enemy, the millionaire Crassus (a distant relation of the orator), and Cinna's former son-in-law Gaius Julius Caesar, now nearly forty but so far prominent only as an anti-senatorial politician. Both, like so many *populares*, were of noble birth, and neither was an ally of Cicero. He fought the bill successfully on its demerits: elected by the people, not by oligarchical influence, so he declared on his first day in office, he would be a 'popular,' i.e. a people's, Consul; but by the term 'popular' had to be understood what was truly for the people's good. And so, as a professed people's man, Cicero could and did oppose a series of 'popular' initiatives, including one to relieve the children of Sulla's victims from their political disabilities. The proposal was just, he admitted, but this was no time to give the establishment another jolt.

It is a reasonable guess that before the elections the Optimates had been given some assurance (and through whom better than Atticus?) about Cicero's official attitude on such issues. At the same time the role of defender of the *status quo* flattered his instincts and hopes. Political life had for him no higher prize than an acknowledged place, second to none, among the 'leaders of the community' (*principes civitatis*) within a constitution functioning traditionally—the place of a Scipio Aemilianus or an Aemilius Scaurus. With the assumptive individual, whether

---

[1] So Sallust and Plutarch, who may be believed as to the essential, though the former may have antedated Catiline's plot.

reformist Gracchus or reactionary Sulla, who took his way with the commonwealth, he was fundamentally out of sympathy. Happy then in his consular role, he played it with vigour, confidence, and address. His unreliable colleague gave no trouble, 'squared' by the transfer of a coveted province which had originally been allotted to Cicero.

But Cicero's term of office ended in a crisis quite outside ordinary political give and take. The conspiracy of Catiline is pretty well documented. Not to mention later sources, we have Cicero's four contemporary speeches (admittedly touched up for publication three years later) and a monograph by the historian Sallust, written about twenty years after the events. Sallust was in his early twenties at the time, and from what we know of him later may easily have come into personal contact with Catiline and his circle. While not the 'popular,' or Caesarian, propagandist he is often represented, his standpoint is definitely not that of Cicero, a political and perhaps a personal enemy; so their substantial agreement as to the character and aims of the conspirators is unlikely to be a *fable convenue*. In concrete terms the plot was an attempt to seize power by violence, principally with a view to the financial benefit of the plotters. In Sallust Catiline promises his followers first and foremost 'new tables' (general cancellation of debts) and 'proscription' of the wealthy, then 'magistracies, priesthoods, plunder, everything that follows from war and the desires of the victors.' After Cinna and Sulla such prospects did not seem fantastic, and many responded, including persons of high birth and official status. But in a shaken and confused society Catiline's appeal was not simply economic. Part of it was to sheer destructiveness. Like Caesar later on, he fascinated explosive youth, in protest against respectability, order, work, and clean shaving.

In July Catiline again stood for the Consulship, and was again defeated. Cicero kept himself informed of his preparations for a coup by private espionage, and convinced the Senate of the reality of the danger; not without difficulty, for Catiline, who was more than an embodiment of the active vices, had friends even among its leaders. Its so-called 'Final Decree,' corresponding to proclamation of martial law, was passed on 21 October; according to Optimate thinking it legitimized any action which the Consuls (effectively Cicero) might judge necessary for the public safety. But Cicero was not prepared to act without more specific authority, not even after the outbreak of armed insurrection in Tuscany, where many of Sulla's old soldiers were spoiling for trouble. Instead, on 5 November, he denounced Catiline in open Senate and called on him to leave Rome; if he would not go quietly into exile, let him put himself where he belonged, with the rebels. As Cicero was one day to do under somewhat similar pressure, Catiline obliged, leaving himself no bridges to burn. The Consul must have been delighted at the success of his tactics, which painlessly deprived the movement of its leader, while forcing his hand. Nothing at this stage could have suited Cicero less than an inconclusive subsidence of the whole ferment, with the plotters left at large and himself unvindicated.

The Catilinarian leader in Rome was now one of the Praetors of the year, Lentulus Sura, a nobleman and an ex-Consul, who had started his official career over again after being expelled from the Senate for private irregularities. He planned arson and massacre, but made the mistake of tampering with a tribal delegation from Roman Gaul (the south of France) in the hope of raising a revolt in that quarter. The Gauls informed, and took Cicero's instructions. As they left Rome, carrying incriminating letters from the chief plotters, they were arrested. Lentulus and four others were brought before the Senate (3 December) and confronted with the evidence. Guilty by their own confession, they were put in custody.

It had been perfectly managed. The problem which the Senate had to deal with when it met on the 5th (the famous Nones of December) was not so easy. The nature of the crime, the confession of the criminals, and the existence of open rebellion outside Rome practically ruled out normal trial procedure. Cicero, always for strong measures against hardened offenders, favoured summary execution. But although many a Roman citizen had been killed for political reasons in the not remote past, formal sentence by the Senate, which was not a court of law, lacked precedent and ran counter to the citizen's legal right of appeal to the People against a death penalty. Earlier in the year a 'popular' politician had brought an elderly Senator to trial for the killing of a seditious Tribune in 100. The Senate might vote for the execution of the five plotters, but as prime mover and executive Cicero would become the target for reprisals. He was alive to the danger, and many years later recalled how he had asked his old Praetor, Peducaeus, what he ought to do. Peducaeus replied with a couple of lines from Homer to the effect that this was Cicero's chance to live in history—let him take it.

Accounts of the debate are inconsistent in detail and unreliable in general. It is certain that Caesar, now Praetor-Elect, spoke powerfully

against a proposal to punish the five by death, which had been supported by the Consulars who had spoken before him; instead he advocated
life imprisonment and forfeiture of property. According to the version
usually accepted, his speech completely turned the tide, until a very
junior Senator, Marcus Cato, turned it back again. But Cicero may
have been right when he maintained in a letter to Atticus nearly
twenty years later that Cato's role was exaggerated in an account
published by his nephew Marcus Brutus; and this account may be
behind the tradition. Cicero himself intervened, after Caesar, and his
speech as he later published it was firm and unequivocal; not so,
according to Plutarch, in the delivery. In the end the Senate voted for
the death motion, as reframed by Cato. The Consul saw to its immediate execution, and announced to an awed crowd: 'They have lived'.

December dark had fallen when he returned to his house through the
narrow streets, surrounded by grandees. Lamps and torches blazed in
his honour from doors and rooftops, and the night was loud with
shouts of 'Saviour' and 'Father of the Fatherland.' It would have been
his apogee, but for that turn of fate which, after twenty years of vanity
and vexation, was to present him with a finer hour.

CHAPTER SIX

After the Fireworks

'It's generally agreed that Pompey is very much my friend.'
Cicero to Atticus (*1 January 61*)

IN the ordinary way of things a Consul went off at the end of his year of office to an allotted province, where for two or three years he would be not only governor but also commander-in-chief of an army, in which latter capacity, provided he could find enemies to fight, he might gain further distinctions—the title of Imperator from his soldiers, a senatorial Vote of Public Thanksgiving (*supplicatio*) in honour of his victories, and (after returning to Italy) the crowning glories of an Ovation or a Triumph. That was normally the end of his regular official career, for it was unconventional in Cicero's day to seek re-election to the Consulship and illegal to do so for ten years. The Consular remained, unless personally inadequate, a leader of the community, available for special assignments such as membership of a state commission or a delegation to a foreign power, but with no prospect of continuous employment. The system helped to maintain equality and solidarity among the ruling oligarchy, but was hard on its abler members; relegated to elder statesmanship at forty-five, they tended to absorb themselves in private luxuries and amusements. Nor did it work in the case of an exceptional individual such as Pompey, standing apart from the oligarchy and ready to defy its rules.

Cicero's position was not that, but it too was peculiar. He had announced that he would not take a province, a decision which may well have been the worst mistake of his career, but for which it was easy to find patriotic excuses. Remaining in Rome, he was a marked man. The suppression of the plot (Catiline was duly liquidated in battle early in the new year) had brought him enormous prestige. At the beginning of each year the new Consuls drew up an order of speaking in the Senate; in 62 Cicero was placed first, above the Optimate leaders (Catulus, Lucullus, Hortensius) and the whole range of senior Consulars. If his head was somewhat turned by such demonstrations, if they led him into dangerous misconceptions, that is not surprising. The climb to the top had proved and exercised his exceptional capacities, but had hardly demanded the political acumen and power of sober personal appraisal which he needed now.

Ever since Gaius Gracchus' reforming Tribunates (123–122), the order of 'Knights' (*equites*), non-senatorial men of wealth and business, had been a recognizable political force often in collision with the governing oligarchy (though not designing to replace it), contending for its own privileges and advantage. In face of Catiline's threat to the economic as well as the political *status quo*, the usual jealousies were suspended. The 'Knights' rallied to Consul and Senate, and on the crucial Nones of December they gathered in numbers on the Capitol with arms in their hands to lend support, headed by none other than Pomponius Atticus. This outbreak of concord among the friends of establishment, the *boni*[1] as they were compendiously called, captured Cicero's imagination. *Concordia ordinum*, 'Harmony of the Orders', became his slogan, its creation his self-proclaimed achievement, its perpetuation his political purpose. By origin a 'Knight' himself, he had owed a great deal to his connexions with the Roman capitalists, especially the great companies farming the collection of state revenues; and his Consulship had made him acknowledged champion of the Senate. The role of mediator was always attractive to Cicero, who liked room for manoeuvre; and in its success he now saw the best guarantee for his own security. There was (there often was) a fatal flaw in his conception: the harmony of 63 could not be expected to last much longer than the situation which produced it. The capitalists had no fundamental interest in maintaining the political creation of their great oppressor Sulla. As Cicero was one day to remark, they were 'never reliable'.

For the time being his main anxiety was Pompey. Shortly after the immortal Nones he sent Pompey a lengthy report on his own actions as Consul and the political situation. The behaviour of Pompey's brother-in-law and lieutenant Metellus Nepos, who had come back from the East to stand for Tribune, was worse than ominous. Upon entering office on 10 December this young nobleman launched a vigorous campaign against Cicero and in favour of recalling Pompey to dispose of Catiline. Cicero had to defend himself. Violent conflicts between Nepos, supported by Caesar (now Praetor), and other

---

[1] Literally 'the good men' (solid citizens, *les gens de bien*). Cicero often referred to their opposites, trouble-makers for the establishment, as *improbi*, 'the rascals'.

Tribunes (including Cato) resulted in another senatorial declaration of martial law and the suspension of both trouble-makers from their offices. Eventually Nepos rejoined Pompey, not before Cicero had received the following from Nepos' brother, Metellus Celer, now (in January) operating against Catiline in his province of Cisalpine Gaul:

In view of our reciprocal sentiments and the restoration of our friendly relations[1] I had not expected that I should be held up by you to ridicule in my absence, or that my brother Metellus would be attacked by you in person or estate because of a phrase. If his personal character did not suffice for his protection, the dignity of our family[2] and my zeal on behalf of you and your friends and the commonwealth should have been support enough. Now it seems that he has been set upon, and I deserted, by those whom it least behoved.

So I wear the black of mourning[3]—I, in command of a province and an army, conducting a war! Well, you and your friends have managed it so, without reason or forbearance. It was not like this in our forebears' time, and it will not be surprising if you all come to be sorry. I did not think to find your own disposition so changeable toward me and mine. In the meanwhile, neither domestic unhappiness nor any man's ill usage shall turn me from the commonwealth.

A spirited but tactful reply from Cicero seems to have smoothed Metellus Celer's aristocratic plumage, for they were afterwards on good terms. More seriously upsetting was a letter from Pompey, in which Cicero's consular achievements (doubtless not diminished in his own telling) were pointedly ignored. He obviously gave a good deal of thought to his answer. After Nepos' behaviour in Rome, Pompey's coldness cannot have taken him altogether by surprise, though he could not ignore so palpable a snub. A break with Pompey, however, was the last thing he wanted. The Optimate ultras might regard Pompey simply as a foe to be fought, but Cicero believed (and here he was right) that Pompey was not really anxious to fight the Senate. For himself such a conflict would be embarrassing, in view of his past record as

---

[1] In his reply Cicero took exception to this expression on the ground that friendly relations had never been interrupted. He also disposed of the other complaints.

[2]
                'In Rome Metelli are ('tis fate)
                elected to the Consulate,'
sang the poet Naevius a century and a half before.

[3] Customary when (e.g.) a near relative was prosecuted on a capital charge. Many people put on mourning for Cicero when Clodius threatened him in 58. There is no reason to take this as a hyperbole on Metellus' part.

Pompey's eulogist, and highly dangerous. The letter he wrote in April 62 made the best of an awkward job:

From Marcus Tullius Cicero, son of Marcus, to Gnaeus Pompeius Magnus,[1] son of Gnaeus, greetings.[2]

I trust all is well with you and the army.[3]

Like everyone else, I was immeasurably delighted with your dispatch, in which you have held out the bright prospect of a peaceful future; such a prospect as I have ever been promising to all and sundry in reliance on your single self. I must tell you, however, that it came as a severe blow to your old enemies, nowadays your friends;[4] their high hopes dashed, they despond.

Your personal letter to me evinces but little of your sentiments toward me, but you may be sure that it gave me pleasure all the same. My chief joy is apt to lie in the consciousness of my services to others. If these fail of a like return, I am excellently well content that the balance of good offices should rest on my side. I have no doubt that if my own hearty goodwill toward you does not suffice to win your attachment, the public interest will join us in confederacy.

Not to leave you in ignorance of the particular in which your letter has disappointed me, let me speak plainly, as becomes my character and our friendly relations. My achievements have been such that I expected to find a word of congratulation upon them in your letter, both for our friendship's sake and that of the commonwealth. I imagine you omitted anything of the sort for fear of giving offence in any quarter.[5] But I must tell you that what I have done for the safety of the commonwealth stands approved in the judgment and testimony of the whole world. When you return, you will find that I have acted with a measure of policy and an absence of self-regard which will make you well content to have me as your political ally and private friend—a not much lesser Laelius to a far greater Africanus.[6]

Pompey's first act on landing in Italy at the end of the year was an

---

[1] Pompey's cognomen Magnus ('the Great'), conferred by his victorious troops in 81 and confirmed by Sulla, was used officially, and in a formal address like this it would have been impolite to omit it. Otherwise Cicero never seems to use it simply as a name without some further implication.

[2] An example of a highly formal letter-heading (headings are normally omitted in this book).

[3] An opening formula in official correspondence. When the writer or addressee is a Proconsul his army is usually included.

[4] A reference to Crassus and Caesar, who, as Cicero implies, would have preferred to see Pompey tied up in the East while they intrigued for power in Rome.

[5] i.e., to people like Caesar who condemned the execution of the conspirators.

[6] Both the elder and the younger Scipio Africanus had a friend called Laelius, but Cicero is doubtless thinking of the younger, destroyer of Carthage in 146.

impressive demonstration of good intent: he disbanded his troops. He
had no desire to be another Marius or Sulla, nor yet the excuses which
they could make for marching Roman legions on Rome. He would not
even use the threat implicit in an army on Italian soil, for the odium of
such a threat might create a situation which would oblige him to
implement it. Let all understand, then, that his objectives were to be
sought from the Senate by constitutional means. These objectives,
immediately, were two: land to settle his disbanded soldiers and the
ratification of his sweeping reorganization of the eastern provinces and
kingdoms. Perhaps he would have obtained them without difficulty but
for the access of confidence given to the Optimates by the events of 63
and the rise of a new spirit of intransigence focused around the stalwart
figure of Marcus Porcius Cato. Cato was still a young man, not much
over thirty, in the earlier stages of an official career. Even with noble
birth and important family connexions in his favour, the authority he
had already begun to command in the Senate is an extraordinary
phenomenon. It was not due to any conspicuous achievement, but to
personal toughness and integrity. Dispirited and drifting Senators
found a rock in Cato—a politician who knew what he stood for and
could neither be terrorized nor bribed. Strict maintenance of constitutional propriety, as seen through Optimate eyes, and the restoration of
standards of conduct in public life, including the government of subject peoples, amounted to something like a political programme, which
gave Cato and his associates a sense of purpose, even if it could not save
the Republic. A skilful tactician, he put principle above expediency.
For him, Pompey was to be opposed and thwarted, not only because of
past affronting of constitutional forms and past and present links with
'popular' elements, but because the individual prominence which
Pompey had acquired, largely in the Senate's teeth, ran counter to
the very essence of an oligarchic régime.

The conflict took time to develop. Cicero, like everyone else,
watched Pompey, at first mistrustfully. One of the Consuls of 61,
Pupius Piso, was Pompey's nominee. He had also been Cicero's
mentor in philosophy, friend, and companion in Athens. It was
provoking, if not disquieting, that Piso elected to demote Cicero from
the first place in senatorial debates to the second. Cicero wrote to
Atticus (now back in Epirus) on 25 January:

... Since you left me there are things that well deserve a letter of mine, but
I must not expose such to the risk of getting lost or opened or intercepted.
First then you may care to know that I have *not* been given first voice in the

Senate, the pacifier of the Allobroges[1] being put in front of me—at which the
House murmured, but I myself was not sorry. I am thereby relieved of any
obligation to be civil to a cross-grained individual, and left free to maintain
my political standing in opposition to his wishes. Moreover, the second place
carries almost as much prestige as the first, while one's inclinations are not
too much fettered by one's sense of the consular favour. Catulus comes third,
Hortensius, if you are still interested, fourth. The Consul himself is of petty
and perverse mentality, given to the sort of peevish sneer that raises a laugh
even in the absence of any wit. His *moue* is funnier than his *mot*. He is
politically inactive and stands aloof from the Optimates, having neither will
to make him useful nor courage to make him dangerous. . . .

And of Pompey in the same letter:

    . . . As to that friend of yours (you know whom I mean? The person of
whom you write to me that he began to praise when he no longer dared to
criticize), he professes the highest regard for me and makes a parade of warm
affection, praising on the surface, while below it (but not so far below that
it's difficult to see) he's jealous. Awkward, tortuous, politically paltry,
shabby, timid, disingenuous—but I shall go more into detail on another
occasion. As yet I am not sufficiently *au fait* with the topic, and I dare not
entrust a letter on such high matters to this who-knows-what of a messenger. . . .

But soon afterwards Pompey spoke in the Senate 'commending in
general terms the decrees of that body,' thus giving the impression,
though with characteristic obliquity, of approval for the Senate's (and
Cicero's) dealings with the Catilinarians. Crassus followed with an
outright eulogy of Cicero (his motive is obscure, but was doubtless
devious). Then:

    . . . As for myself—ye Gods, how I spread my tail in front of my new
audience, Pompey! If ever periods and *clausulae* and enthymemes and
raisonnements came at my call, they did on that occasion. In a word, I
brought the House down. And why not, on such a theme—the dignity of our
order, concord between Senate and Knights, unison of Italy, remnants of the
conspiracy in their death-throes, reduced price of grain, internal peace? You
should know by now how I can boom away on such topics. I think you must

---

[1] Gaius Piso, a kinsman of the Consul. Cicero's periphrasis seems to be sarcastic. The man had been governor of Gaul (see page 28, note 3), and Cicero
had successfully defended him in 63 against a charge of wrongfully executing a
provincial. Such acts of cruelty may have provoked the unrest in Transalpine
Gaul (where the Allobroges were the principle tribe) which the contemporary
governor had to put down.

have caught the reverberations in Epirus, and for that reason I won't dwell on the subject. . . .

Relations with Pompey continued to improve. To Atticus in July:

. . . As for my personal position, it is as follows: With the *boni* I stand as I did when you left, with the dregs of the city populace much better than when you left. . . . There is a further point: this wretched starveling rabble that sucks the treasury dry imagines that I have no rival in the good graces of our Great One. And is it a fact that we have been brought together by a good deal of pleasant personal contact, so much so that these conspirators of the wine-table, our goateed young bloods, have nicknamed him Gnaeus Cicero. Accordingly I get wonderful ovations at games and the gladiators, without a single shepherd's whistle. . . .

Cato and his following will not have looked kindly on this development, though it was not until after Pompey's Triumph, celebrated in September with unprecedented magnificence, that their obstruction of his demands produced a crisis. The divergence between Cicero and his Optimate allies was gradual, and in part the result of events in which Pompey was not primarily involved.

CHAPTER SEVEN

Makings of a Coalition
—and an Exile

'I am defending as best I can the alliance I myself cemented. But as this is all so unreliable, I am building another road, a safe one I hope, to protect my influence. I can't very well explain what I mean in a letter, but a small hint will show: I am on the friendliest terms with Pompey. Yes, I know what you will say. I shall watch the dangers.'

Cicero to Atticus (December 61)

EVEN the name of the mysterious divinity whom Romans called 'the Good Goddess' and Greeks 'the Women's Goddess' was not for masculine ears; and only women might be present at her secret ritual held every year in Rome at the beginning of December. In 62 its locale was the house of Julius Caesar, who was not only City Praetor but had recently been elected head of the state religion (Pontifex Maximus). An untoward incident (how untoward for Cicero time would show) occurred:

> ... I imagine you will have heard that Publius Clodius, son of Appius, was caught dressed up as a woman in Gaius Caesar's house at the national sacrifice, and that he owed his escape alive to the hands of a servant girl—a spectacular scandal. I am sure it distresses you![1] ...

The rumour went that Clodius had come for a rendezvous with Caesar's wife, who was in charge of the ceremonies. Her husband divorced her with the non-committal explanation that 'Caesar's wife must be above suspicion.' But, of course, such an outrage upon a state religious observance called for public action. Clodius was a younger brother of that Appius Claudius to whom Cicero later gave a lesson on the true meaning of nobility, and had powerful friends among his own class; but the Catonians were for bringing him to book, and Cicero agreed, though he had previously been on friendly terms with the young man. After much toing and froing in and out of the

[1] Ironical. Atticus and Cicero both enjoyed a good Roman scandal.

Senate, Clodius was brought to trial in June (61). The case against him was overwhelming, and Cicero himself exploded an alibi put up by the defence (Clodius did not forget). But on account of mismanagement, as Cicero considered, by Cato's connexion Hortensius the jury was open to a different kind of argument. To Atticus in July:

... But if you want to know what sort of trial it was, it was a trial with an incredible outcome; so that others beside myself (who did so from the first) are now criticizing Hortensius' tactics after the event. The challenging of the jury took place amid uproar, with the prosecutor throwing out the most unsavoury characters like an honest Censor,[1] while the defendant put all the more respectable elements on one side like a soft-hearted gladiator-trainer. As soon as the jury took their seats, honest men feared the worst. A more raffish assemblage never sat down in a low-grade music hall—fly-blown Senators, beggar Knights, and Paymaster Tribunes[2] who might better have been called 'Paytakers.' Even so, there were a few honest men whom the accused had not been able to drive off at the challenge. There they sat, gloomy and shamefaced in this incongruous company, sadly uncomfortable at their exposure to such a miasma of disreputability. In these circumstances the strictness and unanimity of the court as various matters were referred to it during the preliminaries was quite astounding. The defendant met with nothing but rebuffs, the prosecutor was repeatedly given more than he asked. In short, Hortensius triumphed in his perspicacity, and nobody but looked on Clodius, not as a man standing his trial, but as one convicted twenty times over. .... Nobody thought the fellow would reply to the indictment.

'Now tell me, Muses nine ... how first the fire did fall.'[3] You know Bald-head, my encomiast, of whose complimentary speech I wrote to you.[4] Inside a couple of days, with a single slave (an ex-gladiator at that) for go-between, he settled the whole business—called them to his house, made promises, backed bills, or paid cash down. On top of that (it's really too abominable) some jurors actually received a bonus in the form of assignations with certain ladies or introductions to youths of noble family. Yet even so, with the *boni* making themselves very scarce and the Forum crowded with slaves, 25 jurors had the courage to take the risk, no small one, preferring to sacrifice their lives rather than the whole community. To 31, on the other

---

[1] The expulsion of bad characters from the Senate and the Order of Knights was a censorial function.

[2] Literally 'not *aerati* ("moneyed") so much as, what they are actually called, *aerarii* ("bribe-takers").' The *tribuni aerarii*, who since 70 had shared the privilege of jury service with Senators and Knights, were originally paymasters to the army. Their functions in Cicero's time are doubtful—it may have been only a matter of a property qualification.

[3] From the Iliad.

[4] See page 40. 'Baldhead' must stand for Crassus.

hand, light purses mattered more than light reputations. Meeting one of them afterwards, Catulus asked him why they wanted us to provide them with a guard—or was it that they were afraid of having their pockets picked? There, then, as briefly as I can manage, you have the quality of the trial and the explanation of the verdict. . . .

The result was felt as a major defeat for the Optimates. No doubt Cicero did not neglect to rub in Hortensius' mistake and his own superior wisdom. A more important difference arose over relations between Senate and Knights, the twin pillars of Cicero's Harmony of Orders. To Atticus in December:

> . . . The state of the commonwealth in which we live here is weak and sad and unstable. I suppose you have heard that our friends the Knights have pretty well broken with the Senate. To begin with, they were greatly annoyed by the promulgation under a senatorial decree of a bill providing for an investigation into the conduct of jurors guilty of taking bribes. I happened to be absent when the decree was voted. Aware that the equestrian order took it amiss, though they said nothing in public, I administered what I felt to be a highly impressive rebuke to the Senate, speaking with no little weight and fluency in a not very respectable cause. Now along come the Knights with another fancy, really almost insupportable—and I have not only borne with it but lent it my eloquence. The tax-farmers who bought the Asiatic taxes from the Censors complained in the Senate that they had been led by over-eagerness into making too high a tender and asked for the cancellation of their contract. I was their foremost supporter, or rather foremost but one, for it was Crassus who egged them on to make such an audacious demand. An invidious business! The demand was disgraceful, a confession of recklessness. But there was the gravest danger of a complete break between Senate and Knights if it had been turned down flat. Here again it was I principally who stepped into the breach. Through my efforts they found the Senate in full attendance and in generous mood, and on the Kalends of December and the day following I discoursed at length upon the dignity and harmony of the two orders. The matter has not yet been settled, but the Senate's attitude was made clear, the only opposing voice being Consul-Designate Metellus.[1] Our doughty champion Cato was to have been another, but dark fell before his turn came. . . .

But Cato persisted. 20 January, 60:

> . . . But all the while, not so much as the shadow of a statesman is to be found. The man who might have been one, my friend (for so he is, let me tell

---

[1] Celer.

you) Pompey, lives up to that lovely embroidered toga of his[1] by holding his tongue. From Crassus not a word that might lose him popularity. The others you know. They seem fools enough to expect to keep their fish-ponds after losing constitutional freedom. The one man who cares for that, with more resolution and integrity, it seems to me, than judgment or intelligence, is Cato. He has now been over two months tormenting the unfortunate tax-farmers, who were his devoted friends, and won't let the Senate give them an answer. . . .

A letter of the following June expands the criticism:

. . . As for our friend Cato, I have as warm a regard for him as you. The fact remains that with all his patriotism and integrity he is sometimes a political liability. He speaks in the Senate as though he were living in Plato's Republic instead of Romulus' cesspool. What could be fairer than that jurors who take bribes should themselves be brought to trial? Cato moved accordingly, and the Senate agreed. Result, the Knights declare war upon the House—not upon me, for I was against it. Could anything be more shameless than tax-farmers repudiating their contract? All the same the loss was worth standing to keep the Order on our side. Cato opposed, and carried his point. So now we see a Consul shut up in gaol[2] and one riot following another, while not one of the men who used to rally round me and the Consuls my successors for the defence of the state lifts a finger. Are we then to keep these fellows as mercenaries? What else, if we can't keep them on any other terms? Or should we take orders from our freedmen, even our slaves? But, as you would say, *trêve de sérieux.* . . .

Cato could have replied that the Harmony of Orders, precarious at best, was not worth a sacrifice of principle. The looseness of the Roman governmental system lent itself only too easily to a *laissez-faire* in which any powerful group could push its interests at the ultimate expense of Rome's subjects. But there was more to divide Cicero and Cato than a disagreement on policy, though in writing to Atticus, a close friend of Cato and his circle, Cicero had to be careful. Cato's prestige was an irritant to him, and Cato's mentality uncongenial. Probably about a year later Cicero published (no doubt with some retouchings) a speech he had made during his Consulship in defence of one of his elected successors on a charge of bribery, Cato being one of

[1] A law passed in 63 at Caesar's instance and against Cato's opposition authorized Pompey to wear triumphal insignia, including the 'painted toga', at the public shows. Pompey was showing his appreciation of the privilege by refraining from any word against Caesar's friends.

[2] Metellus Celer had been hauled off to prison by the Tribune Flavius for obstructing an agrarian bill which Flavius was pressing in Pompey's interest.

the prosecutors. The delicate mockery of Cato's Stoic inflexibilities is one of the best examples of Ciceronian wit. There was laughter in court, and Cato is said to have observed to his neighbours with a smile, 'What an amusing Consul we have!' Perhaps the smile was a trifle sour.

Then there were the 'fish-fanciers'—senior Optimates like Hortensius and Lucullus who 'think they have transcended the summit of human ambition if the bearded mullet in their fish-ponds feed out of their hands.' The parvenu Consular, with his ostentatious new city mansion,[1] his sharp tongue, and his too frequent allusions to his own patriotic services, provoked their 'jealousy' (Cicero's word).

He felt lonely when Atticus was away. His transformation from candidate to premier Consular had not changed their friendship. That says something for them both, though Atticus' original advantage in age, superior wealth, cool temperament, and a formidable quality behind his urbanity, will have helped to maintain an equilibrium. Cicero respected as well as liked him:

> ... What may be called ambition has led me to seek political advancement, while another and entirely justifiable way of thinking has led you to an honourable independence. In the things that really matter—uprightness, integrity, conscientiousness, fidelity to obligation—I put you second neither to myself nor to any other man. . . .

This does not sound like flattery, neither does the following a month or so later (January 60):

> I must tell you that what I most badly need at the present time is a confidant—someone with whom I could share all that gives me any anxiety, a wise, affectionate friend to whom I could talk without pretence or evasion or concealment. My brother, the soul of candour and affection, is away.[2] *[3] is not a *person* at all, only 'sea-shore and air' and 'mere solitude'.[4] And you, whose talk and advice have so often lightened my worry and vexation of spirit,

---

[1] On the Palatine, just bought from Crassus for an enormous sum. The money was largely put up by Publius Sulla, a shady nobleman whom Cicero had defended on a charge of complicity with Catiline. The remark in a letter of January 61 might have made a motto for the gates of Hughenden: 'Folk have begun to realise that it's legitimate to make a respectable show in the world with purchases financed by one's friends.'

[2] Quintus was governor of Asia (the Roman province, western Asia Minor) in 61–58.

[3] The manuscripts have 'Metellus' (i.e., the Consul Metellus Celer). Many editors hold that the name is a copyist's error, but it is just possible that Cicero refers to something in a letter of Atticus, who was a friend of Celer's.

[4] Apparently quoted from a Latin play.

the partner of my public life and intimate of all my private concerns, the sharer of all my talk and plans, where are you? I am so utterly forsaken that my only moments of relaxation are those I spend with my wife, my little daughter, and my darling Marcus. My brilliant, wordly friendships may make a fine show in public, but in the home they are barren things. My house is crammed of a morning, I go down to the Forum surrounded by droves of friends, but in all the multitude I cannot find one with whom I can pass an unguarded joke or fetch a private sigh. That is why I am waiting and longing for you, why I now fairly summon you home. There are many things to worry and vex me, but once I have you here to listen, I feel I can pour them all away in a single walk and talk. . . .

One consolation was to think and write of the glory of 63. To Atticus in March 60:

. . . I am sending you a sketch[1] of my Consulship in Greek. If there is anything in it that may appear un-Greek or unscholarly to a man of Attica, I shan't say what Lucullus said to you, at Panhormus[2] I think, about his history, that he had sprinkled a few barbarisms and solecisms to make his readers more willing to believe that it was written by a Roman. Anything of that sort in *my* work will be unintended and regretted. If I do a Latin version, I shall send it to you. As a third item you may expect a poem, not to leave any form of singing my own praises unattempted. . . .

Atticus too wrote a Greek 'sketch' on the subject which came into Cicero's hands after he had sent off his own:

. . . I was glad when I got it that I had given Lucius Cossinius a piece on the same topic, likewise in Greek, to take to you some time before. Otherwise, if I had read yours first, you would be accusing me of plagiary. Actually though, your piece, which I have read with pleasure, struck me as a trifle rough and unkempt, but it was embellished by its very neglect of ornament and seemed fragrant because odourless, as with the ladies. . . .

Cicero sent his own effort to the great Posidonius in Rhodes 'with the idea that he might compose something more elaborate on the same theme.' Posidonius replied tactfully that 'so far from being stimulated to composition he was effectively frightened away:'

. . . The fact is, I have dumbfounded the whole Greek community, so that the folk who were pressing me on all sides to give them something to dress up are pestering me no longer. If you like the book, please see that it is made

[1] The Greek and Latin words used by Cicero in this connexion signify a memorandum without literary pretensions, raw material for a full-fledged 'history.' In fact Cicero's piece was an elaborate, rhetorical performance.

[2] Modern Palermo.

available at Athens and the other Greek towns. I think it may add some lustre to my achievements. . . .

We hear no more of the prose 'sketch' in Latin, but the poem 'On his Consulship' was completed in three 'books.' Three lines from the conclusion are cited below.

In pique, in policy disagreement, in self-protection, and (as he told himself and Atticus) in regard for the public welfare, Cicero continued his cultivation of Pompey, even when this began to look like a *volte-face*. Atticus was worried, perhaps with memories of his own conciliatory activities in 64, and Cicero tried to reassure him (June 60):

. . . In a mild sort of way you take me to task for my friendly relations with Pompey. I should not wish you to think I had drawn close to him for my own protection. The position, however, was that any dissension which might have arisen between us would inevitably have brought major political conflicts in its train. If I have foreseen and provided against this danger, that does not mean that I have abandoned my own constitutionalist policy, but that *he* has become more constitutionally minded and less inclined to court popularity with the masses at the cost of principle. You may be interested to learn that he eulogizes my achievements, which many persons had prompted him to attack, in far more glowing terms than his own, acknowledging himself as a good servant of the state but me as its saviour. How much *I* gain by his doing so I hardly know, but there is certainly a gain to the commonwealth. Supposing I manage to make a better citizen even of Caesar, who is riding on the crest of the wave just now, am I harming the state so very much? . . .

The logic of their orbits was propelling Pompey and Caesar into conjunction, but not as 'better citizens' under Cicero's suasion. The Senate would not give Pompey what he wanted voluntarily. Caesar (with Pompey's backing) could coerce them in Pompey's interests and his own. He returned in June from a successful spell as governor of Further Spain, to be elected Consul for 59 against strong Optimate opposition. A paragraph in a letter of December foreshadows the future:

. . . I come now to the month of January and *la base de ma politique*. I shall argue thereupon *in utramque partem à la Socrate*, but in the end, according to the practice of the school, shall declare my preference. It is certainly a matter for careful consideration. Either I put up a stout resistance to the agrarian law,[1] which means something of a struggle but an honourable one, or I lie

[1] Caesar's first agrarian law, which he put before the Senate early in his Consulship, mainly to find land for Pompey's soldiers. It proved inadequate, and in April he had to supplement it.

low, which is nearly tantamount to retiring to Antium or Solonium, or I actually lend it my assistance, as they say that Caesar confidently expects me to do. I have had a visit from Cornelius,[1] Balbus I mean, Caesar's intimate. He assured me that Caesar will follow Pompey's and my advice in all things and will try to bring Pompey and Crassus together. This course offers the following advantages; intimate association with Pompey, and with Caesar too if I want it, peace with the populace, tranquillity in my old age. But I can't forget my finale in Book III:

> 'Meantime the paths which thou from earliest days didst seek,
> Aye, and when Consul too, as mood and virtue bade,
> These hold, and foster still thy fame and good men's praise.'

Such was Calliope's[2] own lesson to me in a book which contains many aristocratic sentiments. So I don't think I can hesitate. I must always find 'one omen best: to fight for fatherland.'[3]

But let us keep all this for our strolls together at the Compitalia.[4] Remember the day before. I shall have the bath heated. Terentia invites Pomponia as well, and we shall have your mother over too. Please bring me Theophrastus 'On Ambition' from Quintus' library.

---

[1] Lucius Cornelius Balbus of Gades (Cadiz), who had come to Rome in 71 under Pompey's patronage and obtained Roman citizenship. Subsequently he was closely associated with Caesar as confidential agent and adviser.

[2] The Muse. Cicero (like Propertius after him) put a speech into her mouth addressed to himself, the poet.

[3] Hector's famous saying in the Iliad.

[4] 'Festival of the Crossroads,' held this winter on 1 January.

CHAPTER EIGHT

The Three, and Clodius

'I remember the advice you gave me then through Theophanes and through Culleo, and I have often remembered it with bitter regret.'

Cicero to Atticus (49)

THE coalition between Pompey, Caesar, and Crassus sometimes called the 'First Triumvirate' (though it never had any official status) changed the face of Roman politics. Pompey's prestige and veterans, Caesar's hold on the city populace and authority as Consul, and Crassus' money were combined into a concentration of power before which a Senate majority was helpless. With the aid of a Tribune, Vatinius, Caesar proceeded to push a legislative programme through the popular assemblies. Amongst other things it satisfied the requirements of Pompey and the tax-farmers (patronized by Crassus) and established himself in a five year command covering the Gallic provinces of North Italy and southern France along with the east-Adriatic coastline. His colleague Calpurnius Bibulus, who married Cato's daughter, put up a tough opposition. After nearly losing his life in a Forum riot he shut himself up in his house and imposed a constitutional veto on Caesar's lawmaking by announcing that he proposed to 'watch the skies' (for unfavourable omens) whenever the assemblies could meet for legislative purposes. Caesar and Vatinius took no notice, with the consequence that for Bibulus and his friends their laws were not laws at all.

Cicero could blame Cato for all this, but his own position was unenviable. His efforts to mediate and balance had achieved nothing but his own isolation. The dynasts would have been glad to get him on their side. The trio might have become a quartette. But it was one thing to be Pompey's, or even Caesar's, better angel, another to join a conspiracy against the constitution. Balbus' overtures led nowhere.

During the first three months of 59 we have no letters. Cicero seems to have tried to re-establish himself with the Optimates, and in March publicly attacked Caesar and his associates, naming no names. Retaliation was prompt. Young Publius Clodius was determined to have his revenge for Cicero's part in the affair of the Good Goddess. He was blossoming into a formidable demagogue, leagued with certain proletarian guilds or clubs[1] and able at will to launch gangs of roughs upon the streets. His object was to be elected Tribune, but there was a legal block. The office of Tribune of the Plebs had been created in the early years of the Republic to protect the commons against the ruling patrician nobility, and no patrician could hold it. But Clodius belonged to the patrician Claudii ('Clodius' was a popular variation of the name). For a year past he had been trying in vain to acquire plebeian status one way or another. Now he succeeded, Caesar and Pompey operating the necessary machinery. Cicero had good reason to feel apprehensive at the prospect (duly fulfilled) of Clodius' election to the Tribunate for 58. He went off to his house in Antium (Anzio) determined to retire from politics, at least for the time being, and devote himself to literature. A number of his letters to Atticus reiterate the decision:

... But why ask all these questions, when I want to put all such matters aside and concentrate my whole time and energy on study? Yes, that is what I intend. I wish I had done so from the first. Now, having discovered by experience the emptiness of all the things I prized most highly, I mean to concern myself with all the Muses. ...

He thought of writing a book on geography, but the subject palled:

I promised you in an earlier letter that there would be work to show for this spell away from home, but I am no longer very positive on the point. I have taken so kindly to idleness that I can't tear myself away from it. So I either amuse myself with books, of which I have a goodly store in Antium, or I count the waves—the weather is unsuitable for fishing mackerel. To writing I feel a downright repugnance. The Geography which I had purposed is really a big undertaking. ... And really the material is hard to set out, monotonous, not so easy to embellish as it looked, and (this is the main point) I find any excuse good enough for doing nothing. I had sooner have been Duovir[2] here than Consul in Rome. You were wiser than I in getting a house at Buthrotum.[3] Yet I can assure you there is not much to choose between that town and this community of Antium. One can hardly believe that there could be a place so near Rome where many of the inhabitants have never seen Vatinius, where no member of the Board of Twenty[4] has a single well-wisher

---

[1] These *collegia*, or some of them, had been officially dissolved by the Senate in 64. Clodius restored them in 58.
[2] Chief magistrate. As the word implied, there were two of them at Antium, corresponding (to compare small with great) to the Roman Consuls.
[3] Town near Atticus' estate in Epirus.
[4] Set up to implement Caesar's agrarian laws.

besides myself, where nobody disturbs me and everybody likes me. Yes, this is surely the place to practise politics. In Rome that is impossible, and what is more I am sick of it. So I shall compose *histoires inédites* which I shall read to nobody but you, in the vein of Theopompus[1] or a lot more savage even. And my sole form of political activity now is to hate the rascals, and even that I do without spleen. . . .

From Antium Cicero passed on to Formiae further down the coast —a less tranquil neighbourhood. About 26 April:

. . . You are always urging me to composition, but it's out of the question. It's not a country house I have here but a public exchange, so many of the good folk of Formiae come in. . . . But never mind the multitude—after 10 o'clock the common run doesn't bother me. But my closest neighbour is one Gaius Arrius, or rather room-mate, for that is what he has now become. He actually says he won't go to Rome because he wants to talk literature with me here all day long. Then on the other side there is Catulus' friend Sebosus. Where is a man to turn? I would go to Arpinum right away upon my word, only it's clearly most convenient for me to expect you at Formiae—up to 6 May that is, no longer, for look at the kind of people I am condemned to listen to! What a marvellous opportunity for anyone who might be interested in buying my place here while these fellows are on my carpet! And yet you say, and very fine too, 'Let's attack something big, something that needs plenty of thought and time.' However, I shan't disappoint you nor spare my pains.

A day or two later:

. . . Just as I was writing these lines—there was Sebosus! I had hardly finished when 'Good morning to you' says Arrius. And this is getting away from Rome and people! There's the frying-pan and here's the fire! Well, I shall go to 'my native hills, the cradle of my being.'[2] If the worst comes to the worst and solitude is unattainable, better the society of country folk than of these hyper-sophisticates. . . .

He even toyed with the idea of going abroad. Caesar, who liked Cicero personally, would have co-operated by giving him a public status—a mission to King Ptolemy XII of Egypt was one possibility:

Yes, I am eager and have been for long enough to visit Alexandria and the rest of Egypt and at the same time to get away from this part of the world where people are tired of me and to come back when they have begun to miss me a little. But at the present time, and the authors of the mission being who

[1] Fourth-century Greek historian with a reputation for censoriousness.
[2] Quoted (probably) from Ennius.

they are, 'I fear the Trojans and their long-gowned wives.'[1] What will our Optimates say, if there are any left? Perhaps that I have been somehow bribed to change my views. 'Polydamas will cry me shame the first'[2]—I mean our friend Cato who is 'one worth a hundred thousand'[3] in my eyes. And what will history say of me a thousand years hence? I am far more in awe of that than of the tittle-tattle of my contemporaries. But I think I had better wait and see. If the offer is made, that will give me some sort of latitude, and then will be the time to deliberate. Also, dash it all, there is some glory in not accepting. So if Theophanes[4] happens to say something to you, don't turn it down out of hand. . . .

At the same time Cicero seized avidly on every scrap of political gossip. Reports of trouble between the dynasts and the younger generation, including Clodius himself, were especially stimulating:

. . . You may be interested to hear that young Curio has called on me to pay his respects. What he had to say about Pompey chimed in very well with your letter. He himself 'hates proud grandees'[5] quite remarkably. He told me that the younger set generally are no less incensed and impatient of the present régime. A fine predicament we are in if our hopes rest on them! I think we may as well find other things to think about. *I* am devoting myself to history —except that, though you are welcome to think me a Saufeius,[6] I am the idlest of mortals. . . .

On the way to Formiae:

. . . Now observe a coincidence. I had just come out of the Antium district and joined the Appian Way at Tres Tabernae, on Ceres' day[7] actually, when my young friend Curio runs into me on his way from Rome. At that very point along comes a boy[8] from you with letters. Curio asked me whether I had

[1] From Hector's soliloquy in the Iliad—a favourite quotation. 'Fear' = 'fear what they would say.'

[2] From the same speech.

[3] From a Greek proverb (Cicero quotes it elsewhere in the original, 'One to me is worth tens of thousands') going back to the philosopher Heraclitus.

[4] Theophanes of Mitylene, one of Pompey's intimates. He wrote an account of Pompey's eastern campaigns.

[5] From the satirist Lucilius, who died a few years after Cicero was born, quoted more fully in another letter:

'Granius now
Knew his own worth and hated proud grandees.'

Granius was an auctioneer, celebrated for his tart answers to the great men of his day. In the original the word *reges* ('grandees', literally 'kings') means simply 'great persons', but Cicero gets in a hit at Rome's tyrants, the 'Triumvirs.' The tag was a favourite with Atticus.

[6] This Epicurean friend of Atticus was a busy writer.

[7] 19 April.

[8] i.e., a slave.

heard the news. I said no. 'Publius,'[1] says he, 'is standing for Tribune.' 'No, really?' 'Yes, and as Caesar's deadly enemy, and means to undo everything they've done.' 'What about Caesar?' 'Says he had nothing to do with proposing Publius' adoption.'[2] He went on to declare his own hostility and Memmius' and Metellus Nepos'. I bade the young fellow an affectionate good-bye, in a hurry to get to the letters. What nonsense that is about the living voice![3] I get an infinitely better idea from your letter than from his talk of what is going on—The day-to-day cud-chewing, Publius' plans, with Lady Ox-Eyes[4] to blow the bugle and Athenio[5] carrying the flag, the letter to Gnaeus,[6] Theophanes' and Memmius' talk. And how you whet my curiosity about that dissipated dinner party! I'm ravenous! . . .

It might seem a good moment to try to patch things up with Clodius, and that appears to have been the object of some obscure exchanges between Atticus and Clodius' sister, of whom according to Plutarch Terentia had some reason to feel jealous. But they came to nothing. Cicero affected to take the threat to himself lightly, and Pompey assured him that Clodius would be kept in check. If Pompey broke his word, so much the better, wrote Cicero:

. . . If, however, the bargain as respects myself is not observed, I am *in excelsis*—just wait till our friend from Jerusalem,[7] who manufactures plebeians so easily, learns what a fine return he has made for my toadying speeches![8] You may expect a superlative palinode. . . . It is plain enough to me now to what quarter the wind of unpopularity is veering and where it will set. You can say I have learned nothing from experience and nothing from Theophrastus[9] if you don't soon see people regretting the old days when I was in the saddle. For if the dominance of the Senate was unpopular, what do you think the reaction is going to be now that power has been brought down, not to the people, but to three exorbitant individuals? Let them make Consuls and Tribunes of whom they please, let them drape Vatinius' scrofulous back with a

[1] Clodius.

[2] Clodius had become a plebeian by means of a factitious adoption.

[3] That the 'living voice' was more effective than the written word was a common saying.

[4] Clodius' sister, Clodia. In Homer 'Ox-Eyed' is a stock epithet for Hera, the wife of her brother Zeus. Hence, besides the fact that Clodia did have unusually bright eyes, the point of the nickname.

[5] A nickname. The person meant is probably Clodius' lieutenant Sextus Cloelius (not 'Clodius'; see page 230, note 4). Athenio was a leader in the Sicilian slave revolt of 104–100.

[6] Pompey (Gnaeus Pompeius).

[7] Pompey, whose troops had captured Jerusalem in 63.

[8] Cicero means that he will publicly make Pompey ashamed of his ingratitude.

[9] Greek philosopher, who like his master Aristotle took all knowledge (or a great deal of it) for his province, including politics.

priest's double-dyed toga—you will soon see not only those who never put a foot wrong, but Cato himself, the one who blundered, emerge as national heroes. . . .

How amusing, though, if Clodius' Tribunate were to turn out a thorn in his backers' flesh!

. . . Bibulus' action in holding up the elections may be very noble, but what does it achieve except a personal protest which offers no solution to the country's troubles? Depend upon it, Publius is our only hope. Yes, let him become Tribune, if only to bring you back the sooner from Epirus. I don't see how you could possibly bear to miss him, especially if it turns out that he wants an argument with me. But of course you will hurry back if anything of that sort happens. But even if it doesn't, I promise myself a magnificent show . . .—if only I can watch it with you in the next seat! . . .

All this jauntiness barely disguises his discomfort. While denouncing the dynasts, Cicero lacked the consolation of solidarity with the brow-beaten Optimates. And he could not reconcile himself to his own impotence.

. . . Perhaps Pompey will say: 'I'll keep you all under with Caesar's army.' Oh no you won't! It won't be that army of yours that will keep *me* under so much as the ingratitude of the so-called *boni*, who have never made me the slightest return or recompense, material or even verbal. But if I had urged myself in that direction, I should surely have found some method of opposition before now. . . .

Later (in July) he had found a different excuse:

. . . The truth is that the present régime is the most infamous, disgraceful, and universally odious to all sorts and classes and ages of men that ever was, more so upon my word than I could have wished, let alone expected. These 'popular' politicians have taught even quiet folk to hiss. Bibulus is *in excelsis*, I don't know why, but they laud him as though he were the man who 'singly by his delaying saved our all.'[1] My beloved Pompey, to my great sorrow, has been the author of his own downfall. They hold nobody by goodwill; that they may find it necessary to use terror is what I am afraid of. For my part I do not fight what they are doing on account of my friendship with him, and I do not endorse it, for that would be to condemn all I did in days gone by. I take a middle way. . . .

In the last letter addressed to Atticus (early in May) before he left for

[1] Ennius' famous line on Fabius the Delayer, the first Roman general to check Hannibal in the Second Punic War.

Greece professions of philosophic unconcern end on an incongruous note of anxiety about relations with Pompey:

> I am entirely of your opinion. Sampsiceramus[1] is out for trouble. We can expect anything. He is confessedly working for absolute power. What else signifies this sudden marriage connexion[2] . . . ? If all this were the end it would be worse than bad enough, but in the nature of the case it cannot be the end. They can't like these measures in and for themselves. They would never have come so far if they were not paving their way to other and disastrous objectives. However, as you say, we shall bewail all this at Arpinum on 10 May or thereabouts, or rather *not* bewail it, for that would mean that our studies had been a waste of time and trouble, but talk it over in a tranquil spirit. My spirit, heaven knows, is tranquil enough. Nor is it optimism that consoles me, as in time past, so much as indifference, a state of mind I particularly cultivate in these public and political matters. Indeed a certain foolish vanity to which I am somewhat prone (it's a fine thing to know one's failings) is actually gratified in a way. I used to be piqued by the thought that a thousand years hence Sampsiceramus' services to Rome might be rated higher than mine. I can now rest easy on *that* score. The flop of his reputation makes Curius' 'Girl from Phocis'[3] look like a popular hit. But we will talk over all this when we meet. However, it looks to me as though you will still be in Rome when I get back, and I should really just as soon you were, if you can conveniently manage it. But if you do come as you say you will, would you kindly fish out of Theophanes how our Arabian Prince[4] is disposed toward me? You will of course make your enquiries as a relative, and bring me a doctor's prescription as it were from him on how to conduct myself. We shall be able to get some inkling of the general situation from what he says.

In fact the two friends did not meet in Arpinum, and Atticus seems to have left Rome before Cicero's return at the end of May. But he sent some advice through Theophanes and another friend of Pompey's to the effect that Cicero had better make terms with the dynasts while he could.[5] It was not heeded. Nor did Cicero stick to his resolution to lead a life of study. In August or September he was again the busy advocate:

---

[1] Another oriental nickname for Pompey; actually the ruler of a district in Syria.

[2] Pompey had just married Caesar's daughter Julia.

[3] Perhaps the title of a stage flop.

[4] Pompey again.

[5] The advice may not have been very emphatic or definite (see my edition of the Letters to Atticus, Vol. I, pages 17 f.).

... My present mode of life is such as daily to increase my popularity and resources. I keep absolutely clear of politics, devoting myself industriously to my cases and forensic work, which I perceive to be a fine road to the favour not only of those who use my services but of the general public as well. My house is thronged with visitors, people come up to me recalling my Consulship and professing active good will. I am becoming so sanguine that there are times when the impending struggle seems to me something I ought not to try to avoid. . . .

Caesar had continued to make overtures, but to no purpose. June 59:

... But I have no stomach for more about politics. I'm out of humour with myself, and writing is most painful. I keep my head above water, not so abjectly in view of the general subjugation, but less boldly than befits my past. Caesar is inviting me very handsomely to accept that Commissionership, the one on his staff, and I am also offered a Free Commission in Discharge of Vow.[1] But the protection offered by the latter, resting on Pretty-Boy's[2] sense of decency, is insufficient and it takes me away just when my brother will be coming home. The former is safer and does not prevent my being in Rome when I want. I have this in the bag, but I don't think I shall use it. Still, nobody knows. I have no inclination to run away, I am spoiling for a fight. I have strong public backing. But I make no promises. You will keep this to yourself. . . .

Again in the first half of July:

... When Cosconius[3] died I was invited to take his place. That would have been what is called stepping into the breach—a signal public disgrace, and worse than useless even as regards 'security'. For they are unpopular with the *boni*, I with the rascals. I should have kept my own unpopularity and accepted other people's as well. Caesar wants to have me on his staff. That would be a more respectable evasion of the danger, which however I do not decline. It comes to this, I would rather fight. But my mind is not made up. Again I say, 'If only you were here!' However, if the need arises I shall send for you. . . .

As for Clodius (and Pompey) the letters of July and August speak for themselves:

... Clodius' threats and the combats I have to expect give me only moderate concern, for I think I can either face them with all honour or decline them

---

[1] A senator wishing to travel abroad on private business might apply for a 'Free Commission' (*libera legatio*). The commission was called 'votive' if the business was supposed to be the discharge of a vow at some foreign sanctuary.

[2] Clodius' family surname (cognomen) Pulcher means 'handsome.' Cicero sometimes refers to him with the diminutive Pulchellus.

[3] A member of the agrarian Board of Twenty (see page 51, note 4).

without embarrassment. Perhaps you will say that we have had enough of honour—*le siècle du gland est passé*[1]—and implore me to think of security. Oh dear, why are you not here? Nothing, I am sure would escape you, whereas I perhaps am blind and hold too fast to that which is good. . . . Dear Publius is threatening me, most hostile. The business is looming, and you will naturally make haste back to meet it. I think I have very firm backing in my old consular army of all good men, including the moderately good. Pompey signifies good-will toward me out of the ordinary. He also assures me that Clodius will not say a word about me, wherein he does not deceive me but is himself deceived. . . .

. . . Clodius is still threatening trouble. Pompey says there is no danger, he swears it. He even adds that Clodius will attack me over his dead body. Negotiations proceed. As soon as there is anything definite I shall write to you. If there has to be a fight, I shall send for you to take your share in the work; but if I am let live in peace, I shall not drag you away from Amalthea[2]. . . .

. . . Clodius is hostile. Pompey continues to assure me that he will do nothing against me. It would be dangerous for me to believe that, and I am getting ready to defend myself. I hope to have strong support from all classes. I miss you, and the facts of the case call for your return to meet the crisis. Your presence at the pinch will strengthen me vastly in policy and courage and actual defensive power. I am well satisfied with Varro.[3] Pompey talks marvellously. I hope I shall at least come out of it with much honour, or actually avoid any unpleasantness. . . .

Oh, how I wish you were in Rome! No doubt you would have stayed if we had expected all this to happen. Then it would be easy for us to keep Pretty-Boy in hand, or at least we should be able to find out what he is up to. Now the picture is as follows: He rushes wildly up and down, without any definite programme, threatening numbers of folk with this, that, and the other. Apparently he will take whatever line chance puts in his way. When he notices how the present régime is detested he makes as though to attack its

[1] So Cicero's Greek proverb is rendered (from Voltaire) in an earlier translation.

[2] Atticus had a temple and garden on his estate in Epirus dedicated to the nymph Amalthea.

[3] The famous polymath. As a soldier and politician he was closely attached to Pompey. Cicero explains in a later letter: 'When I praise one of your friends to you, you may take it that I want you to let him know I have done so. The other day you, remember, I wrote to you about Varro's good offices toward me, and you wrote back that you were delighted to hear of it. But I would rather you had written to *him* that I was well content with him, not that this really *was* so but that it might become so. He is a strange person, as you know, "crooked in mind and naught sincere." But I am holding to the old maxim "To bear with rulers . . .".'

authors; then again, when he remembers their power and ruthlessness and the armies behind them, he turns upon the *boni*. Myself he threatens sometimes with violence, sometimes with the law courts. Pompey has spoken to him, strongly, as he himself informed me (I have no other witness), telling him that he, Pompey, would be branded as a traitor and a villain if I were brought into jeopardy by one whose weapons he had himself furnished in allowing his transfer to the plebs. But both Clodius and Appius had given him their words in respect of me. If Clodius did not honour his pledge, he, Pompey, would so react that the pre-eminent importance of our friendship in his eyes would be obvious to all. To this and more of the same kind, said Pompey, Clodius at first made very considerable demur, but in the end capitulated and gave an assurance that he would take no step contrary to Pompey's wishes. But since that conversation he has continued none the less to use most offensive language about me. Even if he did not, I should not trust him a yard and should make all preparations, as I am doing. . . .

. . . As for me (a subject on which I am sure you are anxious to be informed), I take no part in political deliberations, devoting myself entirely to court business and work. In consequence, as may be easily supposed, I hear a good deal of nostalgic reminiscing on my old exploits. But our Lady Ox-Eyes' nearest and dearest[1] flings out formidable threats of wrath to come, denying this to Sampsiceramus but flaunting it ostentatiously before all else. Therefore, if you love me as much as I am sure you do: if you are asleep, wake up! If you are standing still, walk! If you are walking, run! If you are running, fly! You cannot believe how much I rely on your advice and knowledge of the world, and most valuable of all, your affection and loyalty. The importance of the issue perhaps calls for lengthy exposition, but in the unison of our hearts a few words will suffice. It is of the utmost consequence to me that you should be in Rome—if you can't manage it for the elections, then at any rate after he has been returned. Take care of your health.

. . . Pompey tells me not to worry about Clodius, and expresses the most cordial sentiments toward me in everything he says. I very much wish to have you with me to advise me on my tactics, to share my anxieties, to join in everything I have in mind. I have asked Numestius to speak to you about this; and myself ask you likewise, if possible more emphatically, to *fly* to my side. I shall breathe again once I see you.

The last letter of this series, probably written in September, ends with yet another appeal for Atticus' immediate return:

. . . I expect you are already on your way or nearly home after the appeal in my last letter. I am waiting for you impatiently and miss you sorely, but the facts and the hour demand your return no less loudly than I. On affairs here I

---

[1] Clodius, with the usual implication about his relationship with Clodia.

can only repeat what I have so often written. The commonwealth is in truly desperate plight, and the hatred for those responsible is unparalleled. I myself, as I think and hope and forecast, am protected by a powerful bastion of general good will. So make speed. You will either get me out of all unpleasantness or share it. I say less than I might because I hope that we shall soon be able to discuss what we want together. Take care of your health.

But Atticus was in no great hurry—perhaps he felt that too much was expected of him. Shrewder and more detached than Cicero, he will have realized that neither Pompey's assurances nor the support of the *boni* gave safe cover against the gathering storm. No doubt Cicero retained his popularity among the Roman and Italian bourgoisie, but how was it to be mobilized? Cato and his friends could hardly be expected to fight *à outrance* to defend so uncertain an ally as Cicero had proved. Atticus had already recommended prudence; but the line between prudence and humiliating surrender was hard to draw, especially after all his past exhortations to political consistency.

To judge from a letter to his brother written after Clodius' election Cicero's confidence continued to rise—or was he whistling in the dark?

. . . As for my own prospects, I do not think I shall lack general support. It is amazing how people are coming forward with declarations and offers and promises. For my own part, I am in good hope and even better courage— hope, because I am confident I shall win; courage, because in the present state of the country I am not afraid of anything that may betide. Anyhow, this is how things stand: if Clodius takes me to court, all Italy will rally and I shall come off with enhanced credit; if he tries force, I trust to oppose him with force, supported not only by my friends but by outsiders as well. Everyone is pledging his friends, dependants, freedmen, slaves, even money. My old band of *boni* is passionately enthusiastic and loyal. Those who were formerly not so well disposed or not so energetic are now joining the *boni* in their disgust with our present tyrants. Pompey is lavish of promises, and so is Caesar. If I take their word, I do not on that account relax my preparations in the slightest. The Tribunes-Elect are my good friends. The Consuls show every sign of good will. Among the Praetors I can count on Domitius, Nigidius, Memmius, and Lentulus as warm friends and vigorous patriots— others too are well enough, but these are outstanding. Courage then, and good cheer! . . .

What followed is to be made out only dimly, for with Atticus back in Rome the correspondence dries up and later sources tell different stories. We hear of yet another offer by Caesar, presently to set out for

Gaul, of a post on his staff. According to one account Cicero had asked for the position and accepted it, but withdrew his acceptance when Clodius, with his prey on the point of escaping, pretended to be ready for a reconciliation. If so, Caesar's exasperation would be understandable. But Caesar was a man of calculation, and he had an excellent political reason for wanting Cicero out of Rome one way or another. He had already gained a great deal from his alliance with Pompey, but it was essential to keep it going; and Pompey, though he had recently married Caesar's daughter, was never to be depended upon. Caesar had given Pompey results, but by violent and illegal methods little to Pompey's taste. Pompey felt his unpopularity, and had been deeply hurt by scathing manifestos from the Optimate Consul Bibulus. He confided his unhappiness to Cicero, who had written to Atticus late in the summer:

. . . First then I want you to know that our friend Sampsiceramus is bitterly unhappy about his position and longs to get back to where he stood before his fall from grace; he confides his distress to me and sometimes openly casts about for a remedy, but I don't think there is any to be found. . .

Pompey and Cicero always had for one another the basic sympathy that is apt to exist between two mental atmospheres both containing a high percentage of fog. To leave them together during his own absence was a risk Caesar could not afford.

Early in 58 Clodius as Tribune promulgated a bill 'banning from fire and water' (i.e., banishing for life) any person who had put a Roman citizen to death without trial. Nobody was mentioned by name. In executing the Catilinarians Cicero had carried out a mandate of the Senate and could fairly have maintained that if the bill applied to that occasion it applied to every Senator who had voted for the death penalty. But apparently he lost his head, and made the mistake (afterwards regretted) of fitting Clodius' cap. To arouse public sympathy he put on the signs of mourning.[1] Clodius set his rowdies to work, and Cicero was pelted in the streets. Counter-demonstrations followed. First a large number of Knights and then, by decree, the Senate wore mourning in sympathy. Two senior Consulars, Hortensius and the elder Curio, appealed to the Consuls for help; but one of them, Lucius Piso, was Caesar's father-in-law, and the other, Aulus Gabinius, a henchman of Pompey's. Their help was not forthcoming. In fact Gabinius began to take an active part on Clodius' side.

[1] See page 37, note 3.

Pompey's promises had already been belied, and Gabinius' behaviour
was all too obviously symptomatic; but a direct appeal had to be tried.
A deputation of four Optimates went to Pompey's country house at
Alba, where he had retired to avoid embarrassment as best he could,
and pleaded for intervention on Cicero's behalf. But Pompey was not
going to break up the coalition on Cicero's account. He replied that as a
private citizen he could only take action against a Tribune if called upon
by the Consuls, acting under a senatorial decree of martial law. He
knew, of course, that this was out of the question. When Piso, who was
related to Cicero's son-in-law, was approached (Gabinius being
obviously hopeless), he declined to interfere; the best thing, he suggested, was for Cicero to leave Rome. Personal appeals by Cicero both
to Piso and Pompey were equally unproductive. Years later he wrote
to Atticus that when he lay at Pompey's feet, Pompey did not even ask
him to get up, but merely said that he could do nothing against
Caesar's wishes. Despite all warnings, this final rejection came as a
shock. By Cicero's own later admissions alarm and distress now got the
better of his judgment. And those to whom he turned for advice were
nearly all of Piso's opinion: he had better retire from Rome. When
Caesar had left for Gaul perhaps there would be a favourable turn and
he would soon be back again.

Brooding in exile on what he had come to consider a fatal error,
Cicero saw himself as the victim of treachery. From a motive of jealousy supposed friends, especially Hortensius, 'the moment they saw
me a little unnerved and inclined to waver, pushed me forward,
employing all their wickedness and perfidy to bring about my downfall.' His letters are full of such criminations. Cato, however, he
specifically exempted: 'I am so far from thinking him guilty of the
villainy in question that it is one of my principal regrets that the
pretences of others counted more with me than his good faith.' Yet
according to later authorities Cato joined Hortensius in advising him to
leave.

Cicero's charges sound hysterical. But he continued to believe in
them after his restoration, and they will have had this much basis, that
at the crunch the Optimates thought more of their own skins than of
Cicero's. They could surely have mustered enough support in Rome
to counter Clodius' gangs. What then? Caesar seems to have had no
considerable force near the city, his main army being at Aquileia (near
Trieste); and his presence in the north was urgently needed to meet a
grave threat on the frontiers. The Consuls might have called on

Pompey to maintain order with his veterans, but would Pompey have had any stomach for crushing Cicero and the Senate by military force? Such questions may have been no easier to answer then than now. But neither Cicero nor the Optimates were in true fighting mood, and there could only be one decision. On the night of 19 March (the date is not quite certain) he fled from Rome. Clodius' bill was passed in the assembly the next day.

CHAPTER NINE

The Bitter Bread of Banishment

'His exile was a disaster from which he never recovered, politically or psychologically.'

R.G.M. Nisbet, 'Cicero in Pisonem'

'When to my mind rises, darkest of memories,
　　That night, my final hours in Rome,
The night I left behind so many things I loved,
　　Even now the tears roll from my eyes.
It was almost upon me, the day when by Caesar's order
　　I must be out of Italy's boundaries.
Time to prepare had been short and spirit wanting;
　　The long waiting had benumbed my brain.
I took no thought for the choosing of servants and companions,
　　Or clothes and equipment proper for a fugitive.
I was in a daze like a man struck by lightning,
　　Who lives, and does not know he is alive.
But when the very pain cleared the mists from my mind
　　And I finally regained the use of my senses,
I spoke a last word to the sad friends I was leaving
　　(One or two there were, out of the many),
My wife that loved me wept as she held me weeping;
　　Her tears, undeserved, fell faster than mine.
My daughter was far away, over in Africa,
　　And could not be told of what had befallen me.
Wherever one looked was the noise of moaning and wailing;
　　There was a keening, as at a burial.
Men and women, children too, grieved at my burial;
　　Tears were dropping in every corner of the house. . . .'

So (and so on) Ovid, the poet whom Caesar Augustus banished. We have no description of Cicero's last hours in Rome, but we know that his wife, like Ovid's, would have gone with him if he had allowed it. In

Cicero's case the absent member of the family was his brother, still in the East. The seven-year-old Marcus junior understood only too well what was happening; his father wished he had been less intelligent for his age.

Following a period of intense strain upon a nervous temperament, always prone to extremes, the blow was shattering. Cicero had wanted to destroy himself, whether by ordinary suicide or in a desperate sally against Clodius, but was restrained (so he says) by his family and Atticus. He continued to contemplate suicide in the following months. Reports reached Rome of his emaciation, even of mental disturbance— though this was contradicted by himself. His letters, both to Atticus and to his family, point to a condition at least bordering on what would now be called a nervous breakdown.

In company with some friends and servants he made at first for Brundisium (Brindisi) in order to cross over to Greece, but in Campania he changed his plans and travelled down the west of Italy to the toe, intending to go via Sicily to Malta. One incident of the journey is recorded in his dialogue 'On Divination' fourteen years later (Quintus Cicero is supposed to be speaking):

I have heard from your own lips, though our friend Sallustius has told me the story more often, how on your journey into exile (a glory to us, but a disaster to our country) you stopped one night at a house in the Plain of Atina.[1] After staying awake for a great part of the night you fell into a deep sleep towards dawn. So although there was no time to waste, Sallustius gave orders for quiet and would not have you woken. About two hours after dawn you woke up and told him of a dream you had had. You said that you dreamt you were wandering disconsolately in lonely places when Gaius Marius, wearing triumphal insignia, appeared and asked you why you were so sad. You answered that you had been driven out of your country by force; on which he took your right hand, told you to cheer up, and handed you over to the nearest lictor with instructions to take you to his memorial.[2] There, he said, you would regain your rights. Sallustius tells how he exclaimed that a swift and glorious return must be in store for you and says that you yourself seemed pleased with the dream.

About 1 April Cicero reached Valentia in the toe of Italy and stayed at a farm belonging to a friend; but here his plans changed again.

---

[1] Val di Diano, south of Salerno.
[2] i.e., the temple of Honour and Courage, built by Marius out of booty taken from the barbarians. The Senate's decree authorising Cicero's return was in fact passed in this building.

Clodius had lost no time in bringing forward a new bill banning Cicero by name, confiscating his property, and penalizing anyone who harboured him. An amendment fixed the distance within which this applied at 400[1] miles from Rome. Malta was thus ruled out, and furthermore the governor of Sicily, a personal friend, refused permission to land in his province. So once again Cicero headed for Brundisium along the southern coast of Italy, arriving on the 17th, after nearly two months of almost continuous travel. He stayed near the town in the house of one Laenius Flaccus, 'a very worthy gentleman,' he wrote to Terentia, 'who disregarded the danger to his own property and status in his concern for my safety, and refused to be deterred by the penalties of a wicked law from carrying out the established duties of hospitality and friendship. I pray that one day I may be able to show my gratitude. Grateful I shall always be.' On the last day of April he sailed for Greece, intending to travel through Macedonia to Cyzicus on the Asiatic side of the sea of Marmora. Atticus had offered the hospitality of his estate in Epirus, but Cicero had enemies, former Catilinarians in exile, too near by. The same consideration ruled out Athens.

Before sailing he dispatched letters to Atticus and Terentia. To Atticus:

. . . Your exhortation to me to live is only partially effective. You keep me from laying violent hands upon myself, but you cannot keep me from regretting my decision and the fact that I am alive. What is there to hold me, especially if the hope that followed me when I left Rome is no more? I shall not proceed to make a catalogue of all the tribulations on which I have fallen by the signal injury and villainy not so much of those who hated me as of those who were jealous of me. That would only be to bring my grief to the surface and ask you to share my mourning. This I do say flatly, that no one ever suffered so crushing a blow or had greater cause to pray for death. I might have met it with honour, but the moment was let pass. From the time that remains I do not look any longer for a remedy, but only for an end to my misery.

I see you are collecting every item in the political news which you think could afford me some hope of a change. They don't amount to much, but since you wish, let us wait and see. . . . I should write to you more often and more fully, if it were not that my distress has robbed me of all my mental powers and more particularly of this sort of faculty. I long to see you. Take care of your health.

Dispatched 29 April from Brundisium.

[1] So Cicero's text. Later accounts say 500.

To Terentia:

... Ah, what a desperate, pitiful case is mine! How can I now ask you to come—a sick woman, physically and spiritually exhausted? Shall I not ask then? Am I to live without you? Perhaps I should put it like this: if there is any hope of my return, you must build it up, and help in the campaign. On the other hand, if all is over, as I fear, then come to me any way you can. Be sure of one thing: if I have you, I shall not feel that I am utterly lost. But what is to become of my little Tullia? You at home must take care of that—I have nothing to suggest. But assuredly the poor little girl's marriage and good name must be a prior consideration, however matters turn out. Then there is my son. What will he do? I hope that *he* will always be with me, my darling child. I cannot write any more now. Grief clogs my pen. ...

The possibility of a meeting in Greece with Quintus on his way home only aggravated Cicero's distress. He did not really want it. 'I shun my fellow-creatures, I can hardly bear the light of day,' he wrote to Atticus in his letter from Brundisium. To meet the younger brother whom he had always overshadowed in his present abject state would be too painful. Their relations during Quintus' absence had not been entirely smooth. To begin with there had been some unpleasantness between Quintus and his brother-in-law Atticus in which Cicero had mediated—he suspected that Pomponia was at the bottom of it.[1] More-over, Cicero felt that his own prestige was involved in Quintus' performance as Proconsul, and had been generous with his admoni-tions. Quintus was not an unqualified success in that (or indeed in any other) capacity. True, he exercised the primary virtue of honesty. Cicero's testimony to that is corroborated by his brother's anxiety to get back to Rome—the generality of governors stayed in office as long as they could, lining their pockets. When Quintus' term was twice extended, partly through Cicero's fault, he was annoyed. But in other respects he fell short. Two long letters to him in Asia (the first at the beginning, the second at the end of 59) contain criticisms; very delicate in the first, which reads as though intended for publication ('Advice to a Governor'), in the second outspoken. Cicero was especially perturbed by Quintus' irascibility, and the injudicious tone of some of his official letters which were going the rounds in Rome. In writing to a Knight called Catienus, Quintus had undertaken to see that his father was smoked to death to the accompaniment of cheers from the entire province. Another correspondent was exhorted to burn two persons

[1] See further pages 183 f.

alive if he could; if not, let him send them to him, the governor, 'to be burned up in court.' Such verbal ferocities may have been Quintus' idea of humour, but Cicero thought them ill-advised. Nor did he approve of Quintus' efforts to coax one Zeuxis into his power in order to sew him up in a sack—the punishment of parricides. Quintus had already provided two such spectacles in the south of his province and wanted another for the edification of the north. It is worth remembering (the detail comes from a littérateur of much later date) that Quintus Cicero was physically a small man. True, Marcus half-apologizes for his strictures, and apologizes outright for an earlier angry and unbrotherly letter (lost) which Quintus must brother-like forgive.

A deeper source of ill-feeling was the slave Statius, Quintus' confidential secretary, whose influence and arrogance became a scandal both in the province and in Rome. When Quintus gave him his freedom against elder-brotherly dissuasion, Marcus Cicero took it to heart. He wrote to Atticus in July 59:

I have many things on my mind, arising from the grave political crisis and these dangers that menace me personally. They are legion, but nothing distresses me more than Statius' manumission.

'That my commands—no, set commands aside, that my displeasure Should count with him for nothing!'[1]

And yet I don't know what to do, and after all the talk is more than the thing itself. Moreover, I can't even be angry with those I really love. I am only pained, deeply pained. . . .

Nor did he fail to point out to Quintus the damage he was doing his reputation:

. . . You must understand (for it is equally my duty to avoid ill-advised statement and crafty reticence) that Statius has given the gossip of those who want to run you down all the material they have. Previously it could be gathered that certain persons were annoyed by your severity; but now that he has been manumitted, the malcontents have something to talk about. . . .

Cicero's own conscience was not altogether easy. Before leaving Rome he had taken possession on Quintus' behalf of money due to him as Proconsul from the Treasury and applied it to his own use. Far from resenting this misdemeanour, as Cicero himself calls it, Quintus offered to lend more, though himself in money difficulties; and after his brother's return from exile he would willingly have let the debt stand—

[1] From Terence's play, 'Phormio.'

in fact it was paid off gradually. Years later the memory of his own generous behaviour at this time will have added to his bitterness at what he then regarded as Cicero's meanness.

The meeting then did not take place, and in June Cicero wrote a long, lugubriously pathetic letter of apology:

My brother, my brother, my brother! Were you really afraid that I was angry with you for some reason and on that account sent boys to you without a letter, or even did not want to see you? *I* angry with *you?* How *could* I be? As though it was *you* who struck me down, *your* enemies, *your* unpopularity, and not *I* who have lamentably caused *your* ruin! That much-lauded Consul-ship of mine has robbed me of you, and my children, and my country, and my all; I only hope it has robbed you of nothing but myself. Sure it is that you have never given me cause for anything but pride and pleasure, whereas I have given you sorrow for my calamity, fear of your own, loss, grief, loneliness. *I* not want to see *you?* No, it is rather that I did not want to be seen by you! You would not have seen your brother, the man you left in Rome, the man you knew, the man who saw you off and said good-bye with mutual tears—you would not have seen any trace or shadow of *him*; only a likeness of a breathing corpse. . . .

For three weeks Cicero journeyed east through Macedonia. The Quaestor Gnaeus Plancius, a friend who came from a town close to Arpinum, went to meet him and take him under his protection. Together they reached Thessalonica (Salonika) on 23 May, where Plancius gave Cicero lodging in his official residence. Cicero went no further.

In Rome his family and friends were working loyally on his behalf. It was a hopeful sign that Clodius had very soon fallen foul of Pompey. On 1 June the Senate, in Clodius' absence, voted for Cicero's recall, but the motion was blocked by another hostile Tribune. Atticus and others wrote as optimistically as they could, receiving such replies as this of 17 July:

You are at pains to argue what may be hoped for, particularly through the Senate, and yet you write that the clause in the bill which forbids any reference to the subject in the Senate is being posted up. So silence naturally reigns. And in these circumstances you take me to task for tormenting myself, when I am tried beyond any mortal that ever was, as you well know. What does it amount to, with the same Tribune still in office[1] and my enemy[2] Consul-Designate? Then you have given me a blow about the circulation of that

[1] Clodius would remain in office until 10 December.
[2] Metellus Nepos.

speech.[1] Try, as you say, to patch up the damage if you can. I did write it long ago in a fit of annoyance with him because *he* had written against me, but I suppressed it and never expected it to leak out. However, as I have never exchanged a contentious word with him in my life and as it seems to me more carelessly written than my other compositions, I think it may be passed off on internal evidence as a forgery. Would you please see to that, if you think my case is curable? If I am past praying for, I don't so much care.

I am still stuck here, with no one to talk to and nothing to think about. I may have suggested to you, as you say, that you should join me; but I give that up, and realize that you are helping me where you are, whereas you could do nothing even verbally to lighten my load here. I can't write any more, nor have I anything to write about. I am rather waiting for news from your side.

Dispatched 17 July, Thessalonica.

At no time during this dolorous period does Cicero appear to have looked for consolation in philosophy, as he did after Tullia's death in 45. For study and literary work he obviously had no heart. Misery and hope against hope were his only companions, along with endless regret for what he had lost, and the folly (as he now saw it) of the losing, and the villainy of false friends. Even Atticus was not exempt from criticism. Cicero never questioned his good faith, but blamed him for having simply stood by at the crisis instead of offering salutary advice. This, he wrote, must have been because Atticus' affection was inadequate— which meant, of course, that he himself had not done enough to deserve it. Atticus forebore to argue the point.

With Clodius and the Consuls of 58 still in office and Caesar unreconciled, nothing could be achieved. The elections produced a better outlook for the following year. The new Board of Tribunes was at first thought to be unanimously well-disposed. Both of the Consuls-to-be were closely attached to Pompey, but one of them, Lentulus Spinther, was a friend of Cicero's. The other was his old enemy Metellus Nepos, but Atticus went to work to mollify him, apparently with success. Meanwhile Plancius was returning to Rome, and Cicero left Thessalonica for the western coast, arriving at Dyrrachium (Durazzo) in late November. He had good connexions with the town and would get earlier news from Italy. On the last day of the month he wrote to Terentia:

[1] A speech (not delivered) 'Against Clodius and Curio,' written about three years previously in the aftermath of the Good Goddess affair, in which the elder Curio (who is here referred to) had backed Clodius. Some fragments survive.

I have been given three letters by Aristocritus, and almost blotted them out with tears. I am overwhelmed with grief, dearest Terentia; and my own distresses do not torture me more than yours and my family's. But my wretchedness is greater than yours (and yours is bitter enough) because, while we both share in the disaster, the blame for it is mine and mine only. It was my duty either to avoid impending danger by taking a Commissionership, or to oppose it by diligent provision, or to fall bravely. Nothing could have been more miserable, dishonourable, and unworthy of me than *this*. So I am overwhelmed by shame as well as grief. Yes, I am ashamed to have been found wanting in the courage and foresight that my best of wives and most enchanting of children had the right to expect of me. Day and night I have before my eyes the sorry spectacle of my family in mourning and the frailty of your health. The hope of restoration held out to me is very slender. Many are hostile, almost all are jealous. To drive me out took some doing, but to keep me out is easy. However, so long as my family continues to hope, I shall do my part, for I would not wish to seem responsible for *every* fiasco.

You need not worry about my safety. That is no problem now, for even my enemies want me to stay alive in my present utter wretchedness. However, I shall do as you advise. I have thanked the friends you named, and given the letters to Dexippus, and I have written that my information about their good offices has come from you. Our dear Piso's extraordinary zeal and activity on my behalf is evident to me, and everyone talks of it. The Gods grant that I may enjoy the blessings of such a son-in-law in person with you and our children![1] Our last hope now lies in the new Tribunes—and in the first few days; for if novelty is lost, we are finished. I have therefore sent Aristocritus to you straight away, so that you can write me an immediate account of the initial stages and a conspectus of the whole business. Dexippus also has my orders to hurry back at once, and I have written to my brother asking him to send couriers at short intervals. I am staying in Dyrrachium at the present time expressly so that I get the quickest possible news of what goes on. Also I am quite safe, having always been a patron of this town. When my enemies[2] are reported to be on their way, it will be time to go to Epirus.

As regards your offer to join me if I wish, well, I know that a large share of this burden rests upon your shoulders, and so I want you to stay in Rome. If you and the others succeed in your efforts, it is for me to join you. If not— but there is no need to go on. I shall be able to decide what to do from your first letter, or at latest from your second. All I ask is that you write me the most comprehensive and detailed accounts—though it is results rather than letters I should be expecting now. Take care of your health, and rest assured

---

[1] The Gods did not so grant. Piso Frugi died in the first half of 57, before Cicero's return.

[2] The Consul of 58, Lucius Piso, was coming out as governor of Macedonia.

that nobody in the world is more precious to me than you, or ever has been. Good-bye, dearest Terentia. I seem to see you, and my weeping exhausts me. Good-bye.

29 November.

Early in the year fresh efforts were made both in the Senate and the popular assembly, only to be frustrated by a now hostile Tribune and Clodian mobs. Quintus Cicero nearly lost his life in the rioting. The bad news reached Cicero in February and produced a brief, despairing note to Atticus:

From your letter and from the facts themselves I see that I am utterly finished. In matters where my family needs your help I beg you not to fail us in our misery. According to your letter I shall see you soon.

No more letters survive until after Cicero's return to Rome in September. The lapse of correspondence with Atticus is unexplained. One theory, that they were together on Atticus' estate,[1] conflicts with a passage in Cicero's 'Laws,' which seems to prove that in 52 he had never seen it. Another, that Atticus suppressed the letters because they showed a strain in his and Cicero's relations, is only supposition. Probably they disappeared accidentally.

After the fiasco in January the prospect in Rome again brightened. Two pro-Ciceronian Tribunes, Milo and Sestius, hired gangs to fight Clodius with his own tactics and gradually got the upper hand. Pompey decided it was time to move, and Caesar withdrew his opposition, Quintus Cicero having given a personal guarantee for his brother's discreet behaviour in the future. At the beginning of July the Senate carried a decree (Clodius alone opposing) which provided that a law should be put to the People rescinding the sentence of banishment and restoring Cicero's property. Sponsored by the entire body of magistrates, excepting one Praetor (Clodius' brother Appius) and two Tribunes, the bill was passed on 4 August in a crowded, enthusiastic assembly. That same day Cicero took ship home from Dyrrachium.

---

[1] Or at Dyrrachium; but it is hardly credible that Atticus would have stayed there rather than on his own property.

CHAPTER TEN

'A Sort of Second Life'

'My heart is high, higher even than in my palmy days, but my purse is low.'
Cicero to Atticus

To Atticus, a few days after arrival in Rome:

... I left Dyrrachium on 4 August, the very day on which the law for my recall was put to the vote. I landed at Brundisium on 5 August.[1] My little Tullia was there to welcome me. It was her birthday, and also, as it happens, the foundation day of the colony of Brundisium and of your neighbour the Goddess of Weal,[2] a coincidence which attracted popular notice and was joyfully celebrated by the townsfolk. On 11 August, while at Brundisium, I learned by letter from Quintus that the law had been carried in the Assembly of Centuries amid remarkable demonstrations of enthusiasm by all ranks and ages and with an extraordinary concourse of country voters. Thence I set out, after receiving the most flattering marks of regard from the townspeople, and as I travelled along I was joined by congratulatory deputations from all quarters.

So I arrived at the outskirts of Rome. Not a man whose name was known to my nomenclator,[3] no matter what his rank, but came out to meet me, except for enemies who could neither conceal nor deny that they were such. When I reached the Porta Capena[4] I found the steps of the temples thronged by the common people, who welcomed me with vociferous applause. Like numbers and applause followed me to the Capitol. In the Forum and the Capitol itself the crowd was spectacular. In the Senate on the following day, 5 September, I made a speech of thanks to the House. ...

The speech is extant, as is another addressed to a public meeting. They set a pattern for Cicero's public utterances after his homecoming

---

[1] He stayed with his host of the previous year, Laenius Flaccus. It must have been a pleasant reunion.

[2] Atticus' house on the Quirinal (recently inherited from his uncle) was near the temple of Salus.

[3] The slave whose job it was to tell his master the names of the people who came his way.

[4] The gate through which the Appian Way entered Rome.

—extravagant laudation of Pompey and Consul Lentulus, denunciation no less unmeasured of Clodius and the Consuls of 58, rehearsal of
the glorious incidents of his return, presentation of his flight as a
magnanimous self-sacrifice which had saved Rome from civil war. But
this revised conception of that event did not cancel his resentment
against the 'false friends' whose advice he had taken. His speech to the
People refers with conspicuous lack of tact to allies who had betrayed
him out of jealousy or deserted him out of cowardice. His letter ends:

. . . It is a sort of second life I am beginning. Already, now that I am here,
secret resentment and overt jealousy are setting in among those who championed me when I was away. I need you badly.

The 'false friends' were not likely to enjoy public recriminations.
And Cicero's conduct in general at this time did not endear him to the
senatorial leaders. The recall had been too triumphant for his own good.
Three years later he wrote to Lentulus Spinther that some people, the
jealous and hostile, had expected him to come back chastened and
cautious. But now that all the despair and humiliation was behind him,
Cicero could see the whole episode as a glorious demonstration of his
indispensability. The drive to be foremost which had carried him to the
Consulship was as strong as ever, even though his inner confidence was
never quite restored. Almost at once he went into conspicuous political
action.

This was the less fortunate because Roman politics had never been
more complex, and a cooler brain than Cicero's might have taken some
time to get their measure. From sparse evidence we cannot hope to
make out all the cross-currents. It is at least certain that the triple
coalition, whose architect Caesar was busy adding Gaul to the Roman
empire, was in poor repair. The rift between Clodius, its former
instrument, and Pompey had contributed to Cicero's restoration.
Despite that reverse, and Milo's opposition on the streets, Clodius was
still a power there, out to make all the trouble he could for Pompey,
and of course for Cicero. Behind Clodius lurked Crassus, whose
inveterate jealousy and ill will toward Pompey never lay far below
the surface. Cato was away on a mission to Cyprus. He owed it to
Clodius; and Cato's Optimate friends, still regarding Pompey as their
main enemy, viewed their demagogic *Standesgenosse* with a tolerance,
even favour, which scandalized and exasperated Cicero. Pompey's
position was, as usual, uneasy and ambiguous. Caesar's emergence as a
general and empire-builder of the first magnitude had necessarily

changed the relationship between them; the able, if not too respectable, auxiliary had become a potential rival. Though by no means set to break up their alliance, Pompey was tired of marking time, and hankered to exchange private status for some new grandiose responsibility.

As it happened his opportunity came within a day or two of Cicero's arrival in the capital. Further from the letter already quoted:

... Two days later I spoke again. The price of grain had risen very high, and a crowd flocked first to the theatre and then to the Senate, clamouring at Clodius' instigation that the shortage was my doing. The Senate met during those days to consider the grain situation, and there was a general demand, not only from the populace but from the *boni* too, that Pompey be asked to take charge of supplies. He himself was eager for the job, and the crowd called on me by name to propose it. I did so in a full-dress speech. In the absence of all the Consulars except Messalla and Afranius,[1] because as they alleged, it was not safe for them to speak, the Senate passed a decree as proposed by me, to the effect that Pompey should be asked to undertake the matter and appropriate legislation be introduced. The decree was recited immediately, and the people applauded after the silly new-fangled fashion when my name was read out. I then addressed them at the invitation of all magistrates present except for one Praetor and two Tribunes.[2]

The following day there was a large attendance in the House, including all the Consulars. Pompey was given everything he asked. In asking for fifteen Lieutenant-Commissioners he named me first, and said I should be his *alter ego* for all purposes. Messius proposed an alternative bill which gives him control over all moneys and in addition a fleet, an army, and authority in the provinces superior to that of the governors. Our consular bill now looks quite modest; Messius' is felt to be intolerable. According to himself Pompey favours the former, according to his friends the latter. The Consulars are seething, Favonius[3] at their head. I hold my tongue. . . .

To Cicero his own experiences were the hub of the political wheel. If he never got so far as to say *respublica sum ego* (for to him the Republic, the body politic, was really a high and holy thing), he sometimes came near to implying a *de facto* identification. 'I have been restored *to* the Republic,' he told the Senate in his speech of thanks, 'and *with* the Republic; and therefore I shall abate nothing of my old

---

[1] Both adherents of Pompey.

[2] See page 72.

[3] Ironical. Favonius (Cato's Sancho, as Mommsen called him) came of obscure family and had held no office higher than the Tribunate. In Cato's absence he seems to have considered that the mantle had fallen on himself.

free spirit in defending her, no, I shall rather increase it.' To a correspondent six years later he wrote that in attacking himself Clodius had
attacked the entire commonwealth. On this reckoning politics ought to
have been a matter of good men, banding in support of the commonwealth and Cicero, versus bad men, who assailed them. That *is* indeed
the picture painted a few months later in Cicero's speech in defence of
Sestius. Optimates and *populares*, he said, were the abiding components
of Roman political life. But the Optimates ('adherents of the best')
were not a caste. Everybody was an Optimate who was neither a
criminal nor a born rascal nor in financial difficulties. The term
included men of good will in every social stratum, down to freedmen.[1]
This 'consensus of *boni*,' like the 'Harmony of Orders' in 61, ought to
include Pompey, who for all his desertion in 58, had been the prime
author of Cicero's recall. But to the senatorial leaders that event was
not the central fact of their political existence. They continued to
dislike Pompey. And Cicero's eagerness to recommend himself in that
quarter was no more to their taste in 57 than in 61.

On the whole, however, Cicero was at first well satisfied with the
public side of his 'second life.' His private affairs were less flourishing:

... Of my general position it can thus far be said that I have attained what
I thought would be most difficult to recover, namely my public prestige, my
standing in the Senate, and my influence among the *boni*, in larger measure
than I had dreamed possible. But my private affairs are in a very poor way—
you are aware how my property has been crippled and dissipated and
pillaged—and I stand in need not so much of your resources, which I count
as my own, as of your advice in pulling together what is left and putting it on
a sound footing. . . . My financial position, as you know, is in very far from
good order. Moreover, there are certain private matters which I don't trust to
a letter. My brother is a paragon of affection, courage, and loyalty, and I love
him as I ought. . . .

His next letter, at the beginning of October, amplifies:

... As to my private life, my affairs are in a terrible tangle. My house is
being rebuilt, you know at what expense and trouble. My Formian villa is
being reconstructed, and I cannot bear to let it go nor yet to look at it. I have
put up the Tusculum property for sale, though I can't easily do without a
place near Rome. The generosity of my friends was exhausted in a matter
which yielded nothing but disrepute,[2] as you saw in absence and your people

[1] That was very well in theory, but in the Civil War Cicero made fun of his
wife's freedman Philotimus posing as an Optimate.
[2] Probably in hiring toughs to resist Clodius during Cicero's exile.

saw on the spot. Relying on their loyalty and resources, if only my defenders had permitted it, I should have had ample for every purpose; whereas now I am greatly embarrassed in this respect. My other anxieties are more *sub rosa*. I have the affection of my brother and daughter. I look forward to seeing you.

Evidently the 'private matters' had to do with Terentia—the beginning perhaps of the estrangement which ultimately led to divorce. As their later troubles were mainly concerned with money, it is a fair guess that Cicero was dissatisfied with his wife's financial management during his absence. He was the more conscious of money because it was no time for economy. He needed to reassert himself, and a certain amount of display fitted his mood. 'I am building in three different places,' he wrote to Quintus the following spring, 'and refurbishing my other properties. I live in a rather more expensive style than I used. It was called for.' It was about this time that he acquired a handsome villa in the eminently fashionable neighbourhood of Cumae on the Bay of Naples. The town house on the Palatine had been demolished and a temple to Liberty put up on the site, creating a religious sanction against rebuilding. But Cicero took the case before the College of Pontiffs and obtained permission to proceed. The matter of compensation had next to be settled:

> . . . The Consuls with their assessors valued my house, that is the building, at HS 2,000,000[1] and the other properties at very ungenerous figures—the Tusculan villa at 500,000, the Formian at HS 250,000. The valuation is sharply criticized, not only by better-class people but by the populace as well. You may wonder why this happened. *They* say my modesty was the reason, in that I neither refused compensation nor pressed my claim with vigour. But it isn't that. *That* would have been in my favour rather than otherwise. No, my dear Titus Pomponius, those same gentry (you don't need me to tell you their names) who formerly clipped my wings don't want to see them grow back to their old size. However, I hope they *are* growing already. . . .

Clodius did not accept this new defeat easily:

> . . . On 3 November an armed gang drove the workmen from my site, threw down Catulus' portico which was in process of restoration by consular contract under a senatorial decree and had nearly reached the roof stage, smashed up my brother's house by throwing stones from my site, and then set it on fire. This was by Clodius' orders, with all Rome looking on as the fire-brands were thrown, and loud protest and lamentation—I won't say from the *boni*, for I doubt whether they exist, but from all and sundry. Clodius was

---

[1] About £60,000.

running riot even before, but after this frenzy he thinks of nothing but massa-
cring his enemies, and goes from street to street openly offering the slaves their
freedom. . . . On 11 November, as I was going down Holy Street, he came
after me with his men. Uproar! Stones flying, cudgels and swords in evidence.
And all like a bolt from the blue! I retired into Tettius Damio's forecourt, and
my companions had no difficulty in keeping out the rowdies. Clodius himself could have been killed, but I am becoming a dietician, I'm sick of
surgery. When he found that everyone was calling for him to be bundled off
to trial, or rather to summary execution, his subsequent behaviour made
every Catiline look like an Acidinus.[1] On 12 November he tried to storm and
burn Milo's house in the Cermalus, bringing out fellows with drawn swords
and shields and others with lighted firebrands, all in full view at eleven
o'clock in the morning. He himself had made Publius Sulla's house his
assault base. Then out came Quintus Flaccus with some stout warriors from
Milo's other house, the Anniana, and killed off the most notorious bandits
of the whole Clodian gang. He had every wish to kill their principal, but *he*
had gone to earth in the recesses of Sulla's house. . . . On the morning of the
22nd I am writing this between two and three o'clock. Milo is already in
position on the Campus.[2] My neighbour Marcellus (the candidate) is snoring
loud enough for me to hear him. I am told that Clodius' forecourt is pretty
well deserted—a handful of ragamuffins without a lantern. Clodius' party
complain that it's all been my plan. Little do they know my heroic Milo,
what a resourceful as well as gallant fellow he is. His spirit is amazing. I pass
over certain recent brilliancies, but the sum and substance is as follows: I
don't believe there will be any elections. I think Publius will be brought to
trial by Milo, unless he is killed first. If he now puts himself in Milo's way in a
rough-and-tumble I don't doubt that Milo will dispatch him with his own
hands. He has no qualms about doing so, and makes no bones about it. He is
not scared of what happened to me, for *he* is never going to follow anybody's
envious and treacherous advice or put his trust in a sluggish nobility. . . .

Clodius' and Milo's private war on the Roman streets was indeed to
end in the way Cicero here foresaw, but not for another four turbulent
years.

In the early months of 56 much political time was taken up by the
affair of King Ptolemy XII of Egypt, sometimes called Auletes ('the
Flautist'), a typically late-republican tangle of public and private
interests. This unmeritorious ruler (father of the famous Cleopatra) had
been driven out by his subjects, and influential Romans (among them,

---

[1] Consul in 179, a pillar of respectability.
[2] The Campus Martius, where elections were held. Milo, as Tribune, was
blocking Clodius' election as Aedile, which would give him immunity from
prosecution.

according to common report, Pompey and Caesar) to whom he owed vast sums of money wanted him back on his throne. The job of restoring him had been assigned to Cicero's friend and benefactor Lentulus Spinther, who had gone out after his Consulship to govern a province in the south of Asia Minor; but Pompey's friends were active to get it transferred to Pompey—who for his part professed to have no interest in it. Enemies of both found means to obstruct the restoration altogether. Although Cicero considered himself badly treated by Lentulus in the matter of his compensation, he worked for him as in duty bound, and a series of letters to the Proconsul report manoeuvres in and out of the Senate in which Cicero took a leading part. The details of this business, some scandalous and lurid, soon became unimportant, but Cicero's comments on Pompey's attitude have a wider bearing. He wrote to Lentulus on 15 January:

. . . I happened to be dining with Pompey that evening. It was a better moment than had ever come my way before, because I had just had my most successful day in the Senate since your departure. So I talked to him, and I could flatter myself that I led his mind away from all other notions and focused it upon upholding your position. When I listen to him talking, I quite acquit him of all suspicion of selfish aims. But when I look at his friends of all classes, I see what is now plain to everybody, that this whole business has for a long while past been bedevilled by certain individuals, not without the connivance of the King himself and his advisers. . . .

Two days later he told his brother (now on service under Pompey in Sardinia) that he could not make out what Pompey's wishes were. Some years afterwards his young friend Caelius Rufus wrote that Pompey generally talked otherwise than as he felt, but was not clever enough to hide what he really wanted. He managed, however, to baffle Cicero, to whom he was again confiding his troubles. On 7 February he appeared in public on behalf of Milo, who was under prosecution by Clodius on a charge of disturbing the peace. Cicero reported to Quintus:

. . . Milo appeared on 7 February. Pompey spoke—or rather tried to speak, for no sooner was he on his feet than Clodius' gangs raised a clamour, and all through the speech he was interrupted by shouting, even by insults and abuse. When he wound up (and I will say that he showed courage; he was not put off, but delivered all he had to say, sometimes even managing to get silence by his personal authority)—well, when he wound up, Clodius rose. Wishing to repay the compliment, our side gave him such an uproarious reception that he lost command of thoughts, tongue, and countenance. That lasted till half-past one, Pompey having finished just after midday—all manner of insults, ending up with some highly scabrous verse to the address of Clodius and Clodia. Pale with fury, he started a game of question and answer: 'Who's starving the people to death?' 'Pompey,' answered the gang. 'Who wants to go to Alexandria?' Answer: 'Pompey.' 'Whom do you want to go?' Answer: 'Crassus' (who was present as a supporter of Milo, wishing him no good). About 2.15 the Clodians started spitting at us, as though on a signal. Sharp rise in temperature! They made a push to dislodge us, our side counter-charged. Flight of gang. Clodius was hurled from the rostrum, at which point I too made off for fear of what might happen in the free-for-all. The Senate was convened in its House, and Pompey went home. I did not attend, however, not wishing to keep mum about so remarkable an incident nor yet to offend the *boni* by standing up for Pompey, who was under fire from Bibulus, Curio, Favonius, and young Servilius.[1] . . .

The next day:

. . . Cato[2] delivered a broadside against Pompey—a set speech like a prosecuting counsel's with Pompey in the dock. He said many highly laudatory things about me, which I could have done without, denouncing Pompey's treachery toward me. Pompey's ill-wishers listened in rapt silence. Pompey replied warmly, making oblique allusion to Crassus and saying plainly that he intended to take better care of *his* life than Africanus had done, whom Gaius Carbo murdered.[3] So I think big things are on the way. Pompey has information (and talks about it to me) that a plot against his life is on foot, that Crassus is backing Gaius Cato and supplying Clodius with funds, and that both are getting support from Curio, Bibulus, and his other enemies. He says he must take very good care not to be caught napping, with the meeting-going public pretty well alienated, the nobility hostile, the Senate ill-disposed, and the younger generation ill-conditioned. So he is getting ready and bringing up men from the country. Clodius on his side is reinforcing his gangs. . . .

Believing that the 'Triumvirate' was now a thing of the past, Cicero ventured on dangerous ground. During Sestius' trial in early March he clashed with Publius Vatinius, the Tribune whose bill had given Caesar his Gallic command. In the course of a scarifying invective Cicero implied that the bill had been passed illegally, though he was careful to draw a distinction between Caesar and Caesar's instrument. More serious, because more immediately controversial, was the ques-

---

[1] Servilius Isauricus (Consul in 48), at this period a follower of Cato. He later joined Caesar.

[2] Not *the* Cato, but Gaius Cato, a Tribune mentioned below.

[3] The younger Scipio Africanus died suddenly in 129. Foul play was suspected.

tion of state land in Campania, still in process of distribution under a law passed by Caesar as Consul. Money was now needed to finance Pompey's purchase of grain, and at a meeting of the Senate in December 57 one of the new Tribunes, Rutilius Lupus, had aired the possibility of the state resuming possession. Cicero reported to his brother:

> ... Lupus' speech was awaited with interest. He dealt with the Campanian Land very fully, to a most attentive House. You know the material. He covered all my own contributions.[1] There were some barbs to Caesar's address, some insults to Gellius',[2] some complaints to Pompey's—who was not present. It was getting late when he wound up, and he said he would not ask for a debate since he did not wish to put any pressure on members to make themselves enemies. The high words of days gone by and the present silence told him the feeling of the House. Marcellinus[3] observed: 'I must ask you, Sir, not to draw any conclusions as to what we now approve or disapprove of from the fact that we have nothing to say. So far as I myself am concerned, and I imagine the same applies to the rest of the House, I am holding my peace because I do not think the question of the Campanian Land can properly be handled in Pompey's absence.' ...

The validity of Caesar's entire legislation in 59, as well as of his tenure in Gaul, was here involved. Significantly the same Tribune Lupus was active in the Egyptian business in favour of Pompey's appointment. On 4 April, 56 the subject was raised again in the Senate. To his brother Cicero writes merely:

> ... The same day there was a heated debate on the Campanian Land. The shouting in the Senate was like a public meeting. Shortage of funds and the price of grain heightened tension on this issue. ...

Remembering, no doubt, the guarantee which Quintus had given for his own behaviour Cicero did not choose to mention his personal contribution to the proceedings. We hear of it in a letter to Lentulus Spinther two and a half years later:

> ... On 5 April the Senate accepted my motion that the question of the Campanian Land should be debated in plenary session on 15 May. Could I have found a better way to penetrate the citadel of the coalition? Could I have shown myself more oblivious of my present situation or more mindful of my past record? ...

---

[1] Perhaps with reference to Cicero's opposition to Rullus' agrarian bill in 63; see page 31.
[2] A supporter of Clodius.
[3] An Optimate, and Consul-Designate.

In fact his intervention (which came only a few days after an intimation to his brother that he was withdrawing from all political activity
in or out of the Senate) will hardly have been a self-forgetful assertion
of principle. Even if Pompey had not inspired Lupus the previous
December, he had notably failed to come out in Caesar's support. If the
land question could be exploited so as to set the two irretrievably at
loggerheads, Pompey in isolation would inevitably gravitate towards
the Optimates, and Cicero's long cherished dream of playing mediator
might come true. It was encouraging that four days later, when he
visited Pompey after dinner on the eve of the latter's departure overseas, he saw no sign of displeasure. But Pompey did not tell Cicero that
he had arranged to meet Caesar on his way to the coast at Luca (Lucca).
At this conference Caesar succeeded in mending the battered fences. It
was agreed that Pompey and Crassus, reunited, should hold the Consulship in 55 for the second time as colleagues. Both should then receive
five-year military commands, and Caesar's command was to be
extended for the same period. Cicero too was on the agenda. From the
same letter to Lentulus Spinther:

> ... That speech of mine caused a sensation, not only where I had intended,
> but in quite unexpected quarters.[1] After the Senate had passed its decree on
> my motion, Pompey (without giving me any indication of displeasure) left
> for Sardinia and Africa, and joined Caesar at Luca on the way. Caesar there
> complained at length about my motion—he had been stirred up against me by
> Crassus, whom he had previously seen at Ravenna. Pompey was generally
> supposed to be much upset by the affair. I heard this from various sources,
> but my principal informant was my brother. Pompey met him in Sardinia a
> few days after leaving Luca. 'You're the very man I want,' he told him. 'Most
> lucky our meeting just now. Unless you talk seriously to your brother
> Marcus, you are going to have to pay up on the guarantee you gave me on his
> behalf.' In short he remonstrated in strong terms, recalling the many discus-
> sions he had had with my brother himself about Caesar's legislation and the
> pledges my brother had given him concerning my future conduct, appealing
> to my brother's personal knowledge of the fact that his own support for my
> restoration had been given with Caesar's approval. By way of commending
> to me Caesar's cause and position, he made the request that if I could not or
> would not defend them I should at least refrain from attacking them. ...

Cicero also received a message from Pompey himself asking him not
to commit himself on the land question until Pompey's return. Once

---

[1] 'Where I had intended' probably = Caesar; 'in quite unexpected quarters'
probably = Pompey.

more he had miscalculated. The coalition was restored, and he did not want to go on his travels again. The land issue was duly raised in the Senate on 15 May, but Cicero did not attend. 'On this matter,' he wrote to Quintus,' I am muzzled.'

CHAPTER ELEVEN

New Alignment

'Am I then to be a camp follower having refused to be a general?'
Cicero to Atticus

AFTER Luca, with Quintus' letter and Pompey's message to consider, Cicero (as he later told Lentulus Spinther) took stock: 'It was like a dialogue between me and the republic.' What came out of it was a strange new phase in his political life which lasted as long as the alliance between Pompey and Caesar held firm. Before the world at any rate he became a supporter of the coalition, cultivating private relations not only with Pompey but also, and more especially, with Caesar. Senatorial concessions to Caesar of a kind which in March 56 he had called 'monstrous' (in a letter to Quintus) now had his public approval. And in late May or June the House heard a glowing panegyric of Caesar's achievements in Gaul from Cicero's lips in his speech 'On the Consular Provinces:' 'People may think what they like,' he said. 'I cannot be other than friend to any man that does the state good service.' Writing to Atticus he called the speech a 'palinode.'

He was going much further than mere prudence required. For security's sake he need only have avoided provocation: 'If he won't or can't support Caesar, let him at least refrain from attacking him,' Pompey had said to Quintus. Why did Cicero not decide, as in 59, to withdraw from political activity and give himself up to literature and advocacy? In the following year he wrote to Atticus: 'Suppose I choose to fold my hands and seek a haven of refuge in retirement. Vain thought!' But he did not explain why the thought had to be vain. No doubt his position and temperament made reticence hard. Desire to shine, and basic antipathy to a régime in which the rulers 'held everything in their hands and wanted everybody to know it' were constant incitements to indiscretion. In fact Cicero was afraid that, as happened in 59, his impulses might be too much for him: 'The truth is,' he wrote to Atticus with reference to the publication of his 'palinode,' 'I wanted to bind myself irrevocably to this new alliance so as to make it impos-

sible for me to slip back to those people who won't give up their
jealousy even when they ought to be sorry for me.' Atticus and
Quintus had both advised him to conciliate Caesar with something
more positive than bare avoidance of offence. Pride made him receptive
to these suggestions. A relapse into quiescence after Pompey's warning
would save his skin, but it would do nothing for his suffering *amour
propre*. He needed to assert himself somehow, to make the world stare
instead of sneer; and a demonstration in favour of Caesar would
gratify his now almost pathological rancour against the purblind,
supercilious aristocrats who had 'betrayed' him in 58, grudged his
self-glorified renaissance in 57, petted the abominable Clodius, and
rejected his superior statesmanship in jealousy of himself and pigheaded
hostility to Pompey. To Atticus in late June:

> . . . There was also the fact (I might as well stop nibbling at what has to be
> swallowed) that I was not exactly proud of my palinode. But good night to
> principle, sincerity, and honour! You will scarcely credit the treachery of our
> public leaders, as they set up to be and *would* be if they had a grain of honesty
> about them. I had seen it, knew it, led on by them as I was, deserted, thrown
> to the wolves. Yet even so I was disposed to agree with them in politics. They
> proved to be what they had always been. At long last, and by your advice, I
> have come to my senses. . . . I shall give myself more rein if he[1] receives the
> offering cordially and if, on the other hand, it wrings the withers of certain
> gentlemen who object to my owning a villa[2] which once belonged to Catulus
> without recollecting that I bought it from Vettius, and say in the same breath
> that I ought not to have rebuilt my house and that I ought to sell it. But
> what's that compared to the fact that when I made speeches in the Senate on
> lines which they too approved they were delighted none the less that I had
> spoken against Pompey's wishes? *Il faut en finir*. Since the powerless won't
> be my friends, let me try to make myself liked by the powerful. You will say
> that I might have thought of that sooner. I know you wanted me to do so and
> that I have been a prize donkey. But now it's time for me to love myself, since
> *they* won't love me whatever I do. . . .

And to Lentulus in July:

> . . . You felicitate me on the state of my affairs, on Milo's friendship and
> Clodius' irresponsibility and impotence. Well, it does not at all surprise me
> to see a fine artist delighting in his own masterpieces.[3] And yet the perverse-
> ness (not to use a stronger word) of folk is beyond belief. With good will

[1] Caesar.   [2] At Tusculum.
[3] Cicero gracefully implies that he owes everything to Lentulus.

they could have kept me in the common cause; instead their jealousy has estranged me. For I must tell you that their venomous back-biting has pretty well succeeded in turning me away from my old, long-established principles and brought me to the point, not indeed of forgetting my honour, but of paying some attention to my vital interest. The two could have run perfectly well in harness if our Consulars had known the meaning of good faith and responsibility. But the majority are such fribbles that they are less pleased by my steadfastness in public affairs than irritated by my distinction. . . . You enquire about the political situation. There is bitter conflict, but the two sides are unequally matched. The party superior in resources, armed forces, and power has actually contrived (so it seems to me) to gain moral ascendancy as well, thanks to the stupidity and irresolution of their adversaries. Accordingly they have secured from the Senate with very few opposing voices all that they did not expect to obtain even through the People without civil disorder. . . . I tell you this briefly because the present situation is little to my liking; but I tell it all the same, so that I can advise you to learn before you meet with any setbacks a lesson which I myself have learned from experience rather than books (devoted to every class of literature as I have seen since childhood); we must not consider our security without regard to honour, nor honour regardless of security. . . .

Cicero's role in the troubled years that followed was not very conspicuous. Atticus recommended him to lie low, and the dynasts had only occasional need for his services (as in September 56, when he appeared with Pompey and Crassus to defend Caesar's Spanish henchman, Cornelius Balbus, against an Optimate-inspired charge of illegally assuming Roman citizenship). Cato (returned from Cyprus) and his friends kept up a vigorous opposition. Cato's brother-in-law Domitius stood for the Consulship against Pompey and Crassus, whose election was finally forced through in the first month of what should have been their year of office (55). Cicero's relations with Cato, never very easy, were now embittered by a difference about the validity of Clodius' election to the Tribunate in 59; Cicero's contention that it was irregular would have illegalized not only his own banishment but Cato's appointment in Cyprus. As best he could Cicero kept up a semblance of independent statesmanship, making meaningless appeals for concord, pursuing his personal vendetta against Clodius and the Consuls of 58, and even permitting himself a brush with Crassus in the Senate. But a letter from Caesar expressed deep regret, and Pompey patched up the quarrel. In November Crassus left for Syria to launch a disastrous campaign against Rome's chronic enemies in the East, the Parthians; there was some trouble with opposition Tribunes, one of whom solemnly cursed him at the city gates. Cicero spoke in his support, and sent him a singularly fulsome letter. His real sentiments were confided to Atticus:

... They say that our friend Crassus left Rome in uniform with rather less *éclat* than his coeval Lucius Paulus, also Consul for the second time, in days gone by.[1] What a rascal he is! ...

Under similar suasion from Pompey Cicero had let himself be reconciled to Publius Vatinius early in 55, and in the following year actually defended this *bête noire* of the Optimates on a political charge. His defence of Gabinius, who came back from Syria in the autumn of 54 to face a series of prosecutions, was a yet more humiliating reversal. A violent scene took place between them in the Senate, and only prudential considerations restrained Cicero from coming forward as prosecutor himself. He wrote to his brother that Pompey was pressing for a reconciliation: 'but so far he has got nowhere, nor will he if I keep a scrap of personal freedom.' However, at Gabinius' first trial on 23 October Cicero's evidence was given with notable restraint; to have defended Gabinius, as Pompey asked, would have meant 'everlasting infamy'. In December he prays Homerically that the earth may swallow him before he listens to 'most friendly suggestions' on the subject. Shortly afterwards the reconciliation was accomplished, and at his second trial Gabinius was defended, unsuccessfully, by Cicero. Cicero had now reached the point of treading softly *vis-à-vis* Clodius. At a trial in July 54 'I said not a word—my little girl, who is not very well at present, was afraid Publius might be annoyed.'

Hence unease of conscience, abrasion of self-esteem. There were moods of violent revulsion. To Atticus in April 55:

... After all, what could be more ignominious than the life we lead, I especially? For you, though you are a political animal by nature, are not subject to any peculiar servitude, you share the common lot. But as for me, reckoned madman if I speak on politics as I ought, a slave if I say what is expedient, and a helpless captive if I say nothing—how am I to feel? As I do I suppose, and all the more bitterly because I can't even grieve without seeming ungrateful to you. ...

[1] In 168, when Paulus (father of the younger Africanus) set out from Rome during his second Consulship to conduct the war against King Perseus of Macedonia. Livy mentions the unusually large crowd which gathered to see him off.

To Quintus late in 54:

> . . . I would do the poem[1] as best I could, but I am sure you realize that writing poetry calls for a certain mental alacrity of which the times we live in quite deprive me. To be sure I am withdrawing from all political concerns and giving myself over to literary work; all the same, I will tell you something which I assure you I used to want to hide from you of all people. My dearest brother, it wrings my heart to think that there is no Republic any more, no courts of justice, and that those years of my life which ought to have passed in the plenitude of senatorial dignity are dissipated in forensic work or rendered tolerable by my studies at home. As for my childhood dream 'Far to excel, out-topping all the rest,'[2] it has perished utterly. Some of my enemies I have refrained from attacking, others I have actually defended. My mind, even my animosities, are in chains. And of all men Caesar is the only one who cares for me as much as I could wish, or (as others would have it) who wants *me* to care for *him*. And yet none of these thoughts is so painful but that I find many consolations. . . .

He did indeed. In spite of such passages (written perhaps in part as a sop to his own conscience) Cicero's early fifties ought not to be regarded as one of the blacker periods in his life. On the whole he was probably less unhappy than at any time subsequent to his Consulship. The tone of his letters is prevailingly cheerful, even gay. With the outburst to Quintus contrast this to Atticus of about the same date:

> . . . You'll wonder how I take all this. Pretty coolly, I assure you, and I plume myself highly on doing so. My dear friend, not only have we lost the vital essence of the free state—even the outward complexion and aspect it used to wear has gone. There is no Republic any more to give me joy and solace. Can I take that calmly? Why yes, I can. You see, I have the memory of the proud show she made for the short time that I was at the helm, and the thanks I got in return. My withers are unwrung by the spectacle of one man all-powerful, which chokes the persons who found it distasteful that *I* should have any power at all. I have many consolations. All the same, I do not move away from my position, but turn back to the life that is most congenial, to my books and studies. The labour of pleading is compensated by the pleasure that oratory gives me. My house in town and my places in the country are a source of delight. I do not remember the height from which I fell but the depth from which I have risen. If I can have my brother's company and yours, then for aught I care these people can go to the devil. I can philosophize and you can listen. The place in my mental anatomy which used to

---

[1] Cicero was planning to write a poem on Caesar's second expedition to Britain. See page 90.
[2] See page 6.

contain a spleen grew a tough skin long ago. Providing only that my private and domestic circumstances give me pleasure, you will find my equanimity quite remarkable. It largely depends, believe me, on your return. There is nobody in the world with whom I hit it off quite so happily. . . .

The 'labour of pleading' was largely a labour of love. A man cannot be altogether disconsolate when he is busy in work which he and others know he does supremely well. As the premier advocate of his day Cicero's services were in constant demand, and he clearly enjoyed it, despite grumbling such as this to his leisured friend Marcus Marius in the autumn of 55:

. . . As for me, in case you picture me as a free man, if not a happy one, during this holiday, I have pretty well ruptured my lungs defending your friend Caninius Gallus. If only my public were as accommodating as Aesopus,'[1] upon my word I should be glad to give up my profession and spend my time with you and other congenial spirits. I was weary of it even in the days when youth and ambition spurred me forward, and when moreover I was at liberty to refuse a case I did not care for. But now life is simply not worth living. I have no reward to expect for my labours, and sometimes I am obliged to defend persons who have deserved none too well of me at the request of those who *have* deserved well. Accordingly I am looking out for any excuse to live as I please at long last; and your leisured manner of existence has my hearty commendation and approval. I resign myself to the rarity of your visits more easily than I otherwise should because, even if you were in Rome, I am so confoundedly busy that I should not be able to enjoy the entertainment of your company, nor you of mine (if any entertainment it holds). When and if I slacken my chains (for to be loose of them entirely is more than I can ask), then, no question about it, I shall teach you the meaning of civilized living, an art you have been studying these many years past! Only you must go on propping up that frail health of yours, so that you can visit my places in the country and run around with me in my little litter. . . .

But literary work (not, it may be noted, philosophy in a modern sense—that was to come later) was perhaps an even more valuable resource—pabulum for his intellectual energy and hunger for applause. After the political débâcle in April 56 he retired as he had done three years before to his house in Antium, where he set the library in order. To Atticus:

[1] A famous tragic actor. As described earlier in the letter, he had returned to the stage to take part in a show given by Pompey to inaugurate his new stone theatre (the first built in Rome), but his performance was such a failure that 'everyone was willing to let it be his finale.'

... Let me tell you that Antium is the Buthrotum of Rome, as your Buthrotum is of Corcyra—the quietest, coolest, pleasantest place in the world. ... And now that Tyrannio[1] has put my books straight, my house seems to have woken to life.[2] Your Dionysius and Menophilus have worked wonders over that. Those shelves of yours are the last word in elegance, now that the labels have brightened up the volumes. ...

A year later, from Cumae:

... I am feeding here on Faustus' library[3]—*you* perhaps think it's on these Puteolan and Lucrine commodities.[4] Well, I have them too. But seriously, while all other amusements and pleasures have lost their charm because of my age and the state of our country, literature relieves and refreshes me. I would rather sit on that little seat you have underneath Aristotle's bust than in our Consuls' chairs of state, and I would rather take a walk with you at your home than with the personage[5] in whose company it appears that walk I must. ...

To Quintus in February 54:

... I rake together all I can find in order to give you some news, but, as you see, I am simply out of matter. So I go back to Callisthenes and Philistus[6]—I can see you have been wallowing in them. Callisthenes is a vulgarian, a 'bastard'[7] author as certain of his fellow-countrymen have put it. But the Sicilian is capital—full of matter, penetrating, concise, almost a small-scale Thucydides. ...

The greatest poem so far written (perhaps the greatest ever written) in Latin was at this time in Cicero's hands:

... Lucretius' poetry, as you say, sparkles with natural talent, but there is a great deal of craftsmanship in it as well. But we'll talk of it when you come.

[1] Of Amisus in Asia Minor (his real name was Theophrastus). He had settled in Rome about ten years previously, and become a well-known scholar and teacher. A little earlier Cicero had written: 'Tyrannio has made a wonderful job of arranging my books,' and asked Atticus to lend him two library clerks 'to help with the gluing and other operations.' Dionysius and Menophilus were these clerks.

[2] More literally 'had gained a mind' (compare Virgil's *mens agitat molem*). We might rather say 'a soul.'

[3] Either Faustus Sulla (son of the Dictator) had sold his books to Cicero or he possessed a villa in the neighbourhood and let Cicero use his library.

[4] The sea food for which the Bay of Naples was famous.

[5] Pompey.

[6] Two fourth-century Greek historians. Callisthenes wrote on Alexander the Great, Philistus on his native Sicily.

[7] The manuscripts have *notum* ('familiar'). I translate my conjecture *nothum*. In his book 'On the Orator' Cicero remarks that Callisthenes wrote history 'almost in the style of oratory.'

If you read Sallust's 'From Empedocles,'[1] I'll rate you both more and less than ordinary humanity.

Cicero's own compositions (apart from speeches written up for publication) included a poem 'On my Vicissitudes' (i.e., his exile and recall), which was never published. He sent it to Caesar in Gaul, and was not entirely gratified by his comments (August 54):

... But see here, you seem to be keeping me in the dark. Tell me, my dear fellow, how does Caesar react to my verses? He wrote to me that he read the first canto and has never read anything better than the earlier part, even in Greek, but finds the rest, down to a certain point, a trifle 'languid'. The truth please! Is it the material or the style he doesn't like? No need for you to be nervous—my self-esteem won't sink a hairsbreadth. Just write to me *en ami de la vérité* in your usual fraternal way. . . .

The same period produced two of Cicero's most important and least derivative treatises, 'On the Orator' and 'On the Republic.' Cardinal Mai's discovery of considerable portions of the latter in the Vatican in 1820 was the last major addition to extant Latin literature. It treats of the ideal constitution of a state and the ideal citizen; Rome, for Cicero, was naturally the model for the first, Scipio Africanus the Younger for the second. The writing did not go easily, so he tells Quintus from Cumae or Pompeii (May 54):

... I am writing the political book I mentioned earlier, and a pretty sticky, laborious job it is. However, if it turns out to my satisfaction, the time will have been well spent. If not I'll toss it into the sea which is before my eyes as I write, since I can't just rest. . . .

The poem[2] on Caesar's second British expedition in 54 (a response to Caesar's dedication to Cicero of a philological treatise) was eventually finished and may have been published—ephemeral flower of a new-found enthusiasm on which neither fate nor nature smiled. Cicero's personal contacts with Caesar had not been very close in the past (Quintus seems to have had more to do with him), but he must have felt the impression of Caesar's personality, however reluctantly. From beginning to end Caesar liked and, with whatever reservations, admired Cicero, who on his side was not the man to misprize the

---

[1] Presumably a translation from the Greek of the fifth-century philosopher-poet Empedocles of Agrigentum. There is no saying whether the author was the historian or Cicero's friend Gnaeus Sallustius (see page 64) or somebody else of the same name.

[2] See page 88, note 1.

distinguished orator and littérateur, the urbane and tactful correspondent, or even to lack all fellow-feeling for the indomitable architect of
his own fortune (despite patrician origin). The daemonic in Caesar
repelled more than it attracted Cicero; but it did attract him. What
Cicero's flocculent and volatile mentality could never have found
congenial was Caesar's core of adamant. The austerity and authority of
Caesar's literary style he could appreciate, for all its unlikeness to his
own; but the presence of the man who never saw what was not there
made him uncomfortable.

But Caesar was in Gaul, in mid-trajectory of conquest. Cato was not
dazzled; Cicero, the man of words, the Roman from Arpinum, was.
Smarting from the Optimates' rejection, unsure of perennially ambiguous Pompey, conscious of reduced 'dignity', he had been touched
and flattered by the warmth of Caesar's welcome to his overtures.
About the beginning of 54 he wrote to him suggesting that Quintus
might take service as one of his Legates (Lieutenant-Generals) in Gaul.
Cicero's extant letters to his brother since his own return show the
two on excellent terms. Difficulties and misunderstandings—Quintus'
disregard of fraternal advice in certain dealings with their home town,
further trouble with Pomponia, touchiness over Marcus Cicero's
omission to press for his company on a trip to the country—seem to
have been few and fleeting. The tone of the correspondence is relaxed,
sometimes jovial, always friendly. The events of 58–57 had placed them
on a less unequal footing, and as guarantor to Pompey Quintus could
and did offer political advice, which was well received. His proposed
appointment with Caesar would suit Cicero's new orientation and
might redound to the family credit. Quintus was no doubt attracted by
the chance to show what he could do in a sphere where there would be
no elder to overshadow him, no less perhaps by the prospect of another
lengthy separation from Pomponia. Even more important, he was in
debt. For years he had been hankering to escape from financial
stringency, and he hoped to find service under a notoriously liberal
commander a short cut to that elusive goal—even though his brother
might think more of the long-term advantages to be gained from
Caesar's good will.

Caesar could not have been more receptive. Cicero to his brother in
mid-February 54:

. . . I forgot to write to you about Caesar—I can see what sort of a letter
you have been waiting for. Well, he wrote to Balbus that the mail packet
which contained Balbus' letter and mine had been delivered in so waterlogged

a condition that he does not know there *was* a letter from me. But he did make out a few words in Balbus' letter, to which he replied as follows: 'I perceive that you have written something about Cicero which I can't make out; but as far as I can guess it was a thing I could have wished for rather than hoped.' Accordingly I sent Caesar another copy of my letter. Don't be put off by his joke about being hard up. I replied that he had better not spend his last penny in reliance on *my* strong box, and some more banter on the same topic—familiar but not undignified. Everyone brings reports of his special regard for me. . . .

And a day or two later:

. . . As for your Caesar, I have been chanting his praises this while past. Believe me, he is grappled to my heart and *I* have no intention of disengaging. . . .

In June, on receipt of a 'punctilious and charming' letter:

. . . I value such warmth of regard from Caesar higher than all the favours he wants me to expect from him. I was absolutely delighted with the letter I had along with yours, in which he begins by saying how charmed he has been by your arrival and the memory of old affection and goes on to promise that, knowing how sorely I shall miss you, he will make me glad you are with him rather than anywhere else. It is good brotherly advice you give me to make him the one man I exert myself to please, but you are preaching to the converted. I shall do it *con amore*. . . .

And so he did. In conjunction with Caesar's friend Gaius Oppius he managed the expenditure of a vast sum on public buildings in Rome, Caesar's gift to the city. In July and August he wrote to Atticus of Caesar's 'incredible' demonstrations of affection, and as the year drew to its end his language both to Quintus and Atticus became almost lyrical. To the former in September:

. . . I can have no second thoughts where Caesar is concerned. He comes next with me after you and our children. I believe I am doing wisely (it is time for wisdom), but my affection is truly kindled. . . .

To Atticus:

. . . No, no! Hurry back to Rome, come and look at the empty husks of the real old Roman Republic we used to know. For example, come and see money distributed before the elections tribe by tribe, all in one place openly, see Gabinius acquitted, get the smell of Dictatorship in your nostrils, enjoy the public holiday and the universal free-for-all, behold my equanimity, my amusement, my contempt for Selicius'[1] 10%, and, yes, my delectable *rapprochement* with Caesar. That does give me some satisfaction, the one plank left from the wreck. The way he treats my (and your) dear Quintus! Such distinction, such appreciation and favour! I couldn't do more if I were G.O.C. myself. He has just offered him the choice of a legion for the winter, so Quintus writes to me. Wouldn't you love such a man? If not, then which of your fine friends? ...

The cessation of extant correspondence with both Atticus and Quintus at the end of 54 has concealed the exact point at which Cicero borrowed the large sum of 800,000 sesterces (about £25,000) which he owed Caesar in 51.

But Senate, law-courts, and libraries were far from accounting for the whole of Cicero's time. A note to Atticus in the summer of 56 is full of business and social activities:

Egnatius is in Rome, but I took up Halimetus' affair with him strongly at Antium. He assured me that he would speak seriously to Aquilius. So you will see him if you wish. I hardly think I can oblige Macro. There is the auction, you see, at Larinum on the Ides and for the two days following. As you think such a lot of Macro, I must ask you to forgive me. But don't fail to dine with me on the 2nd with Pilia.[2] You really must. On the Kalends I propose to dine at Crassipes'[3] place in the suburbs in lieu of an inn, and thus cheat the decree![4] Then home after dinner so that I can be ready for Milo[5] in the morning. I shall see you there then, and shall warn you beforehand. All my household wish to be remembered to you.

Here is Cicero at the play:

... I returned to Rome for Fonteius' benefit on 9 July, and went to the theatre. To begin with, the applause as I entered was loud and steady—but never mind that, I am a fool to mention it. To proceed, I saw Antipho, who had been given his freedom before they put him on the stage. Not to keep you too long in suspense, he won the prize; but never have I seen such a

---

[1] Selicius was a money-lender. The rampant bribery at the elections this year had raised the monthly rate of interest from $\frac{1}{3}$% to $\frac{2}{3}$% in July. To quote my note on the passage, 'Cicero's *je m'en fichisme* covers both the collapse of the constitution and the financial profiteering which was one of its immediate results.'

[2] At fifty-three Atticus married, apparently for the first time. His wedding to Pilia had taken place in the preceding February.

[3] See next page.

[4] The Senate seems to have passed a decree restricting the cost of meals in public places.

[5] Perhaps in connexion with a prosecution by Clodius, or, possibly, with Milo's engagement to Sulla's daughter Fausta. Cicero came up to Rome in November 55 to attend the wedding.

weedy little object, not a scrap of voice, not a—but don't say I said so![1] As Andromache at any rate he stood head and shoulders above Astyanax. In other roles he didn't have his equal![2] Now you'll want to know about Arbuscula. First rate. . . .[3]

Letters to Quintus too cover a variety of occupations, some of them on Quintus' behalf, such as the supervision of improvements on his property near Arpinum and the buying of books for his library. Glimpses of domestic life are all too rare. About a year after the death of the admirable Piso Frugi, Tullia became engaged to another young nobleman, Furius Crassipes. Marriage followed, but lasted only two or three years; the reasons for its failure are unknown. Not much is heard of Tullia and Terentia at this period, more of the two boys, in whose welfare and education Cicero took an active interest. His own son was not intellectually privileged, and one suspects that Cicero would gladly have exchanged him for his lively and precocious cousin Quintus, who moreover bore a strong physical likeness to himself. It was a remarkable boy of ten of whom his eminent uncle wrote the following (to Quintus senior, April 56):

. . . On 6 April I gave a dinner to Crassipes in honour of the engagement. Your boy (who is also my boy, and a very good one!) could not be at the meal because of a very slight indisposition. On the 8th I went to see him and found him quite fit again. He talked to me at length and in a very under-standing way about the disagreements between our two lady wives. Really it was delightfully amusing. Pomponia, by the way, has been grumbling about you as well. But we'll go into all that when we meet. . . .

This 'charming lad, very fond of his uncle', had one less amiable trait—greed. December 54:

. . . I love young Quintus as you ask, and as he deserves, and as I ought; but I am letting him go both because I don't want to take him away from his tutors and because his mother has left, and without her I am terrified of the young fellow's appetite! . . .

That was jocular, no doubt, but there was prophecy in the joke.

[1] Compare Horace Walpole to Sir H. Mann: 'His acting I have seen, and may say to you, who will not tell it again here, I see nothing wonderful in it; but it is heresy to say so.'
[2] The joke amounts to this: Antipho (otherwise unknown) was the worst actor on the stage, though it could be said that as Andromache he was at least 'bigger' than the colleague who appeared as her small son Astyanax (Latin *maior* can mean either 'physically larger' or 'better in his role.'). The play may have been Accius' 'Women of Troy.'
[3] An actress, also mentioned in Horace's Satires.

CHAPTER TWELVE

Dynasts Diverge

'How can I joke with you in these times, when upon my word I don't think a Roman who can laugh deserves the name?'

Cicero to Curio (53)

THE series of Cicero's extant letters to his brother and to Atticus both break off at the end of 54. There are no more letters to Quintus after that date, and those to Atticus do not resume until the spring of 51, after Cicero had set out to govern a province in Asia Minor. Letters must have been written, for Quintus remained in Gaul for most of the period, and even if Atticus was in Rome for all of it, Cicero doubtless made frequent visits to the country. Their disappearance was probably accidental, like the gap in the Atticus correspondence in 57. Because of the break comparatively little is known about the history of these years and Cicero's part in it. One outstanding fact, the *rapprochement* between Pompey and the Optimates, is certain, but not the means and the timing.

Its causes are hardly in doubt. Pompey's jealousy of Caesar was bound to recrudesce, and two events occurred to loosen the reintegrated coalition. Caesar's daughter Julia was in her early twenties when she married the forty-seven year old Pompey. But what presumably began as a political arrangement became a union of affection almost excessive by Roman ideas. In 54 Julia died in childbirth, and the baby lived only a few days. In the following year Crassus was defeated and killed by the Parthians; his younger son, a brilliant soldier and a particular favourite of Cicero's, died with him. The removal of one of the Three placed the other two in a more obvious posture of confrontation. Meanwhile the hostility of Cato and his friends toward Pompey, though never entirely eradicated, gradually yielded to their recognition of Caesar as a more dangerous enemy. Perhaps even this might not have been enough, if their hands had not been forced by an intolerable sequence of turmoil which brought the machinery of government into paralysis. Electoral scandals and street violence resulted in the magis-

trates of 54 and 53 (like those of 56) going out of office without successors to replace them. Cicero wrote to young Curio in Asia about
half way through 53:

... On one point I hardly know whether to congratulate you or to take
alarm—the extraordinary eagerness with which your return is awaited. It is
not that I doubt your capacity to live up to public expectation, but I am
seriously afraid that when you do come home, you may no longer have
anything to work for. Such is the decay, almost to extinction, of all our
institutions. But perhaps even such remarks as this ought not to be entrusted
to a letter. . . .

The only available answer was to call on Pompey to restore order.
After being appointed in 55 to a five-year command in Spain, he had
stayed behind, biding his time and governing his provinces through
Legates. The crisis was reached in January 52, when Clodius was killed
in a clash with Milo on the Appian Way and the Senate-House burned
down in the ensuing riots. In default of the usual magistrates Pompey
was given authority to call up troops and created Sole Consul. The
motion in the Senate was introduced by Cato's son-in-law Bibulus,
perhaps the bitterest of all Pompey's critics in the past. Pompey's
measures were prompt, stern, and effective. Within a few months
political life returned more or less to normal. But its basis had changed.
Instead of Pompey and Caesar versus the Optimates it was now Pompey and the Optimates versus Caesar; even though there was no open
breach between the dynasts, and in certain matters, such as the banishment of Milo, Pompey and Cato could still take opposite sides.

Cicero's views on the new pattern of politics are not on record. It is
fairly clear that he had no hand in the making of it. His own and his
brother's relations with Caesar were enough to preclude that. Friendly
offices between them continued. A casual reference in a later letter
lets us know that in the winter of 53–52 he met Caesar at Ravenna and
undertook to persuade his friend and former client Caelius Rufus, who
was Tribune in 52, not to oppose a move in Caesar's interests. Shortly
before this Caesar had patched up a quarrel between Cicero and his
lieutenant Mark Antony, whose candidature for the Quaestorship had
Cicero's support. It must have been galling for Cicero to see his own
vain dream of drawing Pompey and the senatorial leaders together
realized by others. But support for Caesar had always gone against his
political grain. His permanent instincts led him in behind the new allies,
who were not disposed to repulse him. Late in 53 he was elected into a
vacancy created by the death of the younger Crassus in the College of

Augurs, whose members had the management of the traditional state system of divination. In the sceptical 1st century B.C. most of them were better qualified to deal with the apolaustic collegiate dinners. But membership, though now by popular election, was normally confined to the nobility, and Cicero had long hankered for this addition to his status.

Put on trial for Clodius' killing, Milo was defended by Cicero and five other counsel, four of them leading aristocrats, including Hortensius and Cato. Cicero lay under a great personal obligation to this man of violence for stemming Clodius in 57, and in his eyes Clodius' elimination could only be cause for patriotic rejoicing. But Pompey and the city mob were hostile, and Cicero was so much unnerved by popular demonstrations and the spectacle of Pompey's soldiers in court that he could hardly stumble through his speech. Milo was found guilty and retired abroad. The speech Cicero published, sometimes reckoned his masterpiece, naturally gives no indication of what actually occurred. He sent a copy to the exile in Massilia (Marseilles). Milo's comment became famous: 'Lucky for me he didn't deliver it! I should never have sampled these remarkable red mullet.' His property was sold for a song to pay his debts, and Cicero, acting through his wife's man of business Philotimus, bought up some of it—for Milo's own sake, as he told Atticus. But Milo was not grateful, and the suspicion cannot quite be put aside that Cicero's Arpinate fondness for a good bargain here got the better of his finer feelings.

Clodius' followers also felt the weight of Pompey's juries. Cicero prosecuted one of them (a very unusual role for him) successfully. He was somewhat nettled when his friend Marcus Marius seemed to belittle the victory.

... I am sure you are pleased about Bursa, but you need not have been so diffident in your congratulations. You say you suppose I don't rate the triumph very high, because he's such a low creature. Well, I ask you to believe that this trial gave me more satisfaction than the death of my enemy. To begin with I prefer to get my revenge in a court of law than at sword-point. Secondly, I prefer my friend to come out of it with credit than with ruin.[1] I was especially pleased with the display of good will toward me on the part of the *boni* in the face of astonishing pressure from a very grand and powerful personage.[2] Lastly, and this may seem hard to credit, I detested this fellow far

---

[1] Cicero apparently means that Milo, who was in banishment for Clodius' murder, had been vindicated by Bursa's conviction. But he may be alluding to some circumstance unknown.

[2] Pompey.

more than Clodius himself. Clodius had a great object in view—he knew that the entire state would be jeopardized in my person; and he acted not of his own volition, but at the instigation and with the assistance of those whose power depended on my downfall. Whereas this little ape selected me for attack just because he felt like it, giving certain ill-wishers of mine to understand that he was ready to be let slip on me at any time. Therefore I tell you to rejoice and be glad. It is a great victory. . . .

The loss of correspondence with Quintus and Atticus is poorly compensated by two series of letters, to Trebatius Testa and the younger Curio. The latter contains little of interest, apart from the notably respectful tone adopted by the fifty-three year old Consular toward this influential young nobleman. By contrast, those to Trebatius show a side of Cicero which it is pleasant and important to recognize, his ease with younger men of his own social type and his readiness to help them. There was some vanity in this, but some genuine kindliness as well. The tact, good sense, and avuncular *camaraderie* of these letters should come out in translation, but the jokes defy it.

Gaius Trebatius Testa was probably in his early thirties. His family home was in Velia, in the far south of Italy, but he had established himself in Rome and was already a leading jurist, a fact to which Cicero often makes facetious reference. His tastes also included wine, swimming, and shows; he needed money. On Cicero's advice, like Quintus and about the same time, he went to find it in Gaul. In April 54 Cicero wrote Caesar a still extant letter of recommendation. Dating from the following May to April 53 there are thirteen letters addressed to Trebatius himself. Here is the first:

Every letter I write to Caesar or to Balbus contains as a kind of statutory bonus a recommendation of yourself, and not the standard sort but phrased with some special indication of my regard for you. Now all *you* have to do is to put aside this foolish craving for Rome and city ways, and by dint of perseverance and energy achieve the purpose with which you set out. I and your other friends will excuse you, as the 'rich and noble dames that dwelt in Corinth, lofty citadel'[1] excused Medea. She persuaded them, hands thick in plaster,[2] not to blame her for living abroad:

'Helping self and helping country, many a rover wide doth roam.
Naught accounted in his staying, sitteth many a stay-at-home.'

Which latter case would surely have been yours, if I had not thrust you forth.

[1] This and the following quotation come from Ennius' version of Euripides' tragedy 'Medea.'
[2] Gypsum, used by actors to whiten their hands.

But I shall be writing more anon. Now you, who have learned how to make caveats for others, enter one for yourself against the tricks[1] of those charioteers in Britain.[2] And since I have started to play Medea, always remember what she says: 'He who cannot help his own case, be he wise, his wisdom's[3] vain.' Take care of your health.

Caesar was busy, and in early August Trebatius' impatience had to be gently rebuked:

Caesar has written to me very civilly, regretting that he has so far been too busy to get to know you very well, but assuring me that this will come. I told him in my reply how greatly he would oblige me by conferring upon you all he could in the way of good will, friendly offices, and liberality. But your letter gave me an impression of undue impatience; also it surprised me that you make so little account of the advantages of a Tribunate,[4] especially one involving no military service. I shall complain to Vacerra and Manilius—I dare not say a word to Cornelius;[5] he is responsible if you play the fool, since you give it out that it was from him you learned your *wisdom*. Now why don't you press this opportunity, this chance?—you'll never find a better. . . .

In October after a reassuring letter from Trebatius:

On the strength of your letter I gave thanks to my brother Quintus, and can at last commend yourself in that you now seem to have fairly made up your mind. Your letters in the first few months disturbed me not a little, for they gave me an impression (if you will forgive me for saying so) at times of irresponsibility in your craving for Rome and city ways, at times of indolence, at times of timidity in face of the labours of army life, and often too, most uncharacteristically, of something not unlike presumption. You seemed to think you had brought a note of hand to the Commander-in-Chief instead of a letter—such a hurry you were in to take your money and get back home. It did not occur to you that people who *did* go with notes of hand to Alexandria[6] have thus far been unable to get a penny.

[1] Cicero facetiously uses legal phraseology. I have had to paraphrase.

[2] Caesar's second expedition to Britain was now in preparation. His 'Commentaries on the Gallic War' describe how the ancient Britons used their war-chariots (*essedae*).

[3] *sapientia* ('wisdom' or 'good sense') and the verb *sapere* can have special reference to juristic lore; Cicero is fond of the *double entendre*. The Euripidean original of this line is quoted in another letter. It is not in our texts of the 'Medea,' so probably comes from a lost play.

[4] i.e. the rank of Military Tribune (staff-officer). There were six to each legion.

[5] Vacerra and Manilius were no doubt fellow-jurists. Quintus Cornelius Maximus is mentioned in the 'Digest' as Trebatius' teacher in law.

[6] Back on his throne, Ptolemy 'the Flautist' was in no hurry to repay his Roman creditors (see pages 78 f.), Cicero's speech in defence of Rabirius Postumus in the following winter is concerned with this matter.

Were I thinking in terms of my own convenience, I should wish you to be with me of all things, for I gained no small pleasure from our intercourse and no small profit from your advice and services. But since from youth upwards you have confided yourself to my friendship and patronage, I have always felt a responsibility not only for your protection but for your promotion and betterment. So as long as I expected to go myself on a provincial assignment I made you certain unsolicited offers, which you doubtless remember. When that plan changed, I hit on another. Observing that Caesar extended to me the most flattering courtesies and held me in exceptional regard, and knowing his extraordinary generosity and punctilious loyalty to his engagements, I commended you to his care in the fullest and most flattering terms I could find. He took my words in the same spirit, and has often intimated to me by letter and made clear to you by word of mouth and by act that he has been greatly impressed by my recommendation. Now that you have got such a patron, if you credit me with any sense or good will toward you, don't let him go. Should some incident occur to ruffle you, should you find him less prompt than you expected through pressure of affairs or some untoward circumstances, be patient and wait for the final outcome. That it will be agreeable and honourable to yourself I will guarantee.

I must not urge you at greater length. I will only point out that if you let slip this opportunity of securing the friendship of a most eminent and generous personage in a wealthy province at just the right time of your life, you will never find a better. In this opinion, as you jurists say in your books, Quintus Cornelius concurs.

I am glad to find that you have not gone to Britain. You are quit of the fatigues, and I shall not have to listen to your account of it all. Please send me full details as to where you will be spending the winter, in what expectations and under what conditions.

This uneasiness out of the way, Cicero's letters become definitely light-hearted, as these of November or December:

You remember the words at the end of the 'Trojan Horse:'[1] 'Their wisdom comes too late.' But yours, old fellow, does *not* come too late. First you sent those turkey-cock letters which were silly enough.[2] Then you showed yourself none too keen a sight-seer in the matter of Britain, for which frankly I don't blame you.[3] *Now* you seem to be well out of harm's way in winter quarters, and so you have no mind to stir. 'Wisdom everywhere befitteth; that shall be thy sharpest arm.'[4]

If I were by way of dining out, I should not have disappointed your friend

[1] A Latin tragedy variously ascribed to Livius Andronicus and to Naevius. The words quoted had become proverbial.
[2] Trebatius seems to have written in martial vein.
[3] Here and elsewhere Cicero jokes upon the reluctance (real or alleged) of the lawyer to risk his skin fighting.　　　　　[4] From an unknown Latin play.

Octavius;[1] though I did say to him after several invitations, 'Do you mind telling me, who *are* you?' But really, in all seriousness, he is a nice fellow. A pity you did not take him with you!

Let me know plainly what you are all about and whether you will be coming to Italy this summer. Balbus has assured me that you are going to be a rich man. Whether he is talking plain Latin, meaning that you will have plenty of cash, or after the manner of the Stoics when they say that all are rich who can enjoy the sky and the earth, remains to be seen. Travellers from Gaul complain of your arrogance—they say you don't *respond* to enquirers.[2] Still you have one satisfaction: everybody agrees that there is no greater legal pundit than yourself in all Samarobriva.[3]

I have read your letter, from which I understand that our friend Caesar is impressed with you as a jurist. You may felicitate yourself on having got to a part of the world where you pass for a man of some *wisdom*! Had you gone to Britain as well, I dare say there would have been no greater expert than you in the whole vast island. But really (you won't mind my jokes—after all you challenged me), I am half inclined to be jealous of you, actually sent for by a personage whom affairs, not arrogance, make inaccessible to the rest of mankind.

But you say nothing in your letter about *your* activities, which I assure you interest me no less than my own. I am terribly afraid you may have a chilly time of it in winter quarters. So I advise you to instal a good stove. Mucius and Manilius[4] concur. After all you are not too well supplied with army greatcoats![5] To be sure, I hear that things are warm enough for you all just now out there, and truly that intelligence made me very nervous about you. However, you are a much safer campaigner than you are a counsel. Keen swimmer though you be, you had no mind for a dip in the ocean; and you didn't care to watch those charioteers, though in the old days we could never do you out of a blindfold gladiator.[6] But enough of banter. . . .

[1] Some nobody who had been pestering Cicero with invitations.

[2] Jurisconsults like Trebatius were said to 'answer' (*respondere*) those who consulted them. Not to answer an ordinary question or greeting was, of course, bad manners. Cicero makes the same joke in a contemporary letter to another lawyer friend abroad.

[3] Modern Amiens, where Caesar had established his winter headquarters.

[4] Both of the two Mucii Scaevolae whom Cicero had known as a young man were eminent jurists, as was the father of the Pontifex, Publius Mucius Scaevola (Consul in 133). Manius Manilius, Consul in 149, was another. Trebatius would catch the echo of these great legal names, but Cicero must be referring primarily to living people. Manilius will be the jurist mentioned in a previous letter (see page 100, note 5). Mucius may be a contemporary Scaevola, a friend of Cicero's. If he was also a friend of Trebatius', Cicero might bring him in for the sake of the associations of his name, even if he was not himself a jurist.

[5] The unsoldierly Trebatius would naturally be short of these.

[6] *andabata*, a special type of gladiator who fought blindfold. Chariot races were a feature of Roman public shows.

The last of the series is dated 12 April (53):

I have received several letters from you in a batch, dispatched at different times. In every respect but one they made pleasant reading. They show that you are now bearing your army life with a stout heart, and that you are a fellow of fortitude and resolution. For a little while I missed these qualities in you, not however putting down your restlessness to weakness of spirit but to your distress at being parted from us. So carry on as you have begun. . . . And please give me an account of the war in Gaul—the less adventurous my informant, the more I trust the information.

However, to get back to your letters: all very nice, except for one feature which surprises me. Is it not unusual to send several identical letters in one's own handwriting?[1] As for the palimpsest, I applaud your frugality. But I wonder what could have been on that scrap of paper which you thought proper to erase rather than not write these screeds. Your forms of procedure perhaps?[2] I scarcely suppose that you rub out my letters in order to substitute your own. Or do you mean to imply that nothing is happening, that you are neglected, without even a supply of paper? Well, that is your fault for taking your modesty away with you instead of leaving it behind with us.

When Balbus sets out to join you, I shall commend you to him in plain Roman style. If you get no further letter from me for some time, don't be astonished. I am going to be away throughout April. I am writing this in the Pomptine country, having turned in for the night at Marcus Aemilius Philemon's house, from which I have already heard the hubbub created by my clients, those, that is, whom you have procured for me—it is common knowledge that a vast crowd of frogs in Ulubrae[3] have bestirred themselves to pay me their respects. Take care of your health.

In the end Caesar seems to have come up to expectations—at any rate Trebatius took his side in the Civil War four years later. He remained a good friend of Cicero's and reappears in Latin literature as Horace's mentor in the poem which prefaces his second book of Satires. The following note of uncertain date may belong to the summer of 44:

You made fun of me yesterday over our cups for saying that it was a moot point whether an heir can properly take action in respect of a theft previously

[1] Important letters were sometimes dispatched in two or more copies (*eodem exemplo*) to ensure safe delivery. In such a case the writing would be done by clerks, though normally it was considered more polite to write in one's own hand. Cicero jokingly implies that Trebatius' letters were so like one another as to be virtually *eodem exemplo*.

[2] As drawn up by jurisconsults for their clients. The joke is in the implication that Trebatius did not know his legal business.

[3] A small place in the Pontine Marshes south of Rome. Trebatius seems to have become its 'patron,' no doubt by legal services.

committed. So when I got home, though late and well in tipple, I noted the relevant section and send you a transcript. You will find that the view which according to you has never been held by anybody was in fact held by Sextus Aelius, Manius Manilius, and Marcus Brutus. However, for my part I concur with Scaevola and Testa.[1]

Under a law passed by Pompey in his third Consulship (52) Consuls and Praetors had in the future to wait five years before proceeding to their provincial commands at the end of their terms of office. The Senate had previously passed a decree to the same effect, which may well have been in aid of Cato's policy, aimed at reducing the cupidity of candidates and the rapacity of governors. Caesar, however, in his 'Commentaries' treats it as a move against himself (for technical reasons it might have resulted in some months' shortening of his own command). Be that as it may, the new regulation temporarily dammed the flow of available governors, and in order to meet the need the Senate called upon ex-magistrates who had not previously served in this capacity. Among these was Cicero, who was now appointed Proconsul in Cilicia, where Appius Claudius was coming to the end of two years' misrule. He took the job with reluctance, for one year only.

The province at this period included not only Cilicia proper, the coastal strip in the south-east of Asia Minor, but the entire southern seaboard and a large part of the interior, as well as the recently annexed island of Cyprus. The newly appointed governor was faced with a serious military situation. Since Crassus' defeat in 53 Rome's eastern frontiers had been under constant threat of a Parthian invasion, and in the summer of 51 the threat materialized; but the target was Syria, not Cilicia, and though that province was overrun, the invaders finally withdrew with loss. This, however, lay in the uncertain future. Lacking military experience of his own, Cicero needed it on his staff. Three of the four Legates he chose were experienced soldiers; one of these, naturally, was his brother Quintus.

Like Trebatius Testa, Quintus Cicero did not find service in Gaul everything he had hoped. Caesar's British campaign in 54, however stimulating as a theme for poetic embellishment, made nobody's fortune. 'I hear there is not an ounce of gold or silver in Britain,' wrote Cicero to Trebatius in June. 'If that is so, you had better lay hands on a war-chariot and hurry back to us at top speed.' In November he received a letter from his brother 'full of spleen and grumbling', and

---

[1] Trebatius himself.

had to urge him to stick it out—and be careful what he put in his letters.[1]

Perhaps the proudest day of Quintus' life was when he received Caesar's public compliments on the defence of his winter camp in the territory of the Nervii (modern Belgium) against Gaulish insurgents; the challenge had been to personal courage and endurance, and Quintus met it nobly. But the following year his carelessness nearly caused a major disaster. All in all, it seems improbable that Quintus emerged from this long military episode with much satisfaction. In 47 one Ligurius, who had been an officer in Gaul himself, told Cicero that to his knowledge Caesar detested Quintus, and had favoured him only as a compliment to his brother. That he was no favourite with his brother officers is suggested by his venomous remarks about two of them in a note to Tiro at the end of 44.[2] Most disappointing of all, Quintus evidently did not come back from Gaul (probably about the end of 52) a rich man.[3] His money difficulties continued to the end of his days. But at least he returned a seasoned commander, and his experience of provincial administration in the East might also be of value.

The first of a new series of letters to Atticus was written in early May (51) from Minturnae on the coast near the northern border of Campania; the brothers had just paid a farewell visit to their home country before setting out for Asia. The letter shows that neither her husband's long absence nor the prospect of another separation had made Pomponia's heart grow fonder:

> ... I come now to the line in the margin at the end of your letter in which you remind me about your sister. This is how the matter stands: When I got to Arpinum, my brother came over and we talked first and foremost about you, at considerable length. From that I passed to what you and I had said between us at Tusculum anent your sister. I have never seen anything more gentle and pacific than my brother's attitude toward her as I found it. Even if he had taken offence for any reason, there was no sign of it. So much for that day. Next morning we left Arpinum. On account of the holiday[4] Quintus had to stay the night at Arcanum. I stayed at Aquinum, but we lunched at

---

[1] Quintus had consoled himself by composing tragedies, from Greek originals. He turned out four in sixteen days.

[2] See below, page 267.

[3] Ligurius indeed spoke of a large sum of money presented by Caesar to Quintus, but this may have been only hearsay.

[4] Probably the festival of the Lares on 1 May, when, as here appears, slaves were entertained by their masters.

Arcanum—you know the farm. When we arrived there Quintus said in the kindest way 'Pomponia, will you ask the women in, and I'll get the boys?' Both what he said and his intention and manner were perfectly pleasant, at least it seemed so to me. Pomponia, however, answered in our hearing 'I am a guest here myself.' That, I imagine, was because Statius[1] had gone ahead of us to see to our luncheon. Quintus said to me 'There! This is the sort of thing I have to put up with every day.' You'll say 'What was there in that, pray?' A good deal. I myself was quite shocked. Her words and manner were so gratuitously rude. I concealed my feelings, painful as they were, and we all took our places at table except the lady. Quintus, however, had some food sent to her, which she refused. In a word, I felt that my brother could not have been more forbearing nor your sister ruder. And I have left out a number of things that annoyed me at the time more than they did Quintus. I then left for Aquinum, while Quintus stayed behind at Arcanum and came over to see me at Aquinum early the following day. He told me that Pomponia had refused to spend the night with him, and that her attitude when she said good-bye was just as I had seen it. Well, you may tell her to her face that in my judgment her manners that day left something to be desired. I have told you about this, perhaps at greater length than was necessary, to show you that lessons and advice are called for from your side as well as from mine. . . .

Perhaps this was the couple's last meeting before Quintus' departure. By custom wives did not accompany their husbands on provincial assignments, but the brothers took their sons, along with their sons' tutor, Atticus' learned freedman Pomponius Dionysius.

After a few days spent in his villas at Cumae and Pompeii Cicero started his journey in real earnest, and wrote to Atticus from stopping places on the road to Brundisium. There was an important halt at Tarentum (Taranto), where Pompey was staying. From Venusia, where the poet Horace had been born fourteen years previously, Cicero had promised to send a full account of his 'Dialogues on the Republic with Pompey.' Serious trouble with Caesar was in the air, over the duration of his command and the question of Roman citizenship for the Italian Gauls north of the Po, and Cicero expected much of the meeting. He wrote from the town:

I got to Tarentum on 18 May. Having decided to wait for Pomptinus,[2] I think it best to spend the days before his arrival with Pompey, especially as I see he would like it. Indeed he has asked me to spend every day with him at his house. I agreed willingly, for I shall have much fine discourse from him on

[1] Quintus' freedman, of whom Pomponia might well be jealous (see page 68).
[2] The senior of Cicero's four Legates.

public affairs and at the same time get some useful advice on this business of my own. . . .

Unfortunately, the promised full account was never written. Atticus was leaving Rome, and Cicero would not risk such a letter miscarrying. Instead a brief note:

> . . . As for me, after spending three days in Pompey's company and in Pompey's house, I am setting out for Brundisium on 22 May. I leave him in the most patriotic dispositions, fully prepared to be a bulwark against the dangers threatening. . . .

At Brundisium he spent about three weeks, held up by a passing illness, the non-arrival of his Legate Pomptinus, and weather. On 14 June he wrote from Actium, on the west coast of Greece:

> We reached Actium on 14 June, after feasting like aldermen both at Corcyra and Sybota on the fare[1] provided by your bounty and assembled for us in most hospitable profusion by Araus and my good friend Eutychides. From Actium we preferred to go by land, though the voyage had been excellent; but rounding Cape Leucata seemed too tiresome. Also I felt it would not be quite *convenable* to land at Patrae from small cargo boats without our luggage. . . .

The letter ends:

> . . . My boy sends you his love. He is a model of good behaviour and engaging manners. For Dionysius I always had a regard, as you know, but I think more highly of him every day, not least, let me add, because he is so fond of you and sees to it that your name is continually cropping up.

Quintus and his son seem to have travelled separately, but the four were together in Athens, where Cicero stayed from 24 June to 10 July. To Atticus, 27 June:

> After reaching Athens on 24 June I have been here four days waiting for Pomptinus, and have still no definite news of his coming. But my thoughts, believe me, are all with you, and though I have no need of such admonitions, the traces of your presence here call you the more vividly to my mind. In fact, you are really our single topic of conversation.
>
> But perhaps *you* prefer to hear something about myself. Here is what I have: Up to date no private or public body has been put to expense on my account or that of any member of my staff. We take nothing under the Julian Law[2] or as private guests. All my people recognize that they must be careful

---

[1] From Atticus' property on the mainland.
[2] Passed by Caesar in his Consulship. Among other things it laid down what travelling Roman officials might require from the places where they stopped.

of my good name. So far, so good. This has not gone unnoticed, and the Greeks are praising and talking about it at large. As for the future, I am taking great pains over this point, as I saw you wished me to do. But let us save the applause till the end of the speech.

The rest is of such a nature that I often blame my unwisdom in not having found some way of escaping this job. It's so hopelessly uncongenial to me. Indeed and indeed 'let the cobbler . . .'[1] Early days, you say, and point out that I am not yet in harness. Too true, and I expect there is worse to come. But even here and now—well, I put up with it, even, as I think and hope, with excellent grace, but in my heart of hearts I am on thorns. Irritability, rudeness, every sort of stupidity and bad manners and arrogance both in word and act—one sees examples every day. I won't give you details, not that I want to keep you in the dark but because they are hard to put into words. So you will admire my self-control when we get safely home again. I am getting plenty of practice in that virtue. . . . What else is there? Why nothing, except this. I have greatly enjoyed Athens, so far as the city is concerned and its embellishments and the affection the people have for you, the good will they seem to have for me. But many things have changed. . . .

Letters followed from the island of Delos in the Aegean, from Ephesus (whose inhabitants gave Cicero a rousing welcome), and from Tralles near the River Meander. He crossed the western boundary of his province on 31 July. The crow would travel about 400 miles to reach its eastern border with Syria.

[1] The Greek proverb, of which Cicero here quotes the first two words, runs: 'Let each man practise the craft he knows.'

CHAPTER THIRTEEN

The Proconsulate

'This colossal bore.'
Cicero to Atticus

i. *Administrative*

A CENTURY and a half after Cicero's death the satirist Juvenal, who hailed from a town only a few miles from Arpinum, crystallized the feelings of such as himself about 'Greeks'—a term which had been extended to cover the more or less hellenized inhabitants of the whole east-Mediterranean area:

Countrymen all, I can't endure a Greek Rome. But after all, the genuine Greeks make up only a small part of the dregs. This long while past Syrian Orontes has been pouring into Tiber. . . . There they come, one from lofty Sicyon, another from Abydos or Andros or Samos or Tralles or Alabanda, heading for the Esquiline or the hill that is named from a withy,[1] the future darlings of great houses: nimble of wit, reckless and bold as brass, their ready tongues wagging fit to beat Isaeus.[2] How is one to place such a fellow? He brings in every character you like to name. Schoolmaster, professor, mathematician, painter, trainer, tight-rope-artist, doctor, magician—your hungry little Greek knows the lot. Bid him mount the sky, and off he'll go. . . . And then your Greek is a past master at flattery. . . . It's a nation of play-actors. If you laugh, he shakes with a louder guffaw. He weeps, quite pain-lessly, at sight of a friend's tears. If you should ask for a bit of fire in winter-time, he dons a woollen cloak. If you say 'I'm sweltering,' he sweats. . . . Furthermore, nothing is safe from his lust—neither the lady of the house, nor her virgin daughter, nor *her* still smooth-cheeked fiancé, nor the once well-conducted son. Failing these, he'll lay his friend's grandmother. . . .

Cicero was an 'outstanding Philhellene', conscious, as he wrote to his brother, that 'all I have achieved, I have gained by those studies and arts which have been handed down to us in the literature and teachings

---

[1] The Viminal (*collis Viminalis*), from *vimen*, 'withy.'
[2] A contemporary declaimer, native of Assyria.

of Greece.' But he was also a burgher of Arpinum, who must needs
maintain (in his 'Tusculans') that the Romans had done everything they
had a mind to do better than the Greeks, and even combat the accepted
truth that Greek is a more resourceful language than Latin. As for
contemporary Greeks, his opinion chimes with Juvenal's. Most of
them, he told his brother, were deceitful, irresponsible, and taught
flattery by generations of servitude. In a variety of contexts he describes
them as cowardly, perjurious, and ungrateful. Such being his estimate
of the more civilized subjects of the empire, (the semi-barbarous
peoples of the west did not interest him at all), he was not overmuch
concerned about their wrongs. In the Verres case he had painted a lurid
picture of a world writhing under its rulers' cruelty and rapacity. But he
was equally ready to defend an ex-governor on trial; and that not all of
his clients in this category were innocent is a fair deduction from his
contemplated defence of Catiline, whose guilt was (on Cicero's own
statement) as clear as daylight. A fortnight after he entered his
province he wrote to Atticus about his predecessor, Appius Claudius:

> . . . I must tell you that on 31 July I made my eagerly awaited entry into
> this forlorn and, without exaggeration, permanently ruined province, and
> that I stayed three days in Laodicea, three in Apamea, and as many at
> Synnada. I have heard of nothing but inability to pay the poll-taxes imposed,
> universal sales of taxes, groans and moans from the communities, appalling
> excesses as of some savage beast rather than a human being. In a phrase these
> people are absolutely tired of their lives. . . .

But the savage beast had daughters. One had married Pompey's son,
the other Cato's nephew, a young nobleman, Marcus Brutus by name,
whom Cicero was anxious to conciliate. As Clodius' brother, Appius
had been Cicero's enemy, but Pompey had arranged a reconciliation.
Moreover, Appius, a complex character, was an authority on augury;
and he had just paid Cicero, now a fellow-member of the College, the
titillating compliment of dedicating to him the first instalment of his
treatise on the science. In a string of letters, most of them written after
his arrival in the province, Cicero addresses him with elaborate regard,
except when provoked by rudeness and suspicion on Appius' side, and
he did all, if not more than all, he decently could to strengthen Appius'
hand against a prosecution in Rome. He wrote to Appius himself in
April 50:

> . . . As for me, I call all the Gods to witness this my solemn pledge, that in
> this province of which you were governor I shall do what in me lies for your

honour (I prefer to say 'honour' rather than 'safety'). On your behalf I shall solicit like an intercessor and work like a blood relation. My influence with the communes, which I flatter myself hold me in affection, and my authority as Commander-in-Chief shall be at your service. I want you to demand all things of me, and to expect no less. My good offices shall surpass anything you can imagine. . . .

Cato's persistent efforts to improve the lot of the governed never seem to have got much backing from Cicero. When in 60 the Senate at Cato's instigation passed a decree to protect provincials against certain forms of financial exploitation, Cicero could only deplore the offence to Roman capitalists. Of course he did not approve of oppression. Governors had a duty to be honest, just, and merciful. But the fact that many were not no more led him to question the existing imperial system than the reign of King James II destroyed an old-style Tory's faith in the Divine Right.

Cicero went out East with the best intentions. Atticus had borne in upon him with almost unflattering emphasis that the Proconsulate must be a model of probity and propriety. He seems to have been particularly exercised about the behaviour of Cicero's staff, who might take advantage of a chief later to be described by Caesar as 'the easiest person in the world.' Cicero was at pains to reassure him. He wrote from Actium in June 51:

. . . Every day I think of how to fulfill your often-repeated exhortations (which fell on willing ears) to get through this abnormal duty with the strictest decency and propriety, and so I impress on my companions, and so in fact I do. . . .

And again from Athens:

. . . So far my journey through Greece has been the admiration of the country, and I must say that I have no complaint to make so far of any of my party. I think they know my position and the understanding on which they come. They are really jealous for my good name. As for the future, if there is anything in the old saying 'like master . . .,' they will certainly keep it up, for they will see nothing in my behaviour to give them any pretext for delinquency. . . .

On the whole he was as good as his word. We do not have to rely solely on his own evidence, though it is impossible to regard his self-applause, much of it in confidential letters, as a smoke-screen—passages like this, for instance:

... You ask what I am doing here. Spending the deuce of a lot of money. I quite revel in this system. My strictness according to your precepts is so remarkable that I am afraid I shall have to raise a loan to meet the bill I negotiated with you. I don't scratch Appius' sores, but they show and can't be hidden. ...

Or this:

... However, it is some relief to the wretched communes that no expense is incurred on my account or that of my Legates or my Quaestor or anyone whosoever. ... Upon my word, the mere fact of my arrival brings them back to life, knowing as they do the justice, the abstinence, and the clemency of your friend Cicero, which has surpassed all expectations. ...

Cato publicly commended him for having 'won back the hearts of our subjects to a loyal support of Roman rule.'

It is true that Cicero later came to believe (perhaps only in a jaundiced moment) that the good conduct of his staff had been 'only veneer.' He personally in the end netted a large sum, 2,200,000 sesterces (about £65,000), most of it probably saved out of his state grant as governor and from military plunder. His casual mention of the money, as 'legally accruing,' to his temporarily not very well-disposed Quaestor suggests that his conscience was quite at ease about it.

Finding the administrative districts of his province deep in a financial morass, he came to the rescue. To Atticus, 13 February, 50:

... I myself left Tarsus for Asia[1] on 7 January amid really indescribable enthusiasm among the communes of Cilicia, especially the people of Tarsus. After crossing the Taurus I found a marvellous eagerness for my arrival in the districts of Asia under me, which in the six months of my administration had not received a single letter of mine or seen a compulsory guest. Before my time that part of the year had regularly been occupied with profiteering of this sort. The richer communes used to give large sums to avoid having troops quartered on them. The Cypriots gave 200 Attic talents.[2] While I am governor the island will not be asked for a penny—that is not hyperbole, it is the naked truth. In return for these benefits, which dumbfound the provincials, I allow none but verbal honours to be decreed to me. I forbid statues, temples, chariots.[3] Nor do I impose myself upon the communes in any other way—but perhaps I do upon you, when I blow my own trumpet like this. Put up with it, if you love me; after all it was you who wanted me to act so. ...

[1] i.e., the Roman province so-called. Three of its administrative districts in the interior of Anatolia had been transferred to the province of Cilicia.

[2] About 4,000,000 sesterces or £120,000.

[3] Four-horse chariots containing a statue of the person honoured, in bronze or marble.

And in late April:

> ... I see that you are pleased with my moderation and disinterestedness. You would be even more so if you were on the spot. At this assize, which I have been holding in Laodicea from 13 February to 1 May for all my Districts except those of Cilicia, I have produced some astonishing results. A great number of communes have been entirely cleared of debt, many others substantially relieved. All have come to life again with the acquisition of home rule under their own laws and courts. I have enabled them to free themselves wholly or partially from debt in two ways. First, no expense whatsoever has been incurred during my term as governor—and when I say 'no expense' I am not speaking in hyperbole, I mean literally none, not a penny. You would hardly believe how much that has helped to drag the communes out of the mire. Then there is another thing. The natives themselves were responsible for an astonishing number of peculations in the communes, committed by their own magistrates. I personally investigated those who had held office in the last ten years. They admitted it quite frankly. So without any open disgrace they put the money back with their own hands into the various public purses. The civic bodies for their part, which had paid the tax-farmers nothing in this present quinquennium, have now without any moaning paid the arrears of the previous quinquennium as well. So I am a prime favourite with the tax-farmers. 'Grateful gentry,' you may say. I have experienced their gratitude.[1] Then the rest of my administration has been sufficiently expert on the one hand and merciful on the other, and my affability makes a great impression. Access to me is not at all after the usual fashion. Nothing is done through my valet. I am up and about in my residence before daybreak, just as in my candidate days. These things are appreciated and thought much of; and being an old campaigner, I have not so far found them irksome. ...

Honest administration under the late Republic was not such a rarity as Cicero's boasts might suggest. He himself told Atticus that his colleagues in the East, the governors of Macedonia, Asia, Bithynia, and Syria were all 'strengthening Cato's policy,' and the governor of Crete and Cyrene would have done equally well if he had had anything to do. But Cicero had advantages over these worthy men; he was a celebrity, and he could charm. Even those earthy characters the Roman tax-farmers (*publicani*), natural enemies of the provincials, responded:

> ... You seem curious to know how I manage about the tax-farmers. I dote upon them, defer to them, butter them up with compliments—and arrange so that they harm nobody. Most surprising of all: the rates of interest specified in their agreements with the provincials were maintained even by Servilius;[2]

[1] Cicero evidently blamed his old allies the capitalists for failing him in 58.

[2] The elder Servilius Isauricus, Proconsul in Cilicia 78–74. 'Even' implies that he was an unusually benevolent governor.

my system is this: I fix a date, giving plenty of time, and say that if they pay before that date I shall apply a rate of 1 %;[1] if not, then the rate in the agreement. So the natives pay a tolerable interest and the tax-farmers are delighted with the arrangement, seeing that they now get verbal compliments and frequent invitations to their hearts' content. In a word, they are all my friends, and each man thinks himself preeminently so. All the same 'in them let not . . .'—you know how it goes on.[2] . . .

Fame, not philanthropy or the beauty of virtue, was Cicero's spur. He did not deeply care what might happen after he had gone. The sooner he went in fact the better, not only because he found it an irksome business on the whole, but to lessen the chances of any tarnish to his fire-new reputation—Scaevola the Pontifex, paragon of governors, spent (he pointed out) only nine months in office. And yet there were times when, to his own surprise, the job well done was its own reward:

. . . Never in all my life have I gained so much pleasure as I do from my integrity here, and it is not so much the *réclame*, which is enormous, as the practice itself that gratifies me. In a word, it has been worth it. I did not know myself, I never quite realized my capabilities in this line. I have a right to a swollen head. It is a fine achievement. . . .

But the good intentions of a Roman governor, who could curb his own appetite and those of his staff, and even sheathe the claws of the tax-farmers, were exposed to other pressures, from Rome itself. Cicero's provincial tedium was enlivened by a series of letters from a younger friend and former client, Marcus Caelius Rufus: man of fashion, distinguished orator, rising politician. An extract or two will illustrate his racy, gaily cynical style, to which Cicero did his at times laboured best to respond in kind. 1 August, 51:

I do envy you. So many surprises landing on your doorstep every day! First, Messalla acquitted; then convicted. Gaius Marcellus elected Consul; Marcus Calidius defeated, and prosecuted by the two Gallii. Publius Dolabella a Quindecimvir.[3] One thing I don't envy you—you missed a really beautiful sight, Lentulus Crus' face when he heard his defeat. He had gone down to the hustings in the highest fettle, he was thought to be a certainty. Even Dolabella had little opinion of his own chances. In fact I may say that but for the sharper eyes of your humble servant, Lentulus would have carried the day, with his opponent practically conceding victory. . . .

[1] i.e., per month.
[2] *We* do not, but the (Greek) saying evidently amounted to 'Don't trust them a yard.'
[3] One of the fifteen custodians of the prophetic Books of the Sibyl. Dolabella was soon to be Cicero's son-in-law; his rival, Lentulus Crus, was Consul in 49.

April–May 50:

... Nothing new has happened really, unless you want to be told such items as the following—which of course you do! Young Cornificius has got himself engaged to Orestilla's daughter. Paula Valeria, Triarius' sister, has divorced her husband for no reason the day he was due to get back from his province. She is to marry Decimus Brutus. ... There have been a good many extraordinary incidents of this sort during your absence. Servius Ocella would never have got anyone to believe he went in for adultery, if he had not been caught twice in two days. Where? Why, just the last place I should have wished—I leave something for you to find out from other informants! Indeed I rather fancy the idea of a Commander-in-Chief enquiring of this person and that the name of the lady with whom such-and-such a gentleman has been caught napping.

August 51:

What a spectacle you have missed over here! If you have made Arsaces[1] prisoner and stormed Seleucia,[2] it was not worth the sacrifice. Your eyes would never have been sore again if you had seen Domitius' face when he heard his defeat.[3] The polling was heavy, and support for the candidates quite on party lines. Only a tiny minority gave their backing in conformity with personal loyalties. Accordingly Domitius is my bitter enemy. He has not a friend in the world he hates more than me![4]—all the more so because he regards himself as wrongfully dispossessed of the prize and me as the author of the outrage. Now he is furious at the general rejoicing over his discomfiture. ...

Caelius was elected Aedile in 51. One of his prospective official functions was to give a show, and for this he needed wild animals, especially panthers. A district in Cicero's province was a well-known source of supply, and Caelius was continually pressing for this and other questionable favours. 2 September, 51:

... In almost every letter I have written to you I have mentioned the subject of panthers. It will be little to your credit that Patiscus[5] has sent ten

[1] i.e., the King of Parthia. These kings bore the name of the founder of the royal line, like the Ptolemies in Egypt.
[2] The Parthian capital, which had supplanted Babylon as the chief city of Mesopotamia.
[3] Domitius Ahenobarbus and Mark Antony had been rival candidates for a place in the College of Augurs, the former as the Optimates' man, the latter as Caesar's. Caelius himself was one of the 'tiny minority' who backed their candidate (in his case Antony) on personal grounds.
[4] Cicero alludes to this same Domitius in a letter of 54 as 'the perpetual enemy of his friends.'
[5] Possibly Quaestor in the neighbouring province of Asia.

panthers to Curio[1] and you not many times as many. Curio has given me these same animals and another ten from Africa—in case you imagine that country estates are the only kind of present he knows![2] If you will but keep it in mind and send for beasts from Cibyra and write to Pamphylia likewise (they say the hunting is better there), the trick will be done. I am all the more exercised about this now because I think I shall have to make all my arrangements apart from my colleague. Do be a good fellow and give yourself an order about it. You usually like to be conscientious, as I for the most part like to be careless. Conscientiousness in this business is only a matter of saying a word as far as you are concerned, that is of giving an order and commission. As soon as the creatures are taken, you have the men I sent in connexion with Sittius' bond to look after their feeding and transport to Rome. Indeed, if you hold out any hope when you write, I think I shall send some more men over.

Marcus Feridius, a Roman Knight, is going to Cilicia on personal business. He is the son of a friend of mine, and is a worthy and energetic young man. May I recommend him to you and request you to admit him to your circle? He hopes that by a kindness which you can render with ease and propriety[3] some lands paying dues in kind to townships in your province will receive exemption from tax. You will be obliging some respectable persons, who do not forget a favour. . . .

Caelius' colleague, Octavius, also wanted panthers and approached Atticus, who gave him no encouragement. Cicero writes (20 February, 50):

. . . As for Marcus Octavius, I answer you once again, your reply to him was right and proper—I could have wished it had been a little more confidently put. Caelius has sent me a freedman and an elaborate letter both about panthers and about raising money from the communes.[4] I replied to the latter point that I was sorry to find that my light was so much under a bushel and that people in Rome were unaware of the fact that in my province not a sixpence is disbursed[5] except in payment of debt; and I told him that I was not entitled to raise money nor he to take it, and advised him (for I really like him) that as one who had prosecuted others he should be more careful of his conduct. As for the panthers, I said it would not help my reputation to have the people of Cibyra hunting publicly on my orders. . . .

[1] Curio (the younger) had given a magnificent show in 53 in memory of his father.
[2] This seems to refer to some incident otherwise unrecorded.
[3] The propriety might be a matter of opinion.
[4] An 'Aediles' tax' was sometimes imposed in the provinces (in the form of 'voluntary' subsidies, voted by the provincials) to raise money for Roman shows. When Quintus Cicero abolished the practice in Asia one nobleman complained that he had been robbed of 200,000 sesterces (£6,000).
[5] i.e., by the provincial communes for the benefit of Romans.

Roman correspondents often put 'I did' or 'I have done' instead of 'I am doing' or 'I intend to do,' adjusting the tense of the verb to the time when the letter would be read by its addressee. Perhaps the letter to Caelius had not yet actually been written. One Cicero wrote subsequently (4 April) suggests that its terms were less austere than his language to Atticus would imply:

. . . About the panthers, the usual hunters are doing their best on my instructions. But the creatures are in remarkably short supply, and those we have are said to be complaining bitterly because they are the only beings in my province who have to fear designs against their safety. Accordingly they are reported to have decided to quit this province and go to Caria. But the matter is receiving close attention, especially from Patiscus. Whatever comes to hand will be yours, but what that amounts to I simply don't know. I do assure you that your career as Aedile is of great concern to me. The date itself is a reminder—I am writing on Great Mother's Day.[1] . . .

The affairs of Marcus Brutus, Cato's nephew and Caesar's future assassin, caused more serious embarrassment. At thirty-four Brutus was a prominent figure in Rome, thanks to his connexions and talents. Atticus' relations with Cato's family circle included Brutus, whose tastes and cultural proclivities he found congenial, and through Atticus Brutus had recently come into closer contact with Cicero. He had served in Cilicia under his father-in-law Appius and left some important financial interests in the area. King Ariobarzanes III of the neighbouring client-state of Cappadocia owed him a very large sum. The king was hard up ('my own honest opinion,' wrote Cicero, 'is that the kingdom is stripped to the bone and the king an absolute pauper'), and Brutus was anxious about his money. Thanks to constant pressure by Cicero he was paid 100 Attic talents (about £60,000) during the year, apparently as interest on the loan. Another loan, to the town of Salamis in Cyprus, carried compound interest at 48 per cent. The nominal creditors were two friends (really agents) of Brutus, who recommended them to Cicero. One of the pair, Scaptius by name, had been allowed to take some mounted troops to Cyprus in Appius' time, with which he shut up the town council in its hall; five councillors died of hunger. Unaware at first of the personal nature of Brutus' concern, Cicero nevertheless did his best; but he had already ordered the troops off the island, and he refused to sanction interest at so high a rate.

---

[1] The festival of the Great Mother (Cybele) began on 4 April. The two Curule Aediles seem to have been responsible for her 'games,' as well as for the 'Roman Games' in September.

Scaptius and representatives of the town met in Cicero's presence, but failed to agree; so, at Scaptius' request, the matter was shelved, interest continuing on the loan at the lower rate authorized by Cicero. Atticus was not satisfied. April 50:

. . . Do you really mean it, Atticus, you, the encomiast of my fastidious rectitude? 'This hast thou dared from thine own lips,' as Ennius says, to ask me to give Scaptius mounted troops to extract the money? You tell me that it sometimes chafes you that you are not here beside me. Well, suppose you *were* with me, would you let me do that if I wanted? . . . Shall I ever dare to read or so much as handle the volumes you praise so warmly[1] if I do anything of the sort? My dearest Atticus, you have really cared too much for Brutus in this matter, and not enough, I fear, for me. However, I have written to Brutus telling him what you have written to me. . . .

Even this was not the end of Cicero's annoyances on Brutus account. May–June 50:

. . . There is a certain Gavius, who, after I had offered him a Prefecture[2] at Brutus' request, often both spoke and behaved in a manner insulting to me— one of the dogs that used to run at Publius Clodius' heels. He omitted to accompany me when I left Apamea and, when subsequently he visited my camp, went off again without taking leave of me and showed quite openly that he bore me some sort of grudge. If I had counted a fellow like that among my Prefects,[3] what would you take me for? As you know, I have never put up with rudeness even from the most powerful personages; was I to tolerate it from this hanger-on? And it is going beyond mere toleration actually to confer something in the way of a favour or distinction. Well, this Gavius, seeing me recently at Apamea as he was leaving for Rome, accosted me in a tone I should hardly dare to use to Culleolus:[4] 'Where am I supposed to apply for my maintenance allowance as Prefect?' I answered more gently than those present thought proper to the occasion, that it was not my practice to give maintenance allowances to persons whose services I had not used. He left in a huff. If Brutus can be affected by what this scum has to say, you are welcome to love him all by yourself, I shall not be your competitor. But I expect he will behave as befits him. However, I wanted you to know the facts, and I have given Brutus a fully detailed account of them. To be sure (I write in confidence), Brutus has never sent me a letter, not even most recently about

---

[1] The six 'books' 'On the Republic.'

[2] The rank of Prefect could be conferred by governors on Romans who wanted an official status, and did not necessarily involve any duties.

[3] It seems clear that Gavius accepted the title, but Cicero apparently took the view that he had forfeited it by his subsequent behaviour.

[4] This evidently contemptible figure cannot be identified.

Appius, that did not contain something arrogant, ungracious. Now one of
your favourite sayings is

'Granius now
Knew his own worth and hated proud grandees.'[1]

But this way of his amuses rather than irritates me. All the same, he should
really take a little more thought about what he writes and to whom. . . .

Willingness to oblige a friend was one of Cicero's most amiable
traits, but it did not assist his ambition to govern like a second Scaevola.

ii. *Military*

A Proconsul was not only head of civil administration in his province
but Commander-in-Chief of an army. Cilicia was garrisoned by two
Roman legions, which should have meant 12,000 men, plus native
auxiliaries. But Appius had let the legions fall below strength by undue
permissiveness in the matter of furlough, and their morale was far from
satisfactory. It was not much of a force to cope with the Parthians,
should they decide to invade, and Cicero was understandably apprehensive. 'Only let the Parthians keep quiet and luck be on my side, I'll
answer for my part,' he wrote to Atticus from Actium; and from Athens:
'Of the Parthians there is not a whisper. As for the future, heaven be
my help.' A letter from Caelius brought some very cold comfort:

How worried *you* may be about the prospects of peace in your province
and the adjacent areas I don't know, but for my part I am on tenterhooks. If
we could so manage that the size of the war should be proportionate to the
strength of your forces and could achieve as much as requisite for glory and a
Triumph, while avoiding the really serious and dangerous clash, it would be
the most desirable thing in the world. But I know that as matters stand any
move by the Parthians will mean a major conflict; and your army is hardly
capable of defending a single pass. Unfortunately nobody allows for this; a
man charged with public responsibility is expected to cope with any emer-
gency as though every item in complete preparedness had been put at his
disposal.

The Roman calendar, soon to be reformed by Julius Caesar, had run
a month ahead of the sun, so that when Cicero entered his province on
the last day of July he still had five months of the campaigning season
in front of him. Travelling eastward, holding assizes as he went along,
he arrived at the main Roman camp near Iconium (Konya) in late

[1] See page 53, note 5.

August. After reviewing the troops, he and they marched east again reaching a town called Cybistra, about 85 miles from Iconium, on 18 September. This place was in the south-western corner of the kingdom of Cappadocia, and Cicero had an opportunity to meet its young king Ariobarzanes, who had been specially commended to him by the Senate. The following account comes from an official despatch to the government in Rome:

. . . While stationed in that spot, I sent a force of cavalry on to Cilicia, so that the news of my arrival might strengthen morale generally in the communes situated in that region, and at the same time I might get early intelligence of events in Syria. I thought it proper to devote the three days of my halt in this camp to an important and necessary duty. I had your resolution charging me to take good care of King Ariobarzanes Eusebes and Philorhomaeus,[1] to defend his welfare, security, and throne, and to protect king and kingdom; to which you added that the welfare of this monarch was a matter of great concern to the People and Senate—something that had never before been decreed by our House with respect to any monarch. I considered it incumbent upon me to convey your mandate to the king, and to promise him my faithful protection and care, adding that, since his personal welfare and the security of his realm had been commended to me by yourselves, I should be glad to hear his wishes, if any.

When I had addressed the king to this effect in the presence of my council, he began his reply with a proper expression of profound gratitude to yourselves, and then proceeded to thank me also. He said he felt it as a most important favour and very high compliment that his welfare should be of so much concern to the Senate and People of Rome, and that I should be at such pains to demonstrate my sense of obligation and the weight attaching to your recommendation. At first moreover, he gave me to understand, to my great satisfaction, that he had no knowledge or even suspicion of any plots against his life or throne. I congratulated him, and said I was delighted to hear it, at the same time urging the young man to remember the end that had overtaken his father;[2] he should guard himself vigilantly and take good heed for his safety, conformably to the Senate's admonition. He then took his leave, and returned to the town of Cybistra.

On the day following, he arrived in my camp along with his brother Ariarathes and some older persons, friends of his father's, in a state of tearful agitation. He appealed to me, as did his brother and friends, in the name of my pledged word and your commendation. When I asked in some surprise what

[1] 'Ariobarzanes the Dutiful and Friend of Rome.' Hellenistic monarchs customarily attached such epithets to their names.
[2] The king's father and predecessor, Ariobarzanes II Philopator ('the Father-loving'), had been murdered by conspirators not long before Cicero's arrival.

had happened, he said that he had received information of a manifest conspiracy, which had been kept secret prior to my arrival because those who might have revealed it were afraid to speak. But now, in the hope of my protection, a number had plucked up courage to come to him with what they knew. Among them was his brother, who loved him dearly and who had a strong sense of family loyalty. He was alleging (and Ariarathes confirmed the king's words in my presence) that he had been invited to aspire to the throne. He had been unable to entertain such a suggestion, his brother being alive, but until now had been too much afraid to bring the facts into the open. Having heard this speech, I admonished the king to take every precaution for his own safety and exhorted the tried friends of his father and grandfather to take warning by the cruel fate of the former and defend the life of their sovereign with every care and safeguard.

The king then asked me for some cavalry and foot regiments from my army. I was aware that under your decree I had not only a right but a duty to agree. But in view of the reports coming in daily from Syria, the public interest demanded that I should conduct the army to the borders of Cilicia as soon as possible. Moreover, now that the plot had been exposed, the king did not appear to me to need a Roman army; his own resources seemed adequate for his protection. I therefore urged him to make the preservation of his own life his first lesson in the art of ruling. He should exercise his royal prerogative against the persons whom he had found organizing a conspiracy against him, punishing where punishment was necessary and relieving the rest of apprehension. He should use the sanction of my army to intimidate the guilty rather than for actual combat. But all would understand, knowing the terms of the Senate's decree, that if need arose, I should come to the king's defence on your authority. So I leave him in good heart. . . .

After this colourful oriental episode Cicero and his army made all possible haste across the Taurus mountains, stimulated by reports of a Parthian invasion of Syria. He reached Tarsus, capital of Cilicia proper, on 5 October, and from there moved on towards the Amanus mountains, the natural barrier between Cilicia and Syria. But as he approached them, he received the good news that the Parthians had already turned back from Antioch and that the Roman commander in Syria, Gaius Cassius (another of Caesar's assassins-to-be), had successfully attacked them as they withdrew. For the current year the danger was over.

These mountains were full of enemies of Rome from time immemorial (as Cicero says with some exaggeration), the 'Free Cilicians' as they were called; brigands in Highlander fashion, harbourers of runaway slaves and deserters, potential allies of a Parthian invader. In a surprise foray on 13 October the Roman army scoured the area in three divisions destroying strongholds and settlements, killing or capturing the inhabitants. Cicero was saluted 'Imperator' by his soldiers—the custom at this period after a successful operation. Some further ravaging followed, but on 21 October the army settled down to the siege of a place called Pindenissum. It lasted eight weeks. To Atticus on 19 December:

... For my part I marched on Pindenissum, a strongly fortified town of the Free Cilicians, which had been in arms as long as anyone can remember. The inhabitants were wild, fierce folk, fully equipped to defend themselves. We drew a rampart and moat round the town, erected a huge mound with penthouses and a high tower, plenty of siege artillery and a large number of archers. In the end, with a great deal of labour and apparatus and many of our men wounded but none killed, we finished the job. The Saturnalia[1] was certainly a merry time, for men as well as officers. I gave them the whole of the plunder except the captives, who are being sold off today, 19 December. As I write there is about HS 120,000 on the stand. I am handing over the army to my brother Quintus, who will take it into winter quarters in unsettled country. I myself am returning to Laodicea. ...

Warfare thus happily concluded, Cicero spent a fortnight in Tarsus before setting out on his return journey to the other end of the province. From his own accounts it is plain enough that his role in the Amanus campaign had been hardly more than titular, and in letters to friends like Atticus, Caelius Rufus, and Papirius Paetus he did not mind poking fun at his military self. When he tells Atticus of his newly won title of 'Imperator' he adds: 'For a few days we encamped near Issus in the very spot where Alexander, a considerably better general (*imperator*) than either you or I, pitched his camp against Darius.' To Paetus (February 50):

Your letter has made a first-rate general of me. I had no idea you were such a military expert—evidently you have thumbed the treatises of Pyrrhus and Cineas.[2] So I intend to follow your precepts, with one addition—I mean to keep a few boats handy on the coast. They say there's no better defensive arm against Parthian cavalry! But why this frivolity? You don't know what sort of a Commander-in-Chief you have to deal with. In my command here I have put into practice the whole 'Education of Cyrus,'[3] a work which I read so often that I wore out the book. But we'll joke another time when we meet, as soon I hope we shall. ...

[1] The traditional Roman week of merry-making, beginning on 17 December.
[2] King Pyrrhus of Epirus (who warred against Rome in 281–275) and his minister Cineas both wrote military treatises.
[3] By Xenophon.

But he had done as much to earn a Triumph as many others so distinguished. That would come (if it came) after his return to Rome. Meanwhile it was important to gain the preliminary honour of a Public Thanksgiving (*supplicatio*). Cicero backed up his official request with personal letters to every member of the Senate (two, for particular reasons, excepted). Certain difficulties had to be negotiated by Caelius and other friends, but the Senate finally passed the decree with only three dissentients. One of these was Cato. In spite of an extremely lengthy letter (extant) appealing for his support, he proposed instead that Cicero should be congratulated on the excellence of his civil administration. His letter of explanation also survives:

Patriotism and friendship alike urge me to rejoice, as I heartily do, that your ability, integrity, and conscientiousness, already proved in great events at home when you wore the gown of peace, are no less actively at work in arms abroad. Accordingly I did what my judgment allowed me to do; that is to say, I paid you tribute with my voice and vote for defending your province by your integrity and wisdom, for saving Ariobarzanes' throne and person, and for winning back the hearts of our subjects to a loyal support of Roman rule.

As for the decree of a Supplication, if *you* prefer us to render thanks to the Immortal Gods in respect of provision taken for the public good by your own admirable policy and administrative rectitude—why, I am very glad of it. If, however, you regard a Supplication as an earnest of a Triumph, and on that account prefer the praise to go to accident[1] rather than to yourself, the fact is that a Triumph does not always follow a Supplication. On the other hand, the Senate's judgment that a province has been held and preserved by its governor's gentle and upright administration rather than by the favour of the Gods or the swords of an army is a far greater distinction than a Triumph; and that is what I proposed in the House.

I have written to you at length on this subject (contrary to my normal habit) so that you may realise, as I most earnestly hope you will, my anxiety to convince you of two things: first, as touching your prestige, I advocated what I conceived to be most complimentary to yourself; secondly, I am very glad that what you preferred has come to pass.

Farewell, remember me kindly, and follow your chosen course, rendering to our subjects and to the state their due of a strict and conscientious administration.

---

[1] It is worth noting that Cato writes as though accident and the favour of the Gods amounted to the same thing. Like Cicero he will have had no more than a conventional respect for official Roman religion, but Stoics believed in a divine providence, which was sometimes equated with Fortune (tyche).

Was this humbug written tongue in cheek? Cicero tried to take it at face value. Cato might still refrain from opposing the Triumph:

I think it is Hector in Naevius who says: 'Glad thy praise doth make me, father, praise from one that praisèd is.' Praise is pleasant, you will agree, when it comes from those who have themselves led honoured lives. Yes, I assure you that the congratulatory terms of your letter and the testimonial you gave me in the House represent to my mind the sum of attainment. I am particularly flattered and gratified to feel that you were glad to accord to friendship what you were clearly according to truth. And if many (not to say all) members of our society were Catos (the marvel being that it has produced *one*), how could I think of comparing the triumphal car and crown with an encomium from you? . . . But I have explained the reason for my inclination (I will not say my desire) in my previous letter. Perhaps you did not find it altogether convincing; it means at any rate that I do not regard the honour[1] as something to be unduly coveted, but that, none the less, if proffered by the Senate, I feel I ought by no means to spurn it. I trust, furthermore, that in view of the labours I have undertaken for the public good, the House will deem me not unworthy of an honour, especially one so commonly bestowed. If it so turns out, all I ask of you is that (to use your own very kind expressions), having accorded me what is in your judgment most complimentary to myself, you should be glad if what *I* prefer comes about. . . .

To Cato's friend Atticus in the following October he described Cato's letter as 'most agreeable.' But when he heard that Cato had proposed a longer Thanksgiving to his son-in-law Bibulus (a man he never liked) his real feelings boiled over:

. . . To me Cato has been disgracefully spiteful. He gave me an unsolicited testimonial for uprightness, justice, clemency, and honourable dealing, while what I asked for he refused. Accordingly Caesar, in a letter of congratulation in which he promises me his full support, is fairly cock-a-hoop at Cato's 'most ungrateful' ill usage. And the same Cato votes twenty days to Bibulus! You must forgive me, I cannot and will not swallow such things. . . .

His next letter reverts to the subject with the acid comment that in thus honouring Bibulus 'Cato made it plain that he confines his jealousy to those whose prestige admits of little or no addition.'

Cicero arrived once more in Laodicea on 11 February, 50. Among the people who (as a customary courtesy) came out to welcome the returning governor, was one Publius Vedius, 'a feather-brained ass, but a friend of Pompey's'—probably the Vedius Pollio who in time to

---

[1] A Triumph.

come displeased the Emperor Augustus by his practice of feeding slaves
to his fish:

> ... This Vedius met me with two gigs, a coach and horses, and a litter and
> a crowd of servants, for which if Curio carries his law[1] he will have to pay
> 100 sesterces per head. There was a baboon as well in one of the gigs, and
> some onagers for good measure. I never saw such a coxcomb. But listen to
> the end of the story. He lodged in Laodicea with Pompeius Vindillus and left
> his belongings there when he set out to meet me. In the meanwhile Vindillus
> dies. Since the Great Pompey was supposed to have a claim on his estate,
> Gaius Vennonius went to the house, and as he was putting everything under
> seal he came upon Vedius' luggage. In this were discovered five ladies'
> portraits in miniature, including one of your friend's sister, you know whose
> wife[2]—they live up to their names both of them, the one by having aught to
> do with the fellow, the other by tolerating such goings-on so easily. I thought
> I'd tell you this *en passant*. We are both fond of a piece of scandal. ...

Cicero stayed in Laodicea holding assizes until early May. Fears of a
Parthian invasion had revived, but they were liars. After spending
June in Tarsus, Cicero and his family set out for home by the sea route,
via Rhodes and Ephesus. On 14 October they were at Athens, on
9 November at Corcyra, where weather imposed a twelve-day halt. On
the 24th, after a perfect crossing, they landed at Brundisium. Terentia
arrived in the town just as their ship came into port, and husband and
wife met in the market square.

iii. *Domestic*

At some time before Cicero left Italy Tullia and Crassipes were
divorced. The choice of a new husband exercised him a good deal, and
several young noblemen (one of them father-to-be of the future
Emperor Tiberius) were considered. At one point he even thought of
'going back to his old gang,' as Atticus put it—i.e., of a young man of
his own 'equestrian' class, from an Arpinum family. However, Tullia
and her mother were left free to make their own selection. They chose
Publius Cornelius Dolabella, a young patrician who had just divorced
an elderly wife, married for her money. His reputation had been murky,

---

[1] Curio was now Tribune, with a programme of legislation. One of his proposed laws, on the use of roads, limited the numbers of travelling attendants, with
a fine of about £3 per man per day (?) for exceeding the permitted maximum.

[2] The lady in question was Brutus' half-sister Junia, who had married Marcus
Aemilius Lepidus (the future Triumvir). The names Brutus and Lepidus mean
'stupid' and 'agreeable' respectively.

but Cicero was not displeased; only somewhat embarrassed, because Dolabella had just brought charges against Appius Claudius, whom he had been at such pains to conciliate. He wrote to Atticus just before leaving the province:

Here I am in my province paying Appius all manner of compliments, when out of the blue I find his prosecutor becoming my son-in-law! 'Good luck to that', say you. So I hope, and I am very sure you so desire. But believe me it was the last thing I expected. I had actually sent reliable persons to the ladies in connexion with Tiberius Nero, who had treated with me. They got to Rome after the *fiançailles*. However, I hope this is better. The ladies are evidently quite charmed with the young man's attentiveness and engaging manners. For the rest, no black paint please! . . .

About the same time a letter of congratulation arrived from Caelius:

I congratulate you upon the connexion you are forming with a very fine fellow, for that, upon my word, is what I think him. In some ways he has done himself little service in the past, but he has already outgrown these failings, and if any traces remain, I feel sure that your association and influence and Tullia's good example will soon remove them. He is not obstinate in bad courses or lacking in the intelligence to perceive a better way. And the capital point is that I am very fond of him. . . .

The composition of a letter to Appius needed finesse, but Cicero's was adequate to the occasion:

. . . As for me, do please for a moment put yourself in my shoes, imagine you are I; and if you have no difficulty in finding what to say, I won't ask you to forgive my embarrassment! I should indeed wish that the arrangement made by my family without my knowledge may turn out well for my dear Tullia and myself, as you are friendly and kind enough to desire. But that the thing should have come about just when it did—well, I hope and pray that happiness may come of it, but in so hoping I take more comfort in the thought of your good sense and kind heart than in the timeliness of the proceeding! And so how to get out of the wood and finish what I have begun to say, I cannot tell. I must not take a sombre tone about an event to which you yourself wish all good luck; but at the same time I can't but feel a rub. On one point, though, my mind is easy—you will not fail to realise that what has been done has been done by others. I had told them not to consult me since I should be so far away, but to act as they thought best.

But as I write the question obtrudes itself: 'What should I have done if I *had* been on the spot?' Well, I should have approved in principle; but as for the timing, I should have taken no step against your wishes or without consulting you. You perceive what a pother I am in all this while, at my wits' end to know how to defend what I must without offending you. Lift the load from my back. I don't think I have ever pleaded a more awkward case. But of one thing you may be sure: though my long-standing zeal to serve you does not seem capable of any enhancement, yet if I had not already settled all matters with the utmost concern for your honour, I should have championed it after the announcement of this connexion, not indeed more zealously, but more ardently, openly, and emphatically. . . . In a phrase, I am no whit the friendlier disposed toward you than I already was, but I *am* much more anxious to show my friendly disposition to the world. Our old variance used to be a stimulus, urging me to guard against any suspicion that the reconciliation was not sincere on my side. Now my new connexion makes me sedulous to avoid any semblance of a falling off in the profound regard I entertain for you.

The wedding seems to have taken place in the autumn. That it did not even temporarily bring about the hoped-for reformation in the bridegroom appears from an ominous reference in a letter to Atticus written about three weeks after Cicero's return to Italy:

. . . Now, let me see. Oh yes, my son-in-law. We all find him charming, Tullia, Terentia, myself. He is as clever and agreeable as you please. Other characteristics, of which you are aware, we must put up with. After all, you know what the rejected suitors were like. Every man of them, except the one in whose case you were intermediary,[1] would have put me into debt— nobody would advance *them* a penny. But of all this when we meet; it will bear a good deal of talking over. . . .

Only one letter to Terentia survives from this period—businesslike in tone, apart from a conventionally affectionate conclusion; and she is barely mentioned in other letters except with Tullia. But two months before he left Cilicia, Cicero had a visit from her freedman and agent Philotimus, who had also been managing some of her husband's affairs, including the purchase of Milo's property. In going through the accounts with him Cicero became convinced that the man had been cheating. However, he made no direct accusation, only charging Atticus (in enigmatic Greek for better security) to see that no more funds of his got into Philotimus' hands. Significantly, he kept his suspicions from his wife; she and Philotimus were to be given the excuse that all spare cash had to be reserved against Triumph expenses. Whether or not Cicero believed her party to Philotimus' dishonesty, he obviously did not trust her any longer.

His family difficulties were not confined to absent members. Quintus' domestic troubles made him a fractious companion. After the tableau

---

[1] The young man from Arpinum, mentioned above.

in the villa at Arcanum it is no surprise to find divorce in the air a year later. A long letter to Atticus of April 50 begins:

Your freedman Philogenes has come to pay his respects to me in Laodicea and says he is returning to you at once by sea, so I am giving him this letter in reply to yours delivered by Brutus' courier. And first I shall reply to your last page, where the account in Cincius' letter to you of his conversation with Statius vexed me deeply. The most vexatious thing about it was that Statius should say that I approve the idea. On that let me say only one thing: so far from wishing the bond between us to be in any way relaxed, I should welcome as many and as intimate links with you as possible, though those of affection, and of the closest, exist already. As for *him*,[1] I have often found that he is apt to speak rather harshly on these matters, and again I have often mollified his irritation. I think you know this. During this foreign trip or rather service of ours I have repeatedly seen him flare up and calm down again. What he may have written to Statius I cannot say. Whatever step he proposed to take in such matter, he ought not to have written to a freedman. I shall do my utmost to prevent any action contrary to our wishes and to what is right. But in a matter of this sort it is not enough to answer for oneself, and a large share of this responsibility falls upon the boy, or young man as he is. This I am in the habit of urging upon him. He does seem to be very fond of his mother, as he should be, and extraordinarily fond of you. But the boy's nature, though gifted, is complex, and I have plenty to do guiding it. . . .

Quintus' outbursts were no doubt directed against Pomponia, but they are consistent with a rising exasperation at his brother's self-interested efforts to keep the marriage going. These were carried to remarkable lengths. May–June 50:

. . . I think, indeed I am sure, that young Quintus has read a letter addressed to his father. He is in the habit of opening them and does so at my suggestion, in case there might be something we ought to know about. This particular letter contained the same item about your sister which you wrote to me. I could see that the boy was dreadfully upset. He cried as he lamented over it to me. In fact I was greatly impressed by the dutiful, affectionate, thoughtful way he spoke. It makes me the more hopeful that nothing untoward will happen. I wanted you to know. . . .

Such schooling in domestic duplicity, however well-intentioned, bore fruit in young Quintus which Cicero had soon to sample. As for Quintus senior, if he ever learned what had been going on he must have wondered what kind of a husband and father his brother took him for. But the immediate results were satisfactory. July 50:

[1] Quintus.

Young Quintus has certainly acted like a good son in reconciling his father's mind toward your sister, not it is true without a good deal of encouragement from me; but I was spurring a willing horse. Your letter too has greatly stimulated him. Altogether, I am satisfied that the matter stands as we wish. . . .

Soon after their arrival in the province the two boys were sent to Galatia in central Anatolia, where they remained while their fathers were campaigning in the south under the care of its king Deiotarus, a good friend to Cicero and to Rome. At sixteen Quintus was old enough to be given his 'manly gown,' and as his father had been left in charge of the army Cicero officiated in his place. Reports of the boy's behaviour had not been entirely satisfactory. To Atticus, 19 December:

. . . I am under instructions to give your nephew Quintus his white gown when I get to Laodicea. I shall keep him on a tighter rein. . . .

From Laodicea, 20 February:

. . . The boys are fond of one another, and are learning and practising.[1] But as Isocrates said about Ephorus and Theopompus, one of them needs the rein, the other the spur. I propose to give Quintus his white gown at the Liberalia,[2] as his father asked me to do. . . . *I* am delighted with Dionysius. The boys say he has a furious temper; but no one could be more learned or high principled or more attached to you and me. . . .

Dionysius was still in high favour when he and Cicero parted in Italy. December 50:

I am sending you Dionysius, who is on fire with impatience to see you; reluctantly I must say, but I had to agree. I have found him not only a good scholar, which I already knew, but upright, serviceable, zealous moreover for my good name, an honest fellow, and in case that sounds too much like commending a freedman, a really fine man. . . .

Soon afterwards the tutor was unmasked, to Cicero's eyes at least, as an ungrateful scoundrel. Quintus senior had never thought much of him, and criticized his brother's partiality. He also seems to have resented aspersions on his son, and when Atticus in his wisdom advised that if the father were left in charge of the province after the Proconsul's

---

[1] i.e., declaiming.
[2] The festival of Liber (Bacchus) and Libera on 17 March, the usual day for a coming of age ceremony.

departure the son should at all events go home, Quintus was parentally annoyed.

This problem of a *locum tenens* gave Cicero much uneasiness during his last few months in Cilicia. He was anxious to leave at the earliest permissible date, the end of July. But the political situation in Rome had prevented the Senate from appointing a successor, so it lay with Cicero to nominate a deputy. His Quaestor, Mescinius Rufus, was notoriously unsuitable—'irresponsible, licentious, and light-fingered,' though Cicero liked him personally. The obvious choice was Quintus in virtue of official rank (as ex-Praetor), experience, and relationship— Pomptinus, the only other Legate who possessed the first two qualifications, had already returned to Rome. Logic and public opinion pointed the same way. Indeed, 'nothing else would look well.' But it was doubtful whether Quintus would accept. He hated the province, a sentiment with which his brother cordially sympathized. In the end the problem was solved by the arrival of a new Quaestor. But even if Quintus was relieved to have the burden shifted, the affair may well have left him with a residue of grievance. It is one thing to decline an unwanted honour, another not to be asked; and for all he might say about Quintus' reluctance, Cicero knew that he would have been persuadable. In confidential explanation to Atticus he gave the real reasons (August 50):

. . . So much for the public ear. For your own, I should never have had a minute's peace of mind for fear of some exhibition of irritability or rudeness or carelessness—these things happen. Then there's his son, a boy and a boy with a fine conceit of himself—any incident involving him would have been *most* distressing. His father was unwilling to send him away and was annoyed at your advising it. . . .

If Quintus sensed the unflattering truth, his feelings are easily imagined.

It may not be an accident that Cicero nowhere expresses any appreciation of his brother's services in Cilicia, not even in his accounts of the Amanus campaign. Quintus' role in the operations of 13 October had been to stand by the Commander-in-Chief in one of the three detachments into which the army was split. A bare mention in a letter to Cato is all the acknowledgment it gets; to Atticus not even that, though Pomptinus is named. Nor does Atticus seem to have been told anything about Quintus' record as deputy-governor of Cilicia proper in charge of the army during winter and spring. Its indiscipline must have made the post no sinecure.

Quintus does not seem to have got much out of the province financially. In the spring of 49 he was unable to repay Atticus a comparatively small loan of 10,000 sesterces (about £300), and it may be— the relevant passage is cryptic and does not quite certainly point this way —that he expressed some disappointment. It is certain that he later asked his brother to lend or give him part of his own large haul and was aggrieved because Cicero would not, or could not, oblige.

Separation from his beloved and trusted Statius may have contributed to Quintus' malaise. His brother was better off. This is as good a point as any to say something of a person who played a notable part in Cicero's private life and was later to do much for his memory. Tiro was probably born a slave in Cicero's father's household. A statement in St. Jerome's Chronicle which would make him only three years younger than Cicero himself is certainly wrong; at this time he will have been at most in his early twenties. As a boy he must have shown talents beyond the ordinary, for Cicero took his education in hand personally and trained him as his confidential secretary and literary assistant. Quintus too was fond of him, and when Tiro was given his freedom in 53 he wrote to his brother from Gaul:

My dear Marcus, as I hope to see you again, and my boy and my little Tullia and your son, I am truly gratified at what you have done about Tiro, in judging his former condition to be beneath his deserts and preferring to have him as a friend rather than a slave. Believe me, I jumped for joy when I read your letter and his. Thank you, and congratulations! If Statius' loyalty gives *me* so much pleasure, how highly you must value the same qualities in Tiro, with the addition of literary accomplishments and culture, gifts worth even more than those! I have all manner of great reasons to love you, but this *is* a reason—the very fact that you so properly announced the event to me is a reason. I saw all that is you in your letter. . . .

Did Cicero remember, and was he not meant to remember, his own violent disapproval of Statius' manumission six years previously?

Cicero accepted slavery, like other existing institutions, as part of natural order. He remarks in his treatise 'On Duties:' 'Admittedly rulers who are holding subjects down by force have to employ cruelty, as masters must toward their domestics if they cannot otherwise be kept under control.' In 61, when he was upset by the death of a slave, he felt (like the epigrammatist Martial 150 years later) that the emotion called for some apology:

. . . I have nothing else to tell you. As a matter of fact I am writing in some distress. My *lecteur* Sositheus, a charming lad, has died, and it has affected me more than the death of a slave perhaps ought to do. . . .

But he can hardly be imagined as other than a kindly master on the whole, and his affection for Tiro comes out even in letters written before his manumission, as this in 53:

Aegypta arrived today, 12 April. He told me that you are quite free of fever and in pretty good shape, but said you had not been able to write to me. That made me anxious, all the more so because Hermia, who ought to have arrived today, has not come. You cannot imagine how anxious I feel about your health. If you relieve my mind on this score, I shall relieve yours of every worry. I should write more if I thought you could read with any comfort at the present time. Put your clever brain, which I value so highly, to the job of preserving yourself for us both. Look after yourself carefully, I repeat. Good-bye.

P.S. Hermia *has* arrived and I have received your letter, shakily written, poor fellow—no wonder, when you are so seriously ill. I have sent you Aegypta to be with you (he is not a bad fellow, and I think he is fond of you), also a cook for your use. Good-bye.

In Cilicia Tiro was still ailing, and he worked too hard. Much to his own distress Cicero had to leave him behind, first at Issus. He wrote to Atticus from Tarsus in July 50:

. . . Tiro would have sent you a letter but for the fact that I left him seriously ill at Issus. But they tell me he is better. Even so I am acutely worried. He is such a well-behaved, conscientious young fellow.

However Tiro recovered sufficiently to travel on the homeward journey as far as Patrae (Patras) on the south shore of the Gulf of Corinth. There, on 2 November, he had to be left behind again. Eight of Cicero's extant letters to him were dispatched from various places *en route* from Patrae to Brundisium. The following specimen, though written in the first person, is headed as from the four—Cicero, his son, and the two Quinti:

I read your letter with fluctuating feelings. The first page upset me badly, the second brought me round a little. So now, if not before, I am clear that until your health is quite restored you should not venture upon travel either by land or water. I shall see you soon enough, if I see you thoroughly strong again.

You say the doctor has a good reputation, and that is what I hear myself; but frankly I don't think much of his treatments. You ought not to have been given stew with a weak stomach. However I have written to him at length, as also to Lyso.[1] To Curius,[2] who is a most agreeable fellow, very obliging and good-natured, I have written a good deal, including the suggestion that, if you agree, he should move you over to his house. I am afraid our friend Lyso is a little casual. It is a Greek national trait, and besides he has not answered a letter he received from me. However, you commend him; so you must judge yourself what is best. One thing, my dear Tiro, I do beg of you: don't consider money at all where the needs of your health are concerned. I have told Curius to advance whatever you say. I imagine the doctor ought to be given something to make him more interested in your case.[3]

Your services to me are beyond counting—in my home and out of it, in Rome and abroad, in private affairs and in public, in my studies and literary work. You will surpass them all, if I see you your own man again, as I hope I shall. If it can be done safely, I think it would be very nice for you to sail home along with Quaestor Mescinius. He is not a bad fellow, and he seemed to me to have a regard for you. But when you have given every possible attention to your health, only *then*, my dear Tiro, attend to sailing arrangements. I do not now want you to hurry in any way. My sole concern is for you to be well.

Rest assured, my dear Tiro, that nobody cares for me who does not care for you. Your recovery is most important to you and me, but many others are concerned about it. In the past you have never been able to recruit yourself properly because you wanted to give me of your best at every turn. Now there is nothing to stand in your way. Put everything else aside, think only of your physical well-being. I shall believe you care for me in proportion to the care you devote to your health. Good-bye, my dear Tiro, good-bye and fondest good wishes. Lepta sends you his, so do we all. Good-bye.

7 November, from Leucas.

Cicero's doubts about Lyso were later confirmed:

... I wish you had stayed away from Lyso's concert—you might have had a fourth weekly attack. However, since you chose to put good manners before your health, do be careful in future. . . .

Nothing in the correspondence suggests that the erotic verses recorded by the younger Pliny[4] were anything more than a *jeu d'esprit*. But it is likely enough that, Tullia apart, Cicero came to care as much for this young man as for anyone in the world, or more.

[1] Cicero's host at Patrae. Tiro had been left in his house.
[2] Manius Curius, a Roman business man resident in Patrae and a friend of Atticus.
[3] The doctor (whose name was Asclepo) seems to have been giving his services gratis.
[4] See page 21, note 3.

CHAPTER FOURTEEN

Rubicon

'Whatever Discord bade, mankind performed.'
Petronius

EVEN before Cicero left Italy for his province signs were plainly visible of coming collision between Caesar and the new league of Pompey and the Optimates. While he was away the storm gathered. In September 50 Caelius Rufus summed up as follows:

> . . . On high politics, I have often told you that I do not see peace lasting for another year; and the nearer the inevitable conflict approaches, the plainer the danger appears. The question on which the dynasts will join issue is this: Gnaeus Pompeius is determined not to allow Gaius Caesar to be elected Consul unless he surrenders his army and provinces; whereas Caesar is persuaded that he cannot survive if he leaves his army. He makes the proposition, however, that both surrender their military forces. So this is what their love-affair, their scandalous union has come to: not covert backbiting, but outright war! As for my own position, I don't know what course to take, and I don't doubt that the same question is going to trouble you. I have ties of obligation and friendship with these people.[1] On the other side I love the cause but hate the men.
>
> I expect you are alive to the point that when parties clash in a community it behoves a man to take the more respectable side so long as the struggle is political and not by armed force; but when it comes to actual fighting he should choose the stronger side and reckon the safer course the better. In the present quarrel Gnaeus Pompeius will evidently have with him the Senate and the people who sit on juries,[2] whereas all who live in present fear and small hope for the future will rally to Caesar. His army is incomparably superior. To be sure, there is time enough to consider their respective resources and choose one's side. . . .

Perhaps no comparable problem in ancient history has produced more print than the constitutional issue between Caesar and the Senate

[1] The Caesarians—Curio, Antony, and Dolabella in particular.
[2] The rich and respectable, from whom juries were empanelled. Pompey himself chose 360 specially for the trials in 52.

which led to civil war in January 49. It turned on two points: first, whether Caesar should be allowed to exercise the privilege granted him by law in 52 of standing for the Consulship in absence, and second, the date on which he should be superseded in his Gallic command. But the war was not fought for the sake of legal or procedural technicalities; and apart from 'face,' neither question was of vital importance.

True, it has been generally held that Caesar *did* have a vital interest in keeping his command right down to the commencement of another year of office as Consul. According to the biographer Suetonius, writing in the second century A.D., Cato had threatened to bring him to trial (the charge is not specified) as soon as he had handed over to a successor. Magistrates in office could not be prosecuted, but in an interval of private status Caesar would be vulnerable; and before a packed or intimidated jury his fate would be as inevitable as Milo's. And Suetonius cites the historian Asinius Pollio, a Caesarian partisan, who reported Caesar's own words as he gazed at the carnage on the battlefield of Pharsalia; 'They would have it so. After all I had done for Rome, I, Gaius Caesar, would have been found guilty as charged if I had not appealed for help to my army.' And when Caelius Rufus told Cicero of Caesar's persuasion that he could not survive if he left his army, he was presumably retailing contemporary propaganda. But there are powerful arguments for denying Caesar the benefit of such a plea. His own 'Commentaries on the Civil War' contain several apologias; but neither in his speech to his troops after crossing the Rubicon nor in his reply to Pompey's messengers nor in his address to the Senate (what was left of it) after his return to Rome is there a word about prosecution or a rigged trial. The same goes for Cicero's letters; in various disquisitions on the war and reports of conversations with Pompey it is always taken for granted that Caesar would infallibly become Consul if he came back and stood for the office in the usual way. After all, if his enemies were so firmly in control of affairs in Rome and so unscrupulously determined to use their power, what good would the Consulship have done him? There were precedents for action against Consuls; and the protection afforded was at best temporary. If Pompey could make a jury convict the conqueror of Gaul, he could also see to it that he was given no more armies to command.

Here, for Caesar, was the hub. He claimed to be defending his *dignitas*, his 'public image' and prestige: his enemies must not be allowed to damage that by depriving him of what he considered his rights. But he must often have asked himself what sort of political future he had to expect after Pompey's defection. Cato's threat would probably end in nothing, as Cato's threats (according to Cicero) often did; Caesar was not Milo, and the situation in 49 was not the same as in 52. Even without Pompey Caesar had a strong following in Rome. The populace was on his side, the rank and file of the Senate might be won over, Pompey himself might not be irreclaimable. Still it would be a difficult game to play, and he might lose. The alternative was tempting: to use the military instrument he had forged in Gaul while it was still in his hands, and make a final reckoning with the Sullan establishment which he had been fighting through most of his career. If he won, he would necessarily become what folk like Cicero called a 'tyrant.' To a man not alarmed by words nor hypnotized by traditional city-state ethics, that prospect would not be too disagreeable.

What of his opponents? On his way back through Italy Cicero found an overwhelming desire for peace, even at the price of concession to Caesar's demands. But the Optimate leaders, who now had Pompey's ear, were war-minded. Some of them, Cicero thought, were looking to war as a way out of their financial difficulties, but this was certainly not true of all. Cato and his friends were convinced that the republican constitution could not assimilate Caesar. The ruthlessness and audacity of his first Consulship and the conquest of Gaul (where he had just crushed the last desperate effort of the natives to shake off the new yoke) had created a sinister mystique around the 'monster,' as Cicero called him, using a Greek word usually applied to weird and terrible creatures of mythology—the hell-hound Cerberus, the Sphinx, the Gorgon's head. Pompey's attitude is defined in a conversation he had with Cicero on 25 December:

... Your forecast that I should be seeing Pompey before I came your way has proved correct. On the 25th he overtook me near Lavernium. We went back to Formiae together and talked privately from two o'clock till evening. The answer to your question whether there is any hope of a pacification, so far as I could perceive from Pompey's talk, which lacked neither length nor detail, is that there isn't even the desire for one. His view is that if Caesar is made Consul, even after giving up his army, it will mean the subversion of the constitution; and he further thinks that when Caesar hears that preparations against him are energetically proceeding he will forego the Consulate this year and prefer to retain his army and province. But should Caesar take leave of his senses, Pompey is quite contemptuous of anything he can do and confident in his own and the Republic's forces. All in all, though I often thought of 'the War-God on both sides,'[1] I felt relieved as I heard such a man, courageous, experienced, and powerful in prestige, discoursing statesmanwise on the dangers of a false peace. We had in front of us a speech made by Antony on 21 December, containing a denunciation of Pompey from the day he came of age, a protest on behalf of the persons condemned, and threats of armed force. Talking of which Pompey remarked: 'How do you suppose Caesar will behave if he gets control of the state when his feckless nobody of a Quaestor[2] dares to say this sort of thing?' In short, far from seeking the peaceful settlement you talk of, he seemed to dread it. . . .

War came because both sides (leaving the helpless, peace-loving majority out of account) wanted war, or at least did not sufficiently want to avoid it. Neither was afraid of the outcome. Caesar's faith in his veteran soldiers and his own military genius needs no explanation. The grounds for confidence in the opposite camp were less simple and obvious. The only troops immediately available to the government in Italy were two legions recently detached from Caesar's army for service in the East, and their loyalty was naturally suspect. The armies in Spain under Pompey's remote command might threaten Caesar's rear, but he had forces enough in Gaul to keep them in check until he was free to deal with them. But Pompey believed the manhood of Italy would come flocking to his banner. He had recently recovered from a long and dangerous illness, which had produced extravagant demonstrations of loyal sentiment from the Italian municipalities. Asked what he would do if Caesar marched on Rome, he answered: 'I have only to stamp my foot anywhere on Italian soil for soldiers, horse and foot, to appear.' And would Caesar's army march against Pompey the Great and the Senate? Pompey thought he had reason to doubt it. Within a few days of the outbreak of war, Caesar's principal lieutenant, Titus Labienus, whose record of independent generalship in Gaul could almost compare with Caesar's own in prejudiced minds, deserted to the republicans.

In certain rare moods Cicero thought, as many still think, that Pompey saw further ahead, that his subsequent retreat from Italy was the operation of a long-preconceived strategy. The present writer has argued against this view elsewhere.[3] Assuredly Pompey's Optimate allies—Cato, Domitius, and the rest—had no such intention, though

---

[1] From the Iliad: 'The God of War / fights on both sides and slayeth him that slays.'

[2] Antony had been Caesar's Quaestor in 51. He had just entered on office as Tribune.

[3] In the fourth appendix to Volume IV of my edition (pages 450 f.).

the consciousness of vast outlying resources will have been a toughen-
ing factor in their minds as well as his. Both he and they were under the
spell of his glorious military past. They did not altogether trust him,
but that too made for bellicosity. A war, of Caesar's starting, was the
Optimates' best guarantee against another Luca.

To the studiously insouciant Caelius, who went over to Caesar at the
last moment, the coming holocaust might present itself in the light of
'a mighty and delightful spectacle, if one could avoid the personal
risk.' To the humane and sensitive Cicero, with his memories of the
eighties and his dedication to the arts of peace, it was hideous and
avoidable. Here he judged better than Cato. Peace was indeed the
lesser hazard for all that both of them wanted to preserve. Caesar
might win a war; and even if he lost, freedom was not guaranteed. No
individual or group was wholly responsible for the Civil War; but none
of those who divided responsibility—not Caesar, nor Pompey, nor the
Catonians—could plead the only admissible excuse, that in war lay the
sole reasonable hope of survival for self or cause.

The accident of absence had absolved Cicero from taking a position
earlier on; but as he travelled homewards the burden of personal
decision weighed upon him, and, as often, he tried to transfer some of it
to Atticus. From Athens, 16 October:

. . . For mercy's sake, put all your affection, lavished on me as it is, and all
your wisdom, remarkable in every field as I do assure you I regard it, into one
single concern, the consideration of my position *in toto*. I fancy I see the
greatest struggle—unless the same Providence that delivered me from the
Parthian war better than I could have dared to hope takes pity on our
country—the greatest that history has ever known. Well, that is a calamity
which I shall have to bear along with the rest of the world. I don't ask you to
think about that. But do pray take up this personal problem of my own. You
see, don't you, that at your prompting I have made friends with both
contestants. And I only wish I had listened to your affectionate admonitions
from the first ('The heart within my breast thou ne'er couldst sway').[1]
However, in the end you persuaded me to make friends with one of them
because of all he had done for me and with the other because of his power. So
I did, and by conciliating them in every possible way I managed to win as
high a place in their several good graces as any other man's. We calculated
that on the one hand joined with Pompey I should never be obliged to go
politically astray, while on the other hand as Pompey's ally I ought not to be
at loggerheads with Caesar—they were so closely linked. Now, as you
represent and as I see for myself, there looms ahead a tremendous contest

---

[1] From the Odyssey.

between them. Each counts me as his man, unless it be that one of them is only pretending—for Pompey has no doubts, judging correctly that I strongly approve of his present politics. Moreover, I received letters from both at the same time as yours, conveying the impression that neither has a friend in the world he values more than myself.

But what am I to do? I don't mean in the last resort—if war is to arbitrate, I am clear that defeat with one is better than victory with the other—I mean in the proceedings that will be set on foot when I get back to prevent his candidature *in absentia* and to make him give up his army. 'Speak, Marcus Tullius!'[1] What shall I say? 'Be so kind as to wait until I see Atticus?' There's no room for fence-sitting. Against Caesar then? 'Where are those close-clasped hands?'[2] For I helped to get him this privilege, as requested by himself at Ravenna in connexion with Caelius who was then Tribune—and not only by him but by our Gnaeus too in that immortal third Consulship of his. Or shall I take a different line? 'I fear' not Pompey only but 'the Trojan men and dames.' 'Polydamas will foremost cry me shame.'[3] Being who? You yourself, of course, the encomiast of my doings and writings.

I escaped this dilemma during the two earlier Marcelline Consulships[4] when the Senate discussed Caesar's command; now I am coming in just at the crisis. Accordingly, 'to let the dunce state his opinion first,'[5] I am strongly in favour of my doing something about a Triumph, and so staying outside Rome with the best possible excuse.[6] Even so they will try to draw a statement of my views. You may laugh when I say it, but I wish to heaven I was still back there in my province. It would really have been better, if this was hanging over us. Not that anything could have been more wretched. . . .

Atticus' position as yet was that of the average Roman conservative, and his advice was to fall into line with respectable opinion; after all, he pointed out, Caesar might have been more generous to Cicero personally. At the same time he need not make himself too conspicuous. He could wait outside the city boundary until the Senate settled the matter of his Triumph, and in general take his cue from his coevals Vulcatius Tullus and Servius Sulpicius—Consulars and good republicans, but men of peace and moderation. Cicero's *amour propre* was not

---

[1] Cicero envisages himself as called upon to speak in the Senate by the presiding Consul.

[2] Probably a (Latin) verse quotation.

[3] See page 52, note 1.

[4] Three members of the Claudius Marcellus family were Consuls successively n 51–49.

[5] A proverbial saying, perhaps from a Latin play, like 'Fools rush in where angels fear to tread.'

[6] If Cicero were to cross the ancient city boundary he would lose his proconsular status and thereby render himself ineligible for a Triumph.

flattered. Writing from the house of a friend about 25 miles east of Pompeii on 9 December, he told Atticus that he was quite right not to doubt his, Cicero's, loyalty to the Republic. *That* would have been proof against any bounties from Caesar, and if the situation were as straightforward as Atticus seemed to think, he, Cicero, would look to play a part worthy of himself. Vulcatius and Servius were hardly the models for *him*. But straightforward it was not. The struggle was really between two individuals, and it was late in the day for Pompey to topple Caesar after taking so long to build him up:

. . . However, since that is the pass we have come to, I shall not in your phrase ask 'Where is the bark of Atreus' sons?'[1] The only bark for me will be the one that has Pompey at the helm. As for your question 'What will happen when the word comes "Speak, Marcus Tullius"?': *tout court*, 'I agree with Gnaeus Pompeius.' Pompey himself, however, I shall privately urge to peace. For my feeling is that things are in a very parlous state indeed. No doubt you people in Rome are better informed. All the same, I see this much: we are dealing with a man who fears nothing and is ready for anything. All persons under legal sentence or censorial stigma, and all who deserve one or the other, are on his side. So are pretty well all the younger people, all the desperate city rabble, some sturdy Tribunes, Quintus Cassius[2] now included, all the debt-ridden, who I find are worth more than I supposed! Caesar's side lacks nothing but a cause, all else they have in abundance. Here I find everyone moving heaven and earth against decision by war, the results of which are always unpredictable and now may be apprehended as more likely than not to turn out the wrong way. . . .

The same letter has a reference (the last of several) to the large loan advanced by Caesar some years previously.[3] When he was leaving for the East in 51 Cicero had tried to arrange for its repayment, but part was still outstanding:

. . . Caesar sends me smooth letters, and Balbus does the same on his behalf. I am determined not to stray an inch from the path of strict honour. But you know how much I still owe him. Don't you think there is a danger of having it thrown in my teeth by someone or other if I take a weak line, or of

---

[1] i.e., 'Which is the side to join?' Atticus had quoted the words from Euripides' 'Women of Troy,' without regard to their original context; and the quotation is inaccurate. The original has 'the general' (Agamemnon) instead of 'the sons of Atreus' (Agamemnon and Menelaus).

[2] To be distinguished from his cousin Gaius Cassius (Caesar's assassin), who took Pompey's side in the war.

[3] See page 94.

payment being demanded if I take a strong one? What do you suggest? 'Pay up,' perhaps. All right, I'll borrow from Caelius![1] But I should like you to give it your consideration. I suppose that if ever I make a fine patriotic speech in the Senate your friend from Tartessus[2] will politely ask me for a banker's draft on my way out! . . .

The next day Cicero met Pompey:

. . . I saw Pompey on 10 December. We were together for something like two hours. He seemed very happy to see me back; encouraged me about the Triumph, promised to do his part, and advised me not to attend the Senate before I had got the matter settled for fear I might make an enemy of some Tribune or other in the course of debate. In fact on this personal matter his language could not have been more forthcoming. On the political situation he talked as though we were certainly in for war—nothing to suggest a hope of agreement. He told me that though he had previously been aware of Caesar's complete estrangement from himself, a very recent incident had confirmed his opinion. Hirtius, a very close friend of Caesar's, had come from him to Rome, but had not approached himself; he had arrived on the evening of 6 December, and Balbus had arranged to call at Scipio's[3] before dawn on the 7th for a talk on the whole situation. But Hirtius had left to join Caesar in the middle of the night. This seemed to Pompey proof positive of estrangement. In short my only comfort is that I don't believe that Caesar, given a second Consulship by his enemies and immense power by grace of fortune, will be mad enough to put all this in jeopardy. But if he does start plunging, then indeed I fear much that I dare not write down. Anyway as matters stand I propose to come to Rome on 3 January.

From Formiae a few days later:

. . . The political situation alarms me more every day. It is not as though the supposed *boni* were agreed. You would hardly credit me if I told you of the Roman Knights and Senators too I have heard using the bitterest language about the conduct of affairs in general and this trip of Pompey's[4] in particular. Peace is what is wanted. Victory will bring many evils in its train, including the certainty of a despot. But we shall talk of this together soon. . . . I am one of those who hold it more expedient to concede his demands than to join battle. It is late in time for us to resist a force which we have been building up against ourselves for ten years. 'What line will you take then?' you may ask.

[1] Since joining Caesar's party Caelius had become affluent; but Cicero is not serious.

[2] i.e., Gades (Cadiz), Balbus' native town.

[3] Metellus Scipio, Pompey's father-in-law.

[4] Pompey had left Rome for Campania on 7 December to take over the two legions stationed there and raise new levies.

None of course which you do not advise and none before I have either settled my own affair[1] or given it up. . . .

More to the same effect on the 19th:

. . . The root of all these things is one and the same. We should have stood up to him when he was weak, and that would have been easy. Now we have to deal with eleven legions, all the cavalry he may want, the Gauls beyond Po, the city populace, our demoralized younger generation, and a leader strong in prestige and hardihood. We must either fight him or allow his candidature as by law authorized. 'Better fight than be a slave,' say you. Fight for what? Proscription if you're beaten; and if you win, slavery just the same? What am I going to do then? What stray cattle do when they follow droves of their own species. As an ox follows the herd, so I shall follow the *boni*, or whoever may be called such, even if they plunge. . . .

Cicero's second interview with Pompey on the 25th had a stiffening effect. The last letter before his arrival on the outskirts of Rome is an elaborate analysis of the possibilities of the situation written from Pompey's point of view, which for the moment seems to be Cicero's. It ends:

. . . Very well, fight we will, in good hope (as the same person[2] says) of victory or of death as free men. War once decided, the time depends on chance, the plan of campaign on circumstances. So I won't take up your time on that question. If you have any views on what I have said, let me know them. For my part I have no peace day or night.

By the time Cicero arrived at the capital the sands had almost run out. He tried to talk Pompey into concessions, not without effect so far as Pompey's own mind was concerned (or so Cicero thought); but the warmongers had their way. On 12 January he wrote to Tiro:

. . . I arrived outside Rome on 4 January. They streamed to meet me on the road—a most flattering welcome. But I found myself plunged into the flames of civil strife, or rather war. I should dearly have liked to heal the mischief, and I believe I *could* have healed it had not the personal desires of certain people (there are warmongers on both sides) stood in my way. To be sure, our friend Caesar has sent a threatening, harsh letter to the Senate and persists in his impudent determination to hold his army and province in defiance of the Senate, and my friend Curio is egging him on. Our friend Antony and Quintus Cassius have gone to join Caesar[3] along with Curio. They were not expelled by violence of any kind, but left after the Senate had charged the

[1] The Triumph.   [2] Pompey.
[3] As Tribunes it was unconstitutional for Antony and Cassius to leave Rome.

Consuls, Praetors, Tribunes, and us Proconsuls to see that the state take no harm. Never was the community in greater peril, never did bad citizens have a leader more ready to strike. Not but what preparations are going very actively forward on our side too. This is taking place by the authority and zeal of our friend Pompey, who late in the day has begun to be afraid of Caesar. . . .

The letter, which Tiro would naturally show to his contacts in Patrae, presents Cicero, fairly enough, as the man of moderation and good will, the personal friend of both Pompey and Caesar, of Curio too and Antony (he might have added Caelius Rufus, who had joined the flight to Caesar's camp). Another letter to Tiro written some three weeks later heightens the colour:

. . . From the day I arrived outside Rome all my views, words, and actions were unceasingly directed towards peace. But a strange madness was abroad. Not only the rascals, but even those who pass for honest men[1] were possessed with the lust of battle, while I cried aloud that civil war is the worst of calamities. Swept along by some spirit of folly, forgetting the name he bears and the honours he has won, Caesar seized Ariminum, Pisaurum, Ancona, and Arretium. So we abandoned Rome—whether wisely or courageously it is idle to argue. . . .

The Senate passed its 'Final Decree,' creating a state of martial law, on 7 January and the two Caesarian Tribunes left for Ravenna that evening. Before day broke on the 11th Caesar crossed the little River Rubicon, which bounded his province, and occupied Ariminum, (Rimini). Although he had only one legion with him, he struck rapidly, seizing towns to the south and east. News of his progress threw Rome into panic, and on the 17th there was a mass exodus, headed by Pompey, the Consuls, and a large part of the Senate. Even the money in the state treasury was left behind in the confusion. Cicero went early on the 18th, first dispatching a hurried note to Atticus:

I have decided on the spur of the moment to leave before daybreak so as to avoid looks and talk, especially with these laurelled lictors.[2] As for what is to follow, I really don't know what I am doing or going to do, I am so confused by the rashness of this crazy proceeding of ours. As for yourself, what can I recommend?—*I* am expecting advice from *you*. What our

---

[1] *boni.*

[2] As long as Cicero retained his proconsular status he was attended by twelve lictors carrying axes and bundles of rods (*fasces*) as emblems of authority. Commanders who had been saluted 'Imperator' had the *fasces* wreathed with laurel in token of victory.

Gnaeus has decided or is deciding I don't yet know, cooped up there in the country towns in a daze. If he makes a stand in Italy we shall all be with him, but if he leaves, it's a matter for consideration. So far anyhow, unless I am out of my mind, there has been nothing but folly and recklessness. Pray write to me often, if only what comes into your head.

He probably arrived at his house near Formiae the following evening.

CHAPTER FIFTEEN

'What to Do? How to Behave?'

'Danger maketh men much pause.'
Sophocles

ABOUT a week before he left Rome Cicero had been asked by Pompey (acting under the Senate's commission) to take over the military governorship of Campania. His first impulse was to accept, but presently he changed his mind,[1] foreseeing that without troops and funds the post was likely to bring him nothing but discredit. Instead he agreed to supervise the coastal area—the playground of the Roman upper classes, where he himself possessed three villas and had many local connexions. To begin with he expected to be much on the move; but in fact he did not find (perhaps did not choose to find) a great deal to do, and spent most of his time in his house near Formiae, until Caesar's victory in Italy at the end of February automatically cancelled his responsibilities. These had indeed been so loosely defined or so merely titular that when convenient he could and did represent himself as taking no part in the war.

To Atticus, who stayed in Rome, he wrote almost every day, and nearly all his letters have been preserved. They let us follow the ups and downs of the war news (mostly downs) and the resulting fluctuations of Cicero's mind and mood. Continually they harp upon the agonizing personal problem to which the events of mid-January had given quite a different turn.

Before arriving in Rome Cicero had thought in terms of a political conflict, in which he was pulled different ways by his personal obligations to Caesar and Pompey respectively, his desire for peace, and his sense of what was expected of him as a loyal citizen of the Republic. If war broke out, it was a matter of course that he would be on the side

[1] This much disputed matter is discussed in Appendix II to Volume IV of my edition.

of Pompey and the Senate. But the manner of its coming compelled him to think afresh. One stumbling-block was out of the way: he no longer had to worry about 'living up to Caesar's friendliness.' Whatever strength there might have been in Caesar's case before the war, his invasion of Italy made him in Cicero's eyes a would-be despot, a brigand, and a moral lunatic. Nothing could justify a Roman general in using the army entrusted to him against the home authorities in assertion of purely personal claims. To Atticus on 21 January:

Pray, what's all this? What is going on? I am in the dark. 'We hold Cingulum, we've lost Ancona, Labienus has deserted Caesar.' Is it a Roman general or Hannibal we are talking of? Deluded wretch, with never in his life a glimpse of even the shadow of the Ideal![1] And he says he is doing all this for his honour's sake! Where is honour without moral right? And is it right to have an army without public authority, to seize Roman towns by way of opening the road to the mother city, to plan debt-cancellations, recall of exiles, and a hundred other villainies, 'all for that first of deities, Sole Power?'[2] He is welcome to his greatness. I would rather a single hour with you, warming myself in that 'bonus' sunshine of yours,[3] than all such autocracies, or rather I had sooner die a thousand deaths than entertain one such thought. You may say 'But supposing you *did* wish for it?' Come! Anyone is free to *wish*. But *I* reckon the mere wish a sorrier thing than crucifixion. There is only one thing sorrier still, and that is for a man in such a case to get what he wishes for. But there's enough. In the midst of these disquietudes I like to make you my lecture class. . . .

This is the language of agitation, but Cicero never in his heart retracted it. Yet he was still for peace, catching eagerly at the news of negotiations in progress between Caesar and Pompey a few days later (like several subsequent attempts they came to nothing). It was easy to condemn Caesar, but the prospect of fighting him had become more forbidding than ever. And if the two dynasts were to negotiate, what better intermediary than Cicero? As he wrote to Caesar about 18 March:

. . . Hope led me towards the notion that, as suits the wisdom which is yours in so admirable and exceptional a degree, you might be desirous of opening negotiations for peace, tranquillity, and civic harmony; and I con-

---

[1] Cicero uses a Greek word, applied by the Stoics to their moral ideal. In his philosophical writing he translates it by the Latin word *honestum*, which I translate '(moral) right' below.

[2] From Euripides' 'Women of Phoenicia.'

[3] To quote my note: Atticus may be supposed to have called the sunshine at his home *lucrativus* ('bonus') because it did not have to be paid for, perhaps poking fun at his own economical housekeeping.

ceived myself to be by nature and public image not ill fitted to help in such an understanding. If I am correct, and if you are at all concerned to maintain our friend Pompey and win him back to yourself and the Republic, you will surely find no more suitable person than myself for that purpose. I advocated peace to him always, and to the Senate as soon as I had opportunity. When arms were taken up, I had nothing to do with the war, and I judged you therein to be an injured party in that your enemies and those jealous of your success were striving to deprive you of a mark of favour accorded by the Roman people. But just as then I not only gave my own support to your position but also urged others to come to your assistance, so now I am deeply concerned for Pompey's. It is some years since I chose you and him as two men to cultivate above all others and as, what you are, my very dear friends. . . .

Such language to the new Hannibal called, in the writer's view, for no apology. To Atticus a fortnight later:

. . . You write that my letter has been broadcast. I am not sorry to hear it, indeed I have let a number of people take copies. In view of what has already happened and of what is coming I want to have my sentiments on peace upon record. In urging this particular person in its favour I saw no readier means of influencing his mind than by representing that the course I was urging upon him befitted his wisdom. If I called the latter 'admirable,' in urging him to the salvation of our country, I had no fear of appearing to flatter; in such a cause I would gladly have thrown myself at his feet. . . . As for my statement that I had taken no part in the war, the truth of it is sufficiently evident; but my object in so writing was to lend weight to my persuasions, and similarly with my approval of his cause.

At the end of February he had asked Atticus to send him a recent Greek treatise 'On Concord' ('you see the sort of brief I am getting up'). These ideas were encouraged by Cornelius Balbus:

I beg you, dear Cicero, put your thoughts and concern upon a design eminently worthy of your character, I mean the restitution of the old happy relations between Caesar and Pompey, now that intriguers have set them at variance. Believe me when I say that Caesar will not only put himself in your hands but will consider himself under the deepest obligation to you if you will bend your mind that way. I only wish that Pompey may do the like: but I rather pray than hope that he may be brought to any sort of accommodation at such a time. But when he settles down and regains a sense of security, *then* I shall begin not to despair of your influence counting heavily with him. Caesar is grateful to you for desiring my friend Consul Lentulus[1] to stay

---

[1] Lucius Cornelius Lentulus Crus, Consul in 49 and Balbus' early patron, from whom he took his name Cornelius. Nothing else is known of Cicero's alleged attempt to persuade him to stay in Rome.

here, and I am indeed more than grateful. . . . If he will listen to you and believe
me about Caesar and serve out the rest of his term of office in Rome, I shall
begin to hope that by the Senate's advice, with you to inspire and him to
propose, Pompey and Caesar may yet be reconciled. If and when that
happens, I shall feel I have lived long enough.

But Cicero had no faith in Balbus' honeyed words. He sent Atticus a
copy of the letter, but only 'so that you can be sorry for me when you
see how I am mocked.' And the treatise on Concord was soon returned
after news of the Consuls' departure for Greece on 4 March.

'I know whom to flee, but I don't know whom to follow'—the
epigram became famous. Cicero left Rome in a ferment of bewilder-
ment and indignation. So this was what had come out of Pompey's cool
confidence! Cicero was not much of a strategist, but the miscalculation
of Caesar's strength which had led to this panic retreat seemed blatant.
To Atticus, 23 January:

> . . . You too remark on our leader's bad generalship. . . . To his lack of
> judgment the facts themselves stand witness. To say nothing of his other
> errors over ten years, would not any terms have been preferable to this fight?
> Nor can I say what his plans are now, though I am continually writing to
> enquire. It is generally agreed that he is in a state of utter panic and confusion.
> Accordingly I see no sign of the defensive force which he was kept at Rome
> to prepare nor of any place or rallying-point for such a force. The whole hope
> lies in two legions kept back not without discredit and scarcely his own.[1] As
> for the levies, the men so far are reluctant and have no stomach for fighting.
> And the time for making terms has been let slip. What will come I cannot fore-
> see, but certain it is that through our own fault or our leader's we have put to
> sea without a rudder and committed ourselves to the mercy of the storm. . . .

What then to do?

> . . . Shall I fling myself whole-hearted into the cause? I am not deterred by
> the risk, but I *am* bursting with indignation at the utter lack of judgment, or
> shall I say the flouting of *my* judgment, in the whole proceedings. Or shall I
> temporize and sit on the fence and offer myself to those in actual possession of
> power? 'I fear the Trojans,'[2] and my obligations not only as a citizen but as a
> friend call me back. And yet pity for the boys often makes me waver. . . .

The question soon became whether or not to go with (or after)
Pompey overseas. For the war continued to go badly for the republi-

---

[1] These were the two legions detached from Caesar's army for service against
the Parthians: see page 137.

[2] See page 53, note 1.

cans. Pompey withdrew to the southwest to join the two veteran legions there. Recruiting went on vigorously, though in Campania Cicero reported an absence of enthusiasm among the population. But Caesar gave his decisive blow at Corfinium in central Italy, where in late February he surrounded and captured a large newly-raised republican force under Cato's brother-in-law Domitius Ahenobarbus; Domitius had refused to retreat while there was time, in defiance of Pompey's warnings and appeals. Cicero, quite unfairly, blamed Pompey for not going to his rescue. He wrote to Atticus on 23 February:

> . . . It seemed to me as though the light of the Ideal[1] had shone before his eyes and the man he should have been had cried aloud:
>
> > 'So let them scheme what they must,
> > And contrive to my bane what they may:
> > Right stands with me.'[2]
>
> But Pompey, waving adieu to the Ideal, is making for Brundisium. As for Domitius, they say that on hearing the news he and those with him have given themselves up. A tragic business! . . .

A fortnight later he remarked that he had already known Pompey for a hopeless failure as a statesman, and now found him no less hopeless a failure as a general. At the same time he harps on his personal ties with Pompey, for whom, as he told Atticus on 17 February, he would gladly die. Such protestations do not ring quite true, for Cicero remembered well enough (without needing Atticus' reminder) that Pompey was the man who 'brought me out of the mess into which he himself had plunged me'—there had been an exile as well as a recall. If he put forward, as he sometimes did, gratitude to Pompey as the only reason for joining him, it was largely because he knew it was a bad reason. Even his cries of stricken conscience when Pompey was shut up in Brundisium in danger of falling into Caesar's hands (he actually escaped with his fleet on 17 March, following the Consuls to Greece) sound falsetto. 18 March:

> I have nothing to write about, having heard no news and having replied to all your letters yesterday. But since my distress of mind is such that it is not only impossible to sleep but a torment to be awake, I have started this scrawl without any subject in view, just in order as it were to talk, which is my only relief.
> I think I have been out of my senses from the start, and the one thing that

---

[1] See page 146, note 1.   [2] From Euripides.

tortures me is that I have not followed Pompey like any private soldier in his drift, or rather plunge, to disaster. I saw him on 17 January, thoroughly cowed. That very day I realised what he was at. Nothing he did thereafter was to my liking. He went on blundering, now here now there. Meanwhile not a line to me, not a thought except for flight. . . . Nothing in his conduct seemed to deserve that I should join him as his companion in flight. But now my affection comes to the surface, the sense of loss is unbearable, books, writing, philosophy are all to no purpose. Like Plato's bird,[1] I gaze over the sea day and night, longing to take wing. Indeed and indeed I am punished for my thoughtlessness. And yet, what thoughtlessness? Was not everything I did most carefully considered? If flight had been the only object, I should have been perfectly ready to fly; but I shuddered at the kind of war intended, savage and vast beyond what men yet see. What threats to the municipalities, to *boni* individually named, to everyone who stayed behind! 'What Sulla could do, I can do'—that was the refrain. . . .

Two or three days later:

. . . Pray consider now of all times what I ought to do. A Roman army is besieging Gnaeus Pompeius, investing him with moat and rampart, stopping his escape; and we go on living, Rome stands, the Praetors sit on the bench, the Aediles prepare their shows, the *boni* book their receipts, I myself sit idle! Shall I make madly for Brundisium, appeal to the loyalty of the municipalities? The *boni* will not follow, the triflers will laugh, the revolutionaries, victorious now with weapons in their hands, will use violence. So what do you think? Have you any sort of advice to offer on how to end this miserable existence? *Now* the pain comes home and I am in torment, just when people think me either wise or lucky in not having gone with Pompey. I think the opposite. I never wanted a share in his victory, but I would rather I had shared his disaster. What use is it now for me to beg you to write, appeal to your wisdom and good will? All is over. No one can help me now. I have nothing even to pray for except that one of my enemies may take pity on me and put me out of my misery.

But the problem could not be narrowed down to one of loyalty to a dubious personal obligation and to a leader whom he saw as an arrant bungler, or occasionally (consistency was even less important than usual to Cicero in this time of stress) as something far worse. 27 February:

. . . Both of the pair have aimed at personal domination, not the happiness

---

[1] In one of his letters Plato writes of how he was kept in Syracuse against his will by the young despot Dionysius II: 'After that we lived together, I and Dionysius, I gazing out like a bird longing to take wing. . . .' He does not mention the sea, but Cicero will have written with the Bay of Gaeta before his eyes.

and fair fame of the community. Pompey has not abandoned Rome because he could not have defended her, nor Italy because he was driven from her shores. His plan from the first has been to ransack every land and sea, to stir up foreign kings, to bring savage races in arms to Italy, to raise enormous armies. He has been hankering for a long while after despotism on the Sullan model, and many of his companions are eager for it. Or would you maintain that no agreement or compromise between them was possible? It is possible today. But neither sees our happiness as his mark. Both want to reign. . . .

He goes on to picture the horrors ahead:

. . . So I prophesy, my dear Atticus, not inspired like the girl[1] whom nobody believed, but by rational forecast. . . . Yes, I can vaticinate in pretty much the same strain on this vast impending Iliad of evils. . . . Yes, you will see our poor Italy trampled over this summer by the bondslaves of one or both the protagonists, scraped together from every species of humanity. It is not so much the proscription of individuals that we have to fear, the threat of which is said to have been common talk in Luceria,[2] as the destruction of the whole country—so enormous will be the power on either side when the clash comes. Such is my forecast. Perhaps you expected some comfort. I can find none. A more miserable, hopeless, horrible situation there could not be. . . .

Caelius Rufus had remarked that he liked the cause of Caesar's opponents but disliked the men. Cicero's position was somewhat similar. Nearly all the leading figures on Pompey's side were anti-pathetic to him. Cato he might respect, but certainly did not love. The business of the Thanksgiving, on top of earlier differences, will still have rankled. Cato had been commissioned in January to take over in Sicily, but preferred to stay and watch the course of the current negotiations with Caesar. 'So,' comments Cicero tartly, 'he does not trouble about going to Sicily, where his presence is urgently needed, but he wants to be in the Senate, where I am afraid he will be a nuisance.' And Cato's conduct when he did get to Sicily comes in for sharp criticism. Nor had Cicero much use for Cato's closer associates, his henchmen Favonius and Postumius and his aristocratic connexions Domitius and Bibulus—both meanly hostile to himself. Even Marcus Brutus was not yet the friend he afterwards became. The Consuls were not worth twopence, 'as flighty as a feather or a leaf.' As for Pompey's personal entourage:

. . . The previous day Crassipes had been with me. He said that he had set out from Brundisium on 6 March and left Pompey there—as was also

---

[1] Cassandra.

[2] In Apulia, where Pompey had established his headquarters.

reported by persons who started from Brundisium on the 8th. All . . . report threatening talk . . . proscriptions and Sulla in every sentence. The language attributed to Lucceius[1] and to the whole Greek set, Theophanes in particular —well! And yet all our hopes of salvation rest on these folk, and I keep constantly on the alert without a moment's respite, longing to be with people utterly unlike myself in my desire to escape the horrors here. Do you suppose there are any criminal lengths over there to which Scipio, Faustus, and Libo will not go?—their creditors are said to be meeting. What do you suppose they will do to their countrymen when they have won? And our Gnaeus' length of view, what of that? They report him as thinking of Egypt and Arabia Felix and Mesopotamia, as having already given up Spain. They tell of monstrous things. These may not be true, but it is certain that there is no hope from this side and no salvation from the other. . . .

It is true that Cicero reprobated many of Caesar's associates—'a gang of desperados.' But they included his son-in-law Dolabella, Atticus' brother(?)-in-law Pilius Celer, and a number of personal friends—Trebatius (still 'a good man and a good citizen'), Caelius, Curio, and others. Then there were the neutrals, including a number of Consulars, who had returned to Rome or had never left it. In the nature of the case their neutrality took on an appearance of inclination toward Caesar. In a letter of 15 or 16 February Cicero says he would be one of them 'if I did not have these confounded nuisances of lictors, and I should not be ashamed to be in company with Manius Lepidus, Lucius Vulcatius, and Servius Sulpicius. None of them is more stupid than Lucius Domitius or more fickle than Appius Claudius.'

After all he was fifty-seven, 'inclined to rest after my long labours and softened by the comforts of domestic life.' Must he again leave his wife and daughter and his beloved Italian homes for a camp in Greece or Spain, with small hope of ever coming back? No wonder he hesitated and tergiversated:

. . . If you complain of my chopping and changing, I answer that I talk to you as to myself. In so great a matter must not any man argue with himself this way and that? . . .

No wonder that when (in mid-February) he finally started off to join Pompey on the other side of the peninsula, he did it with querulous reluctance and turned back, easily convinced that the journey would be too risky. 'Frankly,' he told Atticus, 'I wanted some time to consider what was the right thing to do, the proper thing for me.'

[1] Lucceius and Theophanes were Pompey's intimates; Metellus Scipio, Faustus Sulla, and Scribonius Libo his relations by marriage.

And yet his mind did gradually settle to the necessity of leaving Italy. His family (except his brother, who left the decision to him) were in favour. 11 March:

> . . . I was anxious before and distressed, as one clearly could not but be in such a case, by my inability to think of any solution. But now that Pompey and the Consuls have left Italy,[1] I am not merely distressed, I am consumed with grief:
>
> 'My heart
stands not, I am distraught.'[2]
>
> Yes, I give you my word that I am beside myself at the thought of the dishonour I feel I have brought upon my head. To think that in the first place I am not with Pompey, whatever his mistakes, and that in the second I am not with the *boni*, never mind how ill-advisedly they have managed our cause!— especially as the very ones for whose sake I hesitated to take the plunge, I mean my wife and daughter and the two boys, would have preferred me to have followed the other course and thought this one discreditable and unworthy of me. As for my brother Quintus, he told me that whatever I thought best had his approval and followed it without a qualm. . . .

Was not conviction of duty to the Republic the real determinant, behind the smokescreen of argument and counter-argument? If so, Cicero has made it easy to misjudge him; for this was just what he fought shy of admitting, both at the time and afterwards. To have admitted it at the time would have been to leave himself no further option. And after the republican defeat at Pharsalia he had to find excuses for giving up the fight when others persevered. It was convenient to tell himself and his friends that he ought never to have joined it in the first place, and had only done so because of family pressure or a too sensitive concern for public opinion. Hence his favourite thesis that freedom was doomed whichever side won. To Atticus, 4 March:

> . . . So I ask you, what sort of Optimates are these that thrust me out while they themselves stay at home? And yet, be they what they may, 'I fear the Trojans,' although I am only too well aware with what prospects I shall set out, and although I am allying myself with a man who is better prepared for the devastation of Italy than for victory, and although I expect to find myself a slave. . . .

---

[1] Cicero had been misinformed. Pompey did not sail with the Consuls on 4 March, but later, on the 17th.

[2] From the Iliad.

A week later:

... Believe me, I no longer aim at finding a happy outcome. I realise that we shall never have a free state in the life-time of those two[1] or of either one singly. So I have no longer any hope of a quiet life for myself, and I am ready to swallow every bitter pill. My one fear was of doing, or shall I say of having already done, something dishonourable. ...

So too after the war (for Cicero) was over, for example to Marcus Marcellus (Consul in 51) in 46:

... All power has been handed over to one man;[2] and he follows no counsel, not even that of his friends, except his own. It would not have been very different if *our* leader were in control. In the war, when all of us were united in danger, he followed his own judgment and that of certain persons by no means conspicuous for their good sense. Are we to suppose that he would have been more democratically-minded in victory than he was when the issue hung in the balance? When you were Consul he did not follow your admirable advice; and when your cousin administered the office[3] under your guidance, he would not make you his counsellors. If he were now supreme, do you suppose he would be feeling any need of our opinions? ...

Or to a Pompeian exile in 45:

... Every day I recall how you and I shared each other's views ... and saw with what an infinity of evil that war was charged. All hope of peace being excluded, even victory was bound to prove a most bitter experience, fraught with destruction to the vanquished and slavery to the victors. ...

But in his heart of hearts, a region to which his conscious mind so seldom penetrated, did he believe this? Apart from having Cato to reckon with, Pompey was not made of classical 'tyrant' material; if he had become one, it would have been by mistake. Selfish but not cynical, arbitrary but conventionally-minded, dealer in political small change, he was a man of the moment, of particular situations, not of destiny. The subverter of his own legislation, as Tacitus called him, was not lawless; a disposition to play fast and loose with the constitution, preferably at second hand, did not make him a revolutionary. The laws and the authority of the Senate never lost his respect, even though the wishes of Pompey the Great sometimes had to take precedence. Between such a leader and one of whom Cicero wrote in April 'he no longer objects, in a sense he demands to be called what he really is, a despot (*tyrannus*)' there *was* something for a man of Cicero's outlook

---

[1] Pompey and Caesar.　　　　　[2] Caesar.　　　　　[3] In 50.

to choose. And his choice was clinched by an anxiously awaited personal interview with Caesar on his way back from Brundisium to Rome on 28 March. It took place in Cicero's house at Formiae:

In both particulars I followed your advice. My language was such as to earn his respect rather than his thanks and I stood firm against returning to Rome. But we were wrong in thinking him accommodating; I never found anybody less so. He said I was passing judgment against him, that the rest would be slower to come if I did not. I replied that their position was different. After a lengthy discussion: 'Come along then and work for peace.' 'At my own discretion?' I asked. 'Naturally,' he answered. 'Who am I to lay down rules for you?' 'Well,' I said, 'I shall take the line that the Senate does not approve of an expedition to Spain or of the transport of armies into Greece, and' I added 'I shall have much to say in commiseration of Gnaeus.' At that he protested that this was not the sort of thing he wanted said. 'So I supposed,' I rejoined, 'but that is just why I don't want to be present. Either I must speak in that strain or stay away—and much besides which I could not possibly suppress if I were there.' The upshot was that he asked me to think the matter over, as though seeking a way to end the talk. I could not refuse. On that note we parted. So I imagine he is not pleased with me. But I was pleased with myself, an experience I have not had for quite a long time.

For the rest, Gods! What an *entourage*, what an Underworld, to use your favourite expression! . . . What an unprincipled adventure! What a gang of desperados! . . . But I nearly forgot to mention his disagreeable Parthian shot. If, he said, he could not avail himself of my counsels, he would take those he could get and stop at nothing. . . . But I am waiting to hear from you. It is no longer possible to say now, as formerly, 'see how this turns out.' Our interview was to be the end. I don't doubt that it has put him out of humour with me. All the more reason for rapid action. Do let me have a letter, a political letter. I am eagerly waiting to hear from you now.

From that point on the question was mainly one of ways and means, even though Cicero thought for a time of staying out of harm's way in Athens, Malta, or elsewhere. In the first half of May letters to Atticus contain mysterious allusions to a certain project, which seems to have been to take over the province of Africa (roughly corresponding to modern Tunisia), where there was a temporary governmental vacuum.[1] But it soon collapsed, and in late May or early June the four Ciceros again took ship for the East.

[1] That is the theory advanced in Appendix VI to Volume IV of my edition.

CHAPTER SIXTEEN

Personalia (January–June 49)

'The time I spend writing to you or reading your letters is my only respite.'
Cicero to Atticus (12 March 49)

ALTHOUGH the correspondence is so copious at this period that we hardly lose sight of Cicero for a day,[1] it tells little about his daily activities. The war and his own relation to it almost monopolize his letters; he probably thought and talked of little else. Certainly he was not solitary. His brother and their sons had accompanied him from Rome, and they were joined at Formiae a fortnight later by Terentia and Tullia (perhaps Pomponia also). Outside the family he spent much time with the owner of a neighbouring villa, an elderly Consular of moderate views called Manius Lepidus—*faute de mieux* perhaps ('we spend pretty well all day together, which *he* is very glad to do'). In early March, however, Lepidus went back to Rome. But no doubt the local people crowded in, as they had done ten years before,[2] to exchange news and views. 1 March:

. . . Both town and country people talk to me a great deal. They really think of nothing except their fields and their bits of farms and their investments. . . .

We hear of excursions into the country, but even on these Cicero's mind was on relevant problems of political ethics: 'For as soon as I run out into the country I turn professor, and on the road I meditate my "themes" all the time.'

Sometimes important visitors called at the villa, usually Caesarians, friends or acquaintances more or less welcome. 10 March:

. . . Postumus has paid me a visit, how disagreeable you know from my letter. Another caller was Quintus Fufius (imagine the look of him, the arrogance!), hurrying through to Brundisium, loud against Pompey's

---

[1] See the record in Appendix I to Volume IV of my edition.
[2] See page 52.

wickedness and the Senate's fickleness and folly. If I can't stand this sort of thing under my own roof, shall I be able to stand it in the Senate-House? . . .

Gaius Matius was less objectionable. 20 March:

. . . I also had a visit from Matius on Minerva's Day. I must say he impressed me as a man of moderation and good sense. Certainly he has always been looked upon as an advocate of peace. To me at any rate he seemed very far from approving what is going on, and very apprehensive of the Underworld,[1] as you call them. . . .

We catch a glimpse of Cornelius Balbus' nephew on a secret mission to Brundisium, where he hoped to win over the consul Lentulus Crus to Caesar's side. And in mid-April, at Cumae:

. . . Curio passed my house and left word for me that he would be here shortly. He then rushed off to Puteoli to address a meeting there. He made his speech, returned, and paid me quite a lengthy visit. Horrible! You know what he is like. He kept nothing back. . . .

But Curio was personally friendly and offered Cicero free passage through Sicily, which he was about to take over for Caesar. Early in May the eminent jurist Servius Sulpicius, an old friend whom Cicero always tended to regard as something of an old woman, came to discuss their common situation. The talks did not get far:

A wretched life we lead! To be so long prey to fear is surely worse than the actuality we are afraid of. Servius, having arrived on 7 May, came to my house early next morning. Not to keep you in suspense, we found no future in any plan. Never have I seen a man in such a quaver! Yet I must admit that none of his bogies was imaginary. 'Pompey was angry with him, Caesar no friend. The victory of either was a dreadful prospect, not only because one was cruel and the other unscrupulous, but because of the straits both were in for money, which could only be extracted from private property.' In saying all this he shed so many tears that I wondered such length of misery had not dried them up! . . .

On the following day:

. . . Servius' views take me no further. All manner of quibbles arise against every proposal. He is the only man I have met more timid than Gaius Marcellus,[2] who is sorry he was ever Consul. *Quelle bassesse!* . . .

[1] The Greek term used by Atticus, with a mythological reference, for Caesar's following.
[2] Consul in 50.

Until the end of March Cicero left Formiae only for a few short excursions on business and his abortive attempt to join Pompey in February. The longest of his trips (3–8 February) was to Capua, the chief town of Campania, in obedience to a summons from the Consuls. But when Cicero got there in pouring winter rain, neither had arrived. He found nothing to raise his spirits:

. . . While in Capua I learnt this much, that the Consuls are worthless and that there is no troop-levying anywhere. The recruiting officers dare not show their noses with Caesar in the offing, while our leader by contrast is nowhere and does nothing; and there are no volunteers. It is not loyalty they lack but hope. . . .

After his interview with Caesar on 28 March Cicero left for a tour of his 'little villas', which he never expected to see again; and first to Arpinum, where young Marcus was given his 'manly gown'. Cicero wrote from there on 1 or 2 April:

Rome being impossible, I have given my son the white gown at Arpinum as the next best place, to the gratification of my fellow-townsmen. Not but what I find everyone both at Arpinum and on the road gloomy and downcast; so sad and terrible are the thoughts inspired by this vast mischief. Levies[1] are in progress and men are led off into winter quarters. You can imagine how sorely such proceedings are felt. They are unpleasant enough in themselves, even when carried out with moderation by honest men in legitimate warfare; now they are carried out by ruffians in a wicked civil war with the utmost brutality. You may be sure that every disreputable character in Italy is with Caesar. I saw the whole crew at Formiae, and upon my word I thought them more like beasts than men; and I knew them all, but I had never seen them all in one place. . . .

After a few days on his brother's properties near by, Cicero made his way to the Bay of Naples, and by the middle of the month he was installed in his Cuman villa. There he stayed until shortly before he left for Greece, except for an abbreviated visit to Pompeii in mid-May:

. . . In order to draw off suspicion as to my departure or intentions I left for Pompeii on the 12th, meaning to stay there while the necessaries for the voyage were got ready. On my arrival at the house I had a visit to inform me that the Centurions of the three cohorts stationed at Pompeii desired to meet me next day. Our friend Ninnius discussed this with me, told me they wanted to put themselves and the town in my hands. As for me, I was off and away from the house next morning before daybreak, so that they should not get so

[1] For Caesar.

much as a sight of me. For what was the use of three cohorts, or even more, supposing there had been more? What equipment had they? . . . And besides, it could have been a trap. So I removed all suspicion. . . .

Three years later he recalled this trip in a letter to Marcus Marius:

Considering, as I often do, the general miseries in which we have been living for so many years, and, as I see it, shall continue to live, I am apt to call to mind the last time we were together. I remember the very day—12 May in the Consulship of Lentulus and Marcellus. I had come down to my place near Pompeii that evening, and found you there to meet me in a troubled state of mind—troubled by the thought of the duty, and the danger too, that lay upon me. You were afraid that if I stayed in Italy I should be failing in my duty, whereas if I set off for the war you were disturbed by the risk I should run. No doubt you saw on that occasion that I was in such a state of mental turmoil that I could not work out what was best to do. However, I preferred to yield to the claims of honour and reputation than to calculate for my personal safety. . . .

Naturally the letters of these months breathe trouble, despondency, suspense. Brundisium during Pompey's beleaguerment was Cicero's Dunkirk:

Although by the time you read this letter I expect I shall already know the outcome at Brundisium (for Gnaeus set out from Canusium on 21 February and I am writing this on 6 March, thirteen days after he marched from Canusium), I am tortured none the less by suspense from hour to hour. It is extraordinary that nothing has come through, not even a rumour. The silence is uncanny. But perhaps all this is worry to no purpose, and after all the truth must soon be out. . . .

Only very rarely, after a piece of encouraging news, is there a touch of the jocular, as at the beginning of February in the momentary hope of a negotiated peace:

. . . It looks to me as though you yourself and Sextus[1] can properly stay on in Rome. You certainly have little cause to love our friend Pompey. Nobody has ever knocked so much off property values in town. I still have my joke, you see. . . .

Or just before the débâcle at Corfinium:

. . . Gods above, I am shivering all over with suspense. What is going to happen? Still I am hopeful that there will be great power in our general's name, great[2] terror in his advent. . . . I have just heard that your quartan has

---

[1] Sextus Peducaeus, son of Cicero's old Praetor and a close friend of Atticus.
[2] Cicero seems to be alluding to Pompey's surname Magnus ('the Great').

left you. Hang me if I am not as delighted as if it had happened to me. Tell Pilia it is not fair she should keep hers any longer, nor proper in so united a couple. . . .

Among Cicero's trials were persistent ophthalmia and insomnia ('If I could get any sleep I should not bore you with such long letters'), also worry about Tiro over in Patrae. Of two other private sources of disquiet the letters have a good deal to say. One was the tutor Dionysius, about whom Cicero had developed second thoughts soon after their return to Italy. On 3 February he wrote more in anger than in sorrow:

. . . I forgot to write to you before about Dionysius, but what I have decided to do is to wait for Caesar's reply. If we return to Rome he can wait for us there; if that is postponed, I shall send for him then. To be sure I know what he ought to have done when I fled the capital, what was becoming in a man of his attainments and a friend, especially when he was asked; but I don't expect too much in this way from Greeks. . . .

But when the summons came, Dionysius was recalcitrant. 22 February:

Your (better not say 'our') friend Dionysius, on whose character I preferred your judgment to my own even after I had come to know it pretty well, has not been deterred even by consideration for the testimonials which you have so often given me on his behalf from a display of bumptiousness in what he thought would be my changed fortunes—the vicissitudes of which I intend to govern with some measure of rational calculation so far as that is humanly possible. From me he has had every possible compliment and compliance; I have even recommended this rather dingy figure to others on every occasion, preferring to let my brother Quintus and the world in general find fault with my judgment rather than refrain from singing his praises, preferring that our boys should be taught on the side by my own labour rather than look for another tutor for them. And the letter I sent him, heavens above, what a complimentary, affectionate letter it was! It might have been Dicaearchus or Aristoxenus[1] I was asking to join me, instead of an arrant chatterbox and a thoroughly incompetent teacher. But let it be admitted he has a good memory: he shall find that I have a better! He answered my letter as I should never answer a man whose case I was not going to take. One always says 'if I can manage it,' 'if I am not hindered by a previous commitment.' I have never given any defendant, no matter how humble, how abject, how guilty, how complete a stranger, such a blank refusal as this quite unqualified 'no' I have had from Dionysius. It is the most ungrateful behaviour I ever

---

[1] Two celebrated Greek savants, both pupils of Aristotle.

knew, and ingratitude contains all the vices. But that's more than enough about him. . . .

Later that same day the tutor arrived in person at Formiae, but only to repeat his refusal:

Dionysius having come to me contrary to my expectation, I spoke to him in the most liberal way. I explained the circumstances and asked him to tell me what he had in mind, saying that I was not demanding anything of him against his own free will. He replied that he did not know what shape his investments were in. Some of his debtors were not paying, others were not yet due to pay. He added some stuff about his slaves as a reason why he could not keep us company. I let him have his way and dismissed him. As a teacher for the boys I was sorry to lose him, as an ingrate I let him go without reluctance. I wanted you to know, and to know my opinion of his conduct.

Cicero felt the incident keenly, all the more so because he interpreted it as reflecting his own sunken fortunes. 20 or 21 March:

. . . As for Dionysius, I was surprised. He was treated with more consideration in my house than Panaetius in Scipio's;[1] now he scorns me in my present plight. It is disgusting. I hate the fellow and always shall. I wish I could punish him. But his own character will do that. . . .

Atticus remonstrated:

. . . You say that the harshness of my language about Dionysius is out of character. See how old-fashioned I am! Upon my word I thought you would be more upset by this affair than I. For to leave aside that I think you ought to take a wrong against me to heart, no matter who commits it, there is the further point that his deplorable behaviour toward me is in a way an offence against yourself. But it is for you to judge how seriously you should take that, and do not think that I wish in any way to embarrass you in the matter. For my part I always thought him half crazy, and now think him a blackguardly scoundrel, but no more my enemy than his own. . . .

Dionysius attempted another placatory visit. 5 or 6 April:

. . . I am sorry Dionysius has set out to visit me. Tullia wrote to me about it, but the time is inconvenient and I would rather not parade our embarrassments, serious as they are, before other than friendly eyes. I have no wish for you to be his enemy on my account.

However, the visit took place, though not until over a month later:

I had just sent off a letter to you on various matters when Dionysius

---

[1] The famous Stoic philosopher Panaetius of Rhodes settled in Rome and became one of Scipio Africanus the Younger's circle.

arrived at my place bright and early. I should not only have shown a placable spirit toward him, I should have forgiven the whole episode if he had come in the frame of mind you had led me to expect. You said in the letter which I received at Arpinum that he would come and do what I wanted. Now I wanted, or rather earnestly desired, him to stay with us; and because when he visited Formiae he categorically refused to do that, I used to write you about him rather harshly. However, he had very little to say, and the gist of it was that I must excuse him; he was involved in business of his own, and could not go with us. I did not say much in answer, but I was bitterly hurt. Clearly he scorned us in our present plight. Well, there it is. Perhaps you will be surprised when I tell you that among the distresses of this present time I count this as one of the greatest. I hope you may keep his friendship, and in expressing that wish I am wishing you prosperity; the one will last just so long as the other. . . .

Cicero's bitterness against the man seems justified, and one is almost irritated to find him restored to favour a few years later. Cicero's quarrels needed fuel to keep them going; his mercurial temper was quick to welcome returning amity, or at any rate the façade of it.

The other anxiety was provided by young Quintus. Cicero and his brother were mostly together throughout this time, but the letters have little to say about the latter, apart from the matter of a small debt for which Atticus was pressing him, unduly in Marcus Cicero's opinion. Indeed it is remarkable how often Marcus uses the first person singular about things which concerned them jointly, for example, what to do with the boys. In letters from correspondents (Caesar, Pompey, Caelius, Sulpicius, Mescinius, Antony, Dolabella), all in one way or another canvassing Cicero's attitude and conduct in the crisis, Quintus' name never occurs. Seemingly (despite a contrary opinion later attributed to Caesar) they made no account of him as a factor influencing Marcus' decision. To Pompey on 15 February Cicero actually stated that the only Senator in the coastal area besides himself was one Marcus Eppius—as though his brother had no separate entity. An impression of passivity amounting almost to paralysis on Quintus' part is supported by the few passages in which his future is specifically mooted. On 18 February Cicero asks the question (and does not answer it) whether, if he himself goes abroad, Quintus should go too. But on 6 March:

. . . Then there is my brother, who should not in fairness have been mixed up with me in this predicament. Caesar will be even angrier with him than with me; but I cannot induce him to stay. . . .

A week later this was amplified in a sentence already quoted.[1] No doubt Cicero took his brother's lack of initiative for due confidence and loyalty; in reality (to judge from what was to follow) it was a line of least resistance, travelled in frustration, helplessness, and interior disgruntlement. When Quintus set out for Pompey's camp, he let his hard work in Gaul go for nothing and said good-bye to hopes of favour from Caesar. Why did he not take an independent course, neutral or Caesarian? Perhaps from republican principle, perhaps from lack of enthusiasm for Caesar personally or dislike of his entourage, but chiefly, one imagines, from the habit of a lifetime which made dissociation from his elder brother at such a turning-point a psychological impossibility.

About the beginning of April Marcus Cicero was shocked by a breach of family solidarity amounting, as he feared at first, to arrant treachery, on the part of Quintus junior. The young man had written a letter to Caesar in terms which gravely displeased his uncle and (so Cicero told Atticus) his father. Worse still, he had made an excuse for going to Rome, where he had a meeting with Aulus Hirtius. As a result he was summoned by Caesar to an interview, at which young Quintus spoke of Marcus Cicero's hostility to Caesar's cause and intention of leaving Italy.

Among the obscurities in this odd affair is the source of Cicero's information. He hoped that the report which had reached him was exaggerated, as apparently it was; for about 22 April he wrote:

> ... I gave young Quintus a warm reception. I see it was greed and the hope of a handsome largesse. That is bad enough in all conscience, but I hope there was no such villainy as we feared. I think you will agree that this vice does not proceed from indulgence on our part but from nature. However, I govern him with discipline.

Quintus senior, he believed, was as surprised and dismayed as himself —prostrate with grief in fact; young Quintus had acted in callous disregard of his indulgent parent. The indulgence, however, continued. Marcus Cicero was all for dealing strictly with the culprit, but his disciplinary measures were thwarted by his brother, who also wrote a letter to Pomponia extenuating what had happened.

This letter worried Atticus. He sent an account of it to Cicero, who commented on 4 May as follows:

> ... What you say about my brother no doubt argues a certain infirmity,

---

[1] See page 153.

but nothing treacherous or *fourbe*, nothing that may not be bent over to good, nothing you could not lead where you liked in a single talk. In short, he is fond of his own folk, even those with whom he most often falls out of humour and fonder of me than of himself. I do not think he is to be blamed for writing to you in terms different from those he used to the lad's mother about her son. . . .

Did Atticus suspect that young Quintus' proceedings were not so independent as Cicero supposed? At any rate it seems clear that in writing to his wife (or possibly even to Atticus himself) Quintus senior let slip certain discontents or doubts which Atticus, no mischief-maker as a rule, thought it wise to pass on; but which Cicero, with much else on his mind, chose to dismiss as just another example of Quintus' unstable temper.

The son remained a problem, and Cicero wrote to Atticus about it on 3 May, uncle to uncle:

. . . As for our young man, I cannot help feeling affection for him, but I plainly see he has none for us. I have never met with such a lack of moral constitution, such estrangement toward family, such secretiveness. What an incredible spate of annoyances! But I shall take care that he gets some direction, and am already doing so. His abilities are extraordinary, it is his character that needs attention.

And on the following day:

. . . He has always been indulged by his father, but indulgence does not make a boy untruthful or grasping or wanting in natural affection, though it may make him headstrong, overbearing, and aggressive. Accordingly he has these faults too, the products of over-indulgence, but they are tolerable, at least I suppose I may call them so, young people being what they are nowadays. But the qualities that cause me, fond of him as I am, more pain even than the miseries of our present condition, do not arise from any compliance on our part. They have their own roots. No doubt I should tear them up if I had the opportunity. But the times are such that I must put up with all. I have no difficulty with my own boy, who is the most tractable of beings. . . .

But it is of Tullia, whom he must soon leave behind, that he writes with real emotion:

. . . I have commended to you all my concerns, and your affection for me makes commendation on my part superfluous. I too find nothing to write about—I am just sitting waiting to sail. And yet nothing ever needed writing more than this, that of all your many kindnessess there is none I have valued

more than your tender and punctilious attention to my Tullia. It has given her
the greatest pleasure, and me no less. Her courage and patience in face of
public disaster and domestic worries are really wonderful. How brave she was
when we parted! She combines natural affection with the most delicate
sympathy. Yet she wishes me to do the right thing and to stand well in men's
eyes. But I say less than I might on this subject for fear I end by becoming
my own sympathizer. . . .

That was written at the beginning of May (by the current calendar it
was really only the second week of March).[1] Unfavourable weather
continued, delaying departure. The preparations had to be secret, for
Cicero believed that the Caesarian government (Caesar himself was in
Spain) would not let him go willingly. On the 19th he wrote to Atticus,
the last extant letter before he left Italy:

My Tullia has given birth to a seven-months' child, a boy, on 19 May. For
her safe delivery let me be thankful. As for the baby, it is very weakly.[2] I have
been held up until now by some extraordinary calms which have been a
greater hindrance than the watch set over me. . . . So henceforward I won't
write to you what I am going to do, only what I have actually done. Every
spy in the country seems to have an ear cocked to catch what I say. However,
on your side pray go on sending me news about Spain or anything else you
have, but don't expect to hear from me till we arrive where I hope we shall—
or perhaps I may send something on the voyage. But I hesitate to write even
this much, everything has so far been so slow and sticky. We started badly
and the sequel corresponds.

Now I am for Formiae. Perhaps the same avenging powers will follow me
there. . . . Is there an unluckier fellow in the world? I won't run on for fear of
distressing you too. For myself it is more than I can bear to find that a time
has come when I can no longer act either boldly or wisely.

What happened at Formiae we do not know. Apparently there were
further delays, for a farewell letter to his wife, written on board ship in
the harbour of Gaeta, bears the date 7 June:

All the miseries and cares with which I plagued you to desperation (and
very sorry I am for it) and little Tullia too, who is sweeter to me than my life,
are dismissed and ejected. I understood what lay behind them the day after
our parting.[3] I threw up pure bile in the night, and felt an instantaneous relief
as though a god had cured me. To that god you will make due acknowledgment in piety and purity after your custom.

[1] See page 119.
[2] No more is heard of this infant.
[3] This can hardly have been as long ago as 20 May. Perhaps Terentia and Tullia
had come over to Cumae.

I trust we have a first-rate ship—I am writing this directly after coming aboard. I shall next write many letters to our friends, commending you and our little Tullia most earnestly to their care. I should urge you both to be brave, if I had not found you braver than any man. And after all, I trust things are now in bettei train. You, I hope, will be as well off as possible where you are, and I shall at last be fighting for the commonwealth alongside my peers. First and foremost, I want you to take care of your health. Second, if you agree, use the country houses which will be farthest away from army units. The farm at Arpinum with the servants we have in town will be a good place for you if food prices go up.[1]

Darling Marcus sends you his best love. Once again, take care of yourself and good-bye.

Dispatched 7 June.

[1] Rome's grain supply came largely from Egypt, now controlled by Pompey.

CHAPTER SEVENTEEN

Pompey's Camp

'He did not deny that he regretted coming to Greece, criticizing Pompey's armament and carping at his plans behind his back. He was always sneering and saying amusing things about the foreign contingents, going round the camp with a sour, unsmiling face, but raising laughter in others, who did not want to laugh.'

Plutarch

FOR about seven months after he sailed from Gaeta harbour Cicero escapes from view. Presumably he and his party passed through the Straits of Messina and made their way to Thessalonica (of unhappy memories), the place fixed by Pompey and the Consuls as rendezvous for their expatriate Senate. Though Cicero still kept his proconsular status, with lictors carrying their symbolic rods and axes in attendance, he remained unemployed, whether by his own choice or Pompey's or both. He wrote to Atticus about a year after his arrival in Greece that he had avoided taking any responsibility, 'all the more so as nothing could be done in a manner suitable to my past career'—which seems to mean that as orator and statesman he had no function, and had not been offered a military or administrative post commensurate with his 'dignity.' Young Marcus, however, was appointed to the command of a cavalry regiment and, according to his father, made an admirable showing. As for the Quinti, the record is virtually blank; we only know that Quintus senior spent some time at any rate with his brother in Pompey's camp. His rank and military experience qualified him for an important assignment, but perhaps Quintus himself was not eager to fight his former comrades in the Gallic wars.

Caesar's Spanish campaign in the summer of 49 had been characteristically rapid and triumphant; Pompey's armies there ceased to exist as such. In the beginning of the new year Caesar launched his invasion of Greece, and for the following six months the western coast of Macedonia was the main theatre of war. Cicero spent them in camp, apart from a period of ill health (brought on, as he tells Atticus, by anxiety) in the neighbouring town of Dyrrachium. His few surviving letters (five to Atticus and one to Terentia) say little about the war or his own activities, but what they do say bears out Plutarch's picture of a dismal and sarcastic spectator, at odds with himself and his environment: 'You may ask why I do not write. I am deterred by lack of matter, finding as I do no sort of satisfaction in the happenings or the doings here.' In the summer of 46 he wrote to Marcus Marius:

. . . I came to regret my action, not so much on account of my personal hazard as of the many deplorable aspects of the situation which I found on arrival. To begin with, the forces fell short both in numbers and in fighting spirit. Secondly, apart from the Commander-in-Chief and a few besides, all (I am referring to the principal figures) showed their greed for plunder in the war itself, and talked in so bloodthirsty a style that I shuddered at the prospect of *victory*. Moreover, those of the highest rank were up to their ears in debt. In a phrase, nothing good except the cause. With all this before my eyes, I started by advocating peace, as I had done all along. When Pompey showed himself strongly averse from that policy, I set myself to recommend delaying tactics. At times he tended to favour this course, and seemed likely to make it his policy. Perhaps he would have done, had not the result of a particular engagement[1] given him confidence in his troops. From then on that great man ceased to be a general. With his raw medley of an army he fought a pitched battle against the hardiest soldiers in the world, and was defeated. Even his camp was shamefully lost. He fled alone. . . .

And about the same time to Marcus Marcellus, Consul in 51 and steady, though not fanatical, opponent of Caesar:

. . . I very well remember that I am addressing a man who saw the seeds of these calamities long before they ripened; nor do I forget your fine and splendid record as Consul. But this is not all. I also saw your dissatisfaction, the utter lack of confidence you always felt in the way the civil war was being conducted, in Gnaeus Pompeius' forces, in the type of army he led. I think you remember that I held the same views. Accordingly you took little part in the conduct of operations, and I was always careful to take none.

And to Varro, soldier and savant, who seems to have gone to Greece after surrendering an army to Caesar in Spain:

. . . I know that your heart was always as heavy as mine. Not only did we foresee the destruction of one or the other of the two armies and its leader, an enormous disaster, but we realized that victory in civil war is the worst of all calamities. I dreaded the prospect, even if victory should fall to those we had joined. They were making savage threats against the do-nothings, and your sentiments and my words were alike abhorrent to them. . . .

[1] At Dyrrachium. See page 170.

As a presser of unwelcome counsel and a prophet of calamity ('nothing went badly in the war without my predicting it') Cicero must have been a severe trial to the more zealous of his fellow-campaigners, although in one of his latest speeches he maintains that his personal relations with Pompey continued friendly. They will have been sweetened by the loan of half the proceeds of his proconsulate, which had been left on deposit in Asia. It seemed a prudent gesture at the time, even though he was himself so short of funds that he had to borrow from the manager of Atticus' estate in Epirus. But his main concern was for Tullia and the instalments of her dowry due to his son-in-law. March 48:

... You refer to the dowry. For God's sake take the whole matter into your hands and protect that poor girl, poor through my fault and negligence, with my resources if I have any, and with your own funds so far as you can without inconveniencing yourself. You tell me she is in want of everything; I beg you not to let this continue. What expenses are absorbing the income from my properties? And then the HS 60,000 which you mention, no one ever told me that this had been deducted from the dowry. I should never have allowed it. But this is the least of the injuries I have suffered. Tears of vexation prevent me from writing to you about them. . . .

The complaint about the deduction points to Terentia rather than her man of business Philotimus, of whose fraudulence Cicero had already convinced himself in Cilicia. If he had thought her innocent in the matter he would hardly have written so passionately. Similarly words in a previous letter probably allude to her:

... If I had not thought that I was leaving my credit unembarrassed, trusting to the person whom you know I have trusted too far this long time past, I should have stayed on a little longer and not left my private affairs in a state of embarrassment. . . .

The tone of the letter he wrote to her in July could scarcely have been chillier:

It is not often that I have anyone to take a letter, nor have I anything I want to write about. From the last letter I received from you I understand that it was not possible to sell any property. So I shall be grateful if you and the others will consider how to meet the claim of the person whose claims you know I want met.[1] As to what you say about our girl thanking you, I am not surprised that you should give her good reason to do that. If Pollex has not

[1] Dolabella.

yet left, kindly pack him off as soon as possible. Take care of your health. 15 July.

Dolabella's behaviour as a husband had already been such as to bring the possibility of divorce into consideration. In May he was in Caesar's camp, from where he wrote an extant letter to his father-in-law (perhaps at Caesar's instigation) urging him not to follow Pompey into defeat. At that time the republican army lay under siege, encamped near Dyrrachium; but in July Pompey turned the tables, scoring a considerable success with an attack on Caesar's lines. The blockade was lifted, and Pompey followed his enemy into the interior, to be decisively beaten at Pharsalia on 9 August. Cicero, indisposed again, had remained in Dyrrachium, where Cato was in charge. The whereabouts of the rest of the family are not recorded, but Quintus senior was certainly not with his brother. That much is clear from a passage in the dialogue 'On Divination,' in which he is supposed to be addressing Marcus:

You yourself have told me about an incident of the same sort, no fabrication but actual fact. Your story ran as follows: Gaius Coponius (he was in command of the Rhodian fleet, a very sensible and cultivated person) visited you at Dyrrachium, and told you about a prediction made by one of the crew of a Rhodian man-of-war, to the effect that in less than thirty days Greece would be drenched in blood. There would be looting in Dyrrachium and a panic embarkation; looking back, the fugitives would see the sad spectacle of fires blazing in the town. But the Rhodian squadron was fated to return soon and safely home. You were somewhat disturbed, you told me, and Marcus Varro and Marcus Cato, both highly cultured men, were deeply alarmed. Sure enough, Labienus arrived a few days later fleeing from Pharsalia with news of the destruction of the army. The other items in the prediction were soon fulfilled.

The obvious deduction that Quintus was not himself present is borne out by a later reference in the same dialogue. Marcus Cicero sailed with Cato and the other Senators at Dyrrachium to the republican naval base in Corcyra. There Cato asked him to take command of the forces in being in virtue of his rank and military status. But Cicero had had enough. Already sick of war and inclined to regret his own part in it, he readily convinced himself that there was no sense in further fighting. Cato probably expected no other answer, but Pompey's elder son (a young man of whom Cassius wrote later to Cicero: 'You know what a fool Gnaeus is, how he takes cruelty for a virtue; you know how he thinks we always make fun of him') drew his sword in fury, and Cicero had to be rescued by Cato and got off the island. Now apparently in company with his brother, he sailed south to Patrae.

There he stayed at the house of his and Atticus' friend Manius Curius. Meanwhile (we do not know exactly when) a letter arrived from Dolabella conveying Caesar's invitation to return to Italy. With a haste which he afterwards regretted, Cicero complied, and landed at Brundisium about the middle of October.

CHAPTER EIGHTEEN

Brundisium

'There is really nothing wanting to make me the most miserable of mankind.'
Cicero to Atticus (May 47)

IT was a dolorous year that Cicero spent in Brundisium. The town was
garrisoned by Caesar's troops, and although their commander, his old
enemy Publius Vatinius, was now a friend and treated him kindly, he
was afraid, at any rate to begin with, of what they might do to him. He
landed as inconspicuously as possible, ordering his lictors to carry sticks
instead of the official rods and axes and to mingle with the crowd as he
entered the town. Once inside his residence, he did not go out; it was
probably a rented house—no mention of his host of earlier visits,
Laenius Flaccus.

He would have liked to go nearer Rome, but did not dare without
some guarantee of Caesar's approval. And instead of coming back to
Italy as Cicero had expected, Caesar went to Egypt in pursuit of
Pompey. By the time he arrived in Alexandria, Pompey had been
murdered. The news reached Italy in November:

> ... As to Pompey's end I never had any doubt, for all rulers and peoples
> had become so thoroughly persuaded of the hopelessness of his case that
> wherever he went I expected this to happen. I cannot but grieve for his fate. I
> knew him for a man of good character, clean life, and serious principle...

But in Alexandria Caesar became entangled in a conflict with the native
population and spent months penned up with a small Roman force
inside the town. Meanwhile the republicans still had a stronghold in the
province of Africa, where Curio had been defeated and killed in 49.
Many of the surviving notables, including Cato, arrived to carry on
the fight, and strong forces were organized under Pompey's son-in-law
Metellus Scipio, in alliance with the neighbouring King of Numidia.

Cicero therefore found himself badly out in his assumption that
Pharsalia meant the end of the war, and his letters to Atticus are full of
regret and self-reproach. It was not that he wished to be with the

diehards and their barbarian allies. But he might have retired to some quiet spot in the Aegean area, as Marcus Marcellus and Servius Sulpicius had done, and there waited in less discomfort and, above all, without hopelessly compromising himself in the eyes of the republican militants. When it began to look as if they might after all come out on top, even take over Italy before Caesar extricated himself from the East, Cicero fell into a crisis of anxiety and mental conflict. March 47:

. . . Unbearably painful as my circumstances are, the worst cross of all is to find myself in a situation where my advantage lies only in what I have always wished never would happen[1]. . .

Not that he was certain of Caesar's pardon. At first Balbus and Oppius in the capital were encouraging, and Gaius Matius, like the loyal friend he always showed himself, came over from near-by Tarentum to cheer the depressed and ailing Cicero. But in December (48) Mark Antony, who had returned from Greece to act as viceroy in Italy, sent a copy of a letter from Caesar barring all members of the defeated party from returning there except those whose cases he had personally reviewed. Apologetically Antony pointed out that he was bound to obey orders, and Cicero would have to leave. When he was informed that Cicero did indeed have a mandate from Caesar, conveyed in Dolabella's letter, he published an order in which Cicero (along with one other Senator, an undistinguished person) was exempted by name from the ban. Cicero would have preferred something less invidious: 'I must say,' he wrote to Atticus, 'I wish he had not done that—the *case* could have been exempted without mentioning names.'

His health was poor. The first letter to Atticus from Brundisium speaks of 'mental and physical vexation past belief,' and the last complains of the almost insufferably oppressive climate, which added bodily discomfort to distress of mind. Residence at Brundisium was 'vexatious from every point of view.' In June 47 he thought of sending out his son, suitably accompanied, to plead with Caesar, but soon gave up the idea:

There is as yet no rumour of the man's having left Alexandria, on the contrary he is thought to be deeply entangled. So I am not sending Marcus as I had decided, and I must ask *you* to get me out of here. Any punishment is lighter than staying on in this place. . . . I realised of course from Oppius' talk of which you wrote to me how angry your friends[2] were, but you must

---

[1] Caesar's victory.
[2] Balbus and Oppius. They seem to have been irritated by reports of indiscreet talk on Cicero's part.

mollify them. While I now expect only misery, nothing could be more desperate than the predicament I am in at present. . . .

It was not until August that a reassuring letter from Caesar brought partial relief.

The despairing, self-upbraiding language of the letters of this period, with their occasional hints that the writer was not long for this world, is reminiscent of those from exile ten years before. Then he had at least the comfort of an affectionate family, working loyally on his behalf. It was very different now. The hostility of his brother and nephew (of which more later) was only part of his domestic miseries. Trouble with Terentia, long festering, was now ready to burst. The first of a series of letters, or rather notes, written from Brundisium makes it plain that her husband had no desire for her company:

I hope your joy at our safe arrival in Italy may be a lasting one. But distracted as I was by my unhappiness and the cruel ill-treatment of my family, I am afraid I may have taken a road with no easy outcome. So help me as far as you can—though what you can do I cannot imagine. There is no reason for you to leave home at present. It is a long, unsafe journey, and I do not see what good you can do if you come. Good bye.

Dispatched 4 November from Brundisium.

Those that follow contain nothing more affectionate than the conventional reminders to look after her health, as this of December 48:

I hope you are well, as I am. I would write more often if I had anything to say. As it is, you see how matters stand. Of my own sorry state Lepta and Trebatius will tell you. Be sure to take care of your health and Tullia's. Good-bye.

Or this of July 47:

I hope you are well, as I am. I have nothing definite yet either about Caesar's arrival or the letter which Philotimus is said to have. If anything definite comes along, I shall let you know at once. Take good care of your health. Good-bye.

Some background to this curtness is provided by references in letters to Atticus to Terentia's meanness and dishonesty. 3 June 47:

. . . The last thing I have to beg of you, if you think it right and it is something you feel you can undertake, is to talk to Camillus[1] with a view to your

---

[1] A legal expert who helped Cicero in business matters, apparently something like a modern solicitor.

both admonishing Terentia about her will. The signs of the times are plain to read. She should see that she does justice where it is due. One has heard from Philotimus that she is doing some wicked things. It is hardly credible; but certainly, if there is anything to be done, steps should be taken in time. . . .

The matter of Terentia's will cannot be fully elucidated from this and later allusions, but Cicero seems to have feared that its terms would be unjust to the children. He was also worried about the threat of confiscation hanging over his own and his wife's property, and wanted her somehow to forestall it, perhaps by conveyance to a third party, such as Atticus, who was in no danger. In August we have a more specific complaint:

. . . But here I go back to my own hand, for what follows is confidential. Even at this stage, do see about the will. I wish it had been done when she began to ask questions. . . . As the subject has already been broached between you, you will be able to advise her to trust someone whose fortune lies out of danger in this war. For my part I should like no one better than yourself, if that were her[1] wish too. Poor girl, I am hiding my fears from her. On the other matter, of course I know that nothing can be sold at present, but things *can* be set aside out of the way of the impending débâcle. You write to us that my resources and yours and Terentia's will be available. Yours no doubt; but what resources of mine can there be? As for Terentia, to say nothing of innumerable other incidents, doesn't this cap all? You asked her to change HS 12,000[2] that being the balance of the money. She sent me 10,000, with a note that this was the amount outstanding. When she nibbles such a trifle from a trifle, you can see what she will have been doing where a really big amount was involved. . . .

Even the ever-faithful Tullia was a source of distress at this time. She too was sickly. To Atticus, 27 November, 48:

. . . I am shocked to hear of my Tullia's illness and physical weakness. I can see that you are taking great care of her, and am most grateful. . . .

Her husband Dolabella, unworthy successor of the exemplary Piso Frugi, was becoming a scandal. Promoted Tribune in 47, he launched out into a demagogic programme for debt-cancellation and had to be restrained by Antony. Cicero writes of these 'distinguished activities' with ironic disapproval, and was 'tortured' by the irregularities of his son-in-law's private life. The divorce which had already been mooted

---

[1] Tullia's. She was staying with Cicero at the time.
[2] About £350. Shortage of ready money was among Cicero's minor afflictions at Brundisium.

when Cicero was in Greece was again seriously considered; but was not Dolabella too formidable to be offended? Two letters of July 47 raise the problem. To Terentia:

> As regards what I wrote in my last letter about sending notice of divorce, I don't know how powerful he is at the present time or how excited the state of popular feeling. If he is likely to be a formidable enemy, don't do anything—though perhaps the first move will come from him. You must judge of the whole position and choose whatever you think the least of evils in this wretched situation. Good-bye.
>
> 10 July, 47.

To Atticus:

> ... I implore you to think about this poor girl, both as to the matter on which I wrote you in my last letter, how to raise something to keep the wolf from the door, and also as to the will itself. I wish the other thing too had been taken in hand sooner, but I was afraid of everything. That would have been doing something like a man—whether on the score of the debt-cancellation or his nocturnal housebreaking[1] or Metella[2] or the whole chapter of delinquencies. I should have saved the money and given some evidence of manly resentment. Now he seems to be threatening it on *his* side—I have heard about Clodius' statue.[3] To think that my son-in-law of all people should be advocating this, or debt-cancellation either! Accordingly I am in favour, and so are you, of sending notice of divorce. He may ask for the third instalment,[4] so consider whether we should send the notice when he himself takes the initiative or before. ...

In fact, no action was taken for the time being. But with her marriage on the rocks, her family quarrelling, and the looming danger of a penniless future, Tullia became her father's most heartfelt anxiety. To Atticus, 17 December, 48:

> ... Another reason why I don't want you to leave Rome is that you say you are being pressed. Oh dear, what am I to write or wish? I'll cut short, the tears have come pouring from my eyes. I leave it to you. You decide for the best. Only don't let anything harm *her* at this time. Forgive me, I beg. Tears and grief stop me from dwelling on this topic longer. I shall only say this much, that nothing is more grateful to me than your affection for her. ...

[1] For amatory purposes.
[2] Perhaps the daughter of Metellus Celer and Clodia ('Lady Ox-Eyes'), married to the son of Cicero's old friend Lentulus Spinther. Another of her affairs, with the actor Aesopus' son, is hinted at by Horace.
[3] Dolabella seems to have proposed putting up a statue to this earlier patrician demagogue.
[4] Of Tullia's dowry.

3 January, 47:

... So I am beset on all sides. I can hardly stand it; or rather I just *cannot* stand it. Worse than all the rest of my afflictions put together is the thought that I shall leave that poor girl despoiled of father, inheritance, all that was hers. On that account I should indeed like to see you, as you promise. I have no one else to whom I can commend her, since I perceive that the same fate is in store for her mother as for me. ...

On 12 June she joined him:

The couriers to whom I am giving this letter are not my own and they are in a hurry. That is why it is so short, and also because I am going to send my own men. My Tullia joined me on 12 June. She told me a great deal about your attentiveness and kindness to her, and gave me three letters. Her own courage, thoughtfulness, and affection, far from giving me the pleasure I ought to take in such a paragon of daughters, grieve me beyond measure when I consider the unhappy lot in which so admirable a nature is cast, not through any misconduct of hers but by grave fault on my part. Therefore I do not expect consolation from you any longer, though I see you are anxious to supply it, nor advice, for the case does not admit of it, and I realise that you have tried everything, both in your many previous letters and in those I have just received.

But the reunion was painful, and two days later Cicero was proposing to send his daughter back as soon as she herself was willing ('I see no reason why I should keep her with me for long when we are both so heavily afflicted'). But she was still with him at the end of August.

So the dreary months trailed by until the end of September when, like a god from a belated machine, Caesar landed at Tarentum. Plutarch narrates:

When the word came that Caesar had disembarked at Tarentum and was travelling by road from there to Brundisium, Cicero went out to meet him, not quite expecting the worst, but embarrassed at the prospect of testing his all-powerful enemy's disposition before many witnesses. But he found he had no need to do or say anything below his dignity. For when Caesar saw him advancing along the road far ahead of others, he got down and gave him a friendly greeting. Then he walked for many hundred yards with Cicero in private conversation.

On 1 October Cicero was already on the road to Rome, and penning the bleakest of notifications to the wife he had not seen for over two years:

I think I shall get to Tusculum either on the 7th or on the following day. Kindly see that everything is ready. I may have a number of people with me, and shall probably make a fairly long stay. If there is no hip-bath in the bathroom, get one put in; likewise whatever else is needed for comfort and health. Good-bye.

1 October, from the district of Venusia.

CHAPTER NINETEEN

Brothers' Quarrel

'I am writing to you on my birthday. I wish I had never been let live that day, or else that my mother had never borne another child.'

Cicero to Atticus (*3 January 47*)

AT the end of his first extant letter to Atticus after his return to Italy Cicero writes:

... Quintus was most unamiably disposed toward me at Patrae. His son joined him there from Corcyra. I imagine they left with the rest.

In a later letter he refers to the bitterness of Quintus' language to him 'at the beginning of the voyage,' which so upset him that he was laid up afterwards. Apparently this relates to the journey from Corcyra to Patrae, since Quintus was not at Dyrrachium when Cicero sailed. In that case they must have met in Corcyra, and Quintus junior must have arrived there some time after they left. That is all quite possible, though Cicero's words *could* apply to the outward voyage from Italy in 48. At all events it is clear that the brothers parted at Patrae on bad terms, after 'many harsh words and actions' on Quintus' part. During the following months at Brundisium Cicero was appalled by the reports he heard of Quintus' behaviour. In December he wrote to Atticus that Quintus had sent his son to Caesar in Egypt

... not only to make his own peace but to accuse me as well. He is going about saying that I am traducing him to Caesar, which Caesar and all his friends contradict. And wherever he is he never stops heaping all manner of abuse upon me. It is the most unbelievable thing that has ever happened to me, and the bitterest of my present woes. Persons who professed to have heard him at Sicyon with their own ears using scandalous language about me before a large company have repeated it to me. You know the style, you may even have experienced it. It has all been turned on me. But I make the pain worse by dwelling on it, and give you pain also. ...

Confirmatory evidence came accidentally a few days later:

... My ruin is my own work. Nothing in my adversity is due to chance, I am to blame for all. When I saw the kind of war it was, nothing but weakness and improvisation against excellently prepared enemies, I made up my mind what to do and resolved upon a course which may not have been courageous but was particularly allowable in my case.[1] Then I yielded to my family, or rather I obeyed them. What one of them really felt, the one for whom you put in your good word, you will see from his own letters to yourself and others. I should never have opened them but for an accident. It was like this: A package was brought to me. I undid it to see whether there was a letter for me. There was nothing, but there was a letter to Vatinius and another to Ligurius.[2] I gave instructions for these to be forwarded to the addressees. They promptly arrived on my doorstep, burning with indignation, clamorous against the 'damned scoundrel', and read me the letters, which were full of all manner of slanders against me. At this Ligurius lost his temper completely, exclaiming that he knew Caesar detested the person concerned, but had not only shown him favour but had given him all that money in compliment to me. After this painful discovery I wanted to know what he had written to the others, for I thought it would be highly damaging to himself if this infamous behaviour of his were to become public property. I found it was in the same strain. I am sending the letters to you. If you think their delivery will be in his own interest, then deliver them. It does me no harm. As for the broken seals, I think Pomponia has his seal. . . .

January 47:

Reports reaching me about the Quinti have dropped new bitterness into my overflowing cup. My friend Publius Terentius had a job as managing director of the Customs and Pasture Rents Company in Asia. He saw Quintus junior at Ephesus on 8 December, and was at pains to be hospitable because of his friendship with me. He says that when he asked about me Quintus told him that we were on the worst possible terms and showed him a roll containing a speech which he was going to make against me in Caesar's presence. Terentius says he tried to talk him out of his folly. He adds that later on at Patrae Quintus senior spoke much to him in similarly outrageous fashion. The letters which I sent you will have enabled you to judge of his unbalanced state of mind. I am sure that all this gives you pain. It tortures me, all the more because I do not expect even to have the opportunity of remonstrating with them. . . .

What made Quintus' conduct all the less excusable was that Cicero had been at pains to defend him to Caesar:

[1] i.e., to stay in Italy (or at all events not to join Pompey). Cicero's own contemporary letter (see page 153) shows that *Quintus* at any rate did not urge him to the contrary.
[2] A friend of Caesar's and a fellow-officer of Quintus' in Gaul.

. . . Cornelius Balbus junior wrote to me that Caesar thought my brother Quintus had 'sounded the clarion for my departure.' Not yet knowing what Quintus had written about me to all and sundry, though I had had many harsh words and actions from him face to face, I wrote to Caesar as follows notwithstanding:

'For my brother Quintus I am no less anxious than for myself, but in my present situation I do not venture to intercede for him with you. This much, however, and no more I shall venture to ask you (and I beg it of you), not to hold him responsible for any short-comings of mine in respect to yourself or for any want of regard for you, and on the contrary to believe that he was always in favour of our connexion, and that he was the companion of my journey, not the guide. Accordingly in other respects you will doubtless grant him such indulgence as your natural kindness and the friendship between you make appropriate. All I ask, as I do again most earnestly, is that *I* may not count against him with you.'

This letter to Caesar is certainly to Cicero's credit, even if R. Y. Tyrrell went rather far in characterizing it as an act 'of large nobleness and truly chivalrous feeling, quite startling when one remembers the times in which Cicero lived.' Leaving aside the implication that the virtue of magnanimity was alien to the first century B.C., and without denying that Cicero here showed more than a trace of it, one may fairly remember that the opinion he contradicted was unflattering to his own *amour propre* ('the last thing I wanted Caesar to think was that on such a matter I had followed anybody's judgment but my own'), and that a generous attitude was more likely to impress Caesar favourably than the contrary.

Atticus tried to make peace. March 47:

. . . Quintus excuses himself to me by letter in terms much more offensive than those he used in his bitterest attacks. He says he gathers from your letter that you do not approve of his writing harshly about me to all and sundry; therefore he is sorry to have vexed you, but considers that what he did was justified. Then he enumerates in the most indecent language his reasons for doing it. But he would not have flaunted his hatred of me either now or previously were it not that he sees I am totally ruined. . . .

April and May brought further reports of Quintus' evil tongue, also a letter 'of extraordinary malignity' from Quintus junior. But in July, probably thanks to Atticus' continuing efforts, a comparatively friendly letter came to hand from Quintus, and in August Cicero could express qualified pleasure at the news of his brother's pardon by Caesar. His resentment of Quintus' villainy had been put aside, but it revived in force when he saw a copy of another injurious letter written by him to Caesar some time previously. At this point the correspondence with Atticus again breaks off. When it resumes in the following year, both brothers were back in Rome, amity superficially restored.

If the letter in which Quintus enumerated his grievances had been preserved, much would be certain that is now guesswork. Cicero does indeed mention one of them incidentally. Quintus had expected to benefit, whether by gift or loan, from the Cilician money which his brother had withdrawn from Asia and lent to Pompey (who of course never repaid it), apparently in fulfilment of a promise made before the outbreak of the war.[1] Cicero's excuses to Atticus on this point do not altogether convince. He does not comment on the justice of Quintus' expectations, but says, first, that Quintus had not asked him and, second, that he never touched the money himself, was indeed in difficulties at the time. Quintus might perhaps have retorted that he ought not to have needed to ask (or knew it would be no use, since the loan to Pompey had already been agreed), and that Cicero had not been obliged to earmark the money without consulting him.

Perhaps, as has sometimes been asserted, Quintus blamed his brother for the situation in which he found himself as a result of the part they had taken against his former Imperator. As has been seen, he accused Marcus of putting the blame on *him*; and though this was untrue, the fact that Caesar did apparently at this time hold Quintus responsible suggests that Quintus made his charge in good faith (mischief-makers, including his son, may have been at work). Further suspicion and resentment may have arisen from the discrimination implied in Marcus Cicero's warrant from Caesar to return to Italy. We have only the bare facts to go on, but it is on the cards that Quintus, who does not seem to have been mentioned in Dolabella's letter, felt deserted.

But whatever grounds Quintus *alleged*, the causes surely went deep. His temper was naturally irritable, and his sojourn in the Peloponnese may have been as disagreeable as his brother's in Brundisium; but grudges of long standing, probably unsuspected by the elder brother and in part perhaps not consciously realized by the younger, will have lain beneath an eruption which so thoroughly shattered the surface of family concord. That seems to have been Marcus Cicero's own belief, implicit in his words to Atticus after reading Quintus' letter of accusa-

---

[1] See page 169. In January 49 Cicero told his former Quaestor, Mescinius, that Pompey had taken the whole of the money, which was not strictly true. But he may have promised Pompey to keep it at his disposal if needed.

tion: 'he would not have flaunted his hatred of me either now or previously, were it not that he sees I am totally ruined.' If Quintus (in Marcus' opinion) would have concealed his hatred in different circumstances, it looks as though (in Marcus' opinion) he *had* concealed it before the circumstances of 48 existed.

It is in this connexion that the story of Quintus' quarrel with Atticus in 61[1] makes instructive reading. We know about it from Cicero's letter to the latter in December of that year:

Your letter in which you enclose copies of my brother Quintus' letters argues, I agree, a remarkable change of feeling and inconstancy of judgment and opinion on his part. Naturally, in view of my deep affection for you both, I am very much distressed, and also puzzled to imagine what can have happened to offend my brother so seriously as to bring about such a revulsion of sentiment. I had already perceived, and saw that you too suspected at the time you left us, an undercurrent of grievance; evidently his feelings had been hurt, and some disagreeable suspicions had sunk into his mind. I tried to counteract them on many occasions, more especially after the allotment of his province, but I did not realise he had taken umbrage to the extent revealed by your letter, nor did I make as much headway as I wished. However, I took comfort in the assurance that he would be seeing you at Dyrrachium or somewhere else over there. I trusted, and indeed convinced myself, that once this happened a frank talk, or even the mere meeting and sight of one another, would set all to rights between you. I need not tell you, for you already know, what a kindly, amiable fellow my brother is, how impressionable he is both in taking offence and in laying it aside. But most unfortunately you did not see him at all. The notions implanted by certain designing persons had more influence upon him than his sense of family and friendship or your former affection for one another, which ought to have been paramount. Where the blame for this unhappy rift may lie is easier for me to judge than to put into writing. I am afraid that in defending my own relations I might have some hard things to say of yours. For it is plain to me that even if his domestic circle did nothing to cause the damage, they could at least have counteracted it when they found it. But it will be better for me to explain the whole thing when I can talk to you—it's a malaise which goes rather further even than appears on the surface.

With regard to the letter he sent you from Thessalonica and the things you believe he said in Rome in the hearing of friends of yours and *en route*, whether or not some grain of reason for them may exist is outside my knowledge; but my hopes of alleviating this unpleasantness lie entirely in your good nature. . . .

[1] See page 67.

So for at least a year Quintus had carried a smouldering grudge; suddenly it broke out, not only in letters to its object but in talk to outsiders. And on that occasion Cicero clearly did not have the full confidence of his 'most candid of brothers.'

The conditions of correspondence in those days made for reticence on delicate domesticities, and Cicero had other and to himself more interesting things to write about than his brother's psychology. Any relation of what happened between them in 48–47 to past history must contain a large element of inference and surmise. Still the quarrel is a datum, and the letters offer clues, which have been noticed in their place. The deplorable marriage, which Marcus Cicero had made and striven to keep in being for his own reasons, friction over Statius, disappointments in Gaul, untoward incidents in Cilicia, Quintus' strange passivity in the early months of the Civil War—all this and much more of which we are not informed may have gone to nourish the ulcer in Quintus' mind: the mind of a small man, irritable, querulous, and weak; a severe magistrate, who spoiled his son and let himself be run by a slave; a good man in a battle or a riot, but a rabbit in front of his wife; ambitious, but inhibited by distrust of his talents, which were not of the first order, and handicapped by the unlucky accident of birth, which had made him a bigger man's younger brother.

Cicero's biographers and commentators have been blind to the significance of this affair, treating it as an unfortunate episode without lasting consequence. Most of them simply pass it by. The general underlying assumption was expressed by Strachan-Davidson: 'Though the evidence looks black against Quintus, the complete reconciliation which followed allows us to hope that what looked like baseness proved to have been only ill-temper and indiscretion.' But the 'complete reconciliation' is a comfortable myth. Poisoned wounds do not heal so easily. Apart from some hostile and contemptuous remarks in a letter of July 46, Quintus virtually disappears from the correspondence until the middle of 45. When Tullia died in February of that year Cicero could look to Atticus and to Brutus for consolation, but of Quintus never a word. Stray references in later letters attest a certain amount of intercourse, but their tone is either neutral or coolly ironic. In public, no doubt, appearances were kept up, as by Quintus' roles in certain literary dialogues or polite references in the Senate; the extent to which even in private Cicero was prepared to hide his real feelings will be seen from his self-confessedly hypocritical reconciliation with the distrusted and despised Quintus junior. As for the father, not a phrase or nuance in the confidential letters of the period can fairly be set in evidence of a return to the affection, let alone the intimacy, of earlier days.

Cicero's relationship with his brother was his oldest emotional attachment, and its traumatic dissolution a loss of major psychological importance. His reactions to the death of his daughter, the one member of the family for whom he still deeply cared, and to other events of these closing years, might not have been just what they were if the bond with Quintus had held, and if he had not known in whatever unacknowledged recesses of his mind that Quintus was not alone to blame.

CHAPTER TWENTY

Under Caesar (1)

'I enjoy things while I am able. I pray I may always be able.'
Cicero to Papirius Paetus

OF Cicero's homecoming in October 47 and of his life for some six months afterwards practically nothing is recorded. Only one of a very few letters which can be assigned to the first quarter of 46[1] is of personal interest. It was to Marcus Varro, who like Cicero had given up the republican cause after Pharsalia and seems to have been on his way home:

The letter which you sent to Atticus and which he read to me informed me of your doings and whereabouts, but as to when we were to see you, I could not so much as make a guess from that letter. However, I am coming to hope that your advent is not far away. I wish I may find some comfort in it, though our afflictions are so many and so grievous that nobody but an arrant fool should hope for any relief. And yet you may be able to help me, or perhaps I may somehow be able to help you. For I should tell you that since my return I have restored my relations with my old friends, I mean my books. Not that I had renounced their companionship because I had any complaint against them—it was because they gave me a feeling of shame. I felt that in casting myself into a turmoil of events with altogether untrustworthy associates I had failed in obedience to their precepts. They forgive me. They call me back to the old intercourse, and tell me that you, in staying faithful to it, were wiser than I. And so I have made my peace with them, and we are together again. That is why I think I may properly hope that, once I see you, I shall find both present and impending troubles easy to bear. Whatever venue you favour—Tusculum or Cumae, my house or yours, or (what would be my last choice) Rome—I can promise you that it will be judged the most convenient for both of us, only provided we are together.

For a year and a half Cicero lived at his house in Rome or Tusculum

---

[1] This was the year of Julius Caesar's sorely needed reform of the Roman Calendar. By the sun the year began on 14 October. To put the reckoning straight, three extra ('intercalary') months were inserted, one between February and March, two between November and December. To keep it straight, ten days were added to the normal year.

near by. In another letter to Varro, written toward the end of April after news of Caesar's crushing victory over the republicans in Africa, he says he was afraid of raising suspicion if he went away:

... To you I have the same advice to offer as to myself. Let us avoid men's eyes, even if we cannot easily escape their tongues. The jubilant victors regard us as among the defeated, whereas those who are sorry for the defeat of our friends feel aggrieved that we are still among the living. Perhaps you will wonder why, with all this going on in Rome, I am not, like you, elsewhere. Well, and have you yourself, a shrewder man than I or any other, foreseen everything, has *nothing* turned out contrary to your expectations? I can hardly believe that. Whose eyes are so preternaturally sharp as to avoid every obstacle, every pitfall, in darkness such as this? In point of fact it did cross my mind long ago that it would be nice to get away somewhere, so as not to see or hear what was being done and said in Rome. But I made difficulties for myself. I thought that whoever met me would suspect, or, even if he did not suspect, would say (as might suit his individual purpose), 'Aha! He took fright, that's why he ran away; or else he's up to something, has a boat all ready.' Even the most charitable (and perhaps the best acquainted with the kind of man I am) would have thought that I was leaving because I could not stand the sight of certain persons. With all this in mind I stay in Rome. And, after all, long custom has imperceptibly anaesthetized my spleen. . . .

Another and perhaps stronger reason appears in a letter of January 45:

... My Tullia's confinement has kept me in Rome. But even now that she has, as I hope, fairly well regained her strength, I am still kept here waiting to extract the first instalment[1] out of Dolabella's agents. And in point of fact I am not the gadabout I used to be. My buildings and the freedom from distraction were what I used to enjoy. Well, I have a town house as pleasant as any of my country places, and as perfect freedom from distraction as anywhere in the wilds. So even my literary work is not hampered, and I employ myself in it without any interruptions. I fancy therefore that I shall see you here before you see me there. . . .

From April 46 to the next major event in Cicero's life, the death of his daughter in February 45, we have between sixty and seventy letters, excluding letters of recommendation and introduction, but only a dozen are to Atticus. His other correspondents could be called friends, more or less close, but not intimates with whom he could think aloud. In reading what he writes to them, whether on public or

---

[1] Of Tullia's dowry, she and Dolabella having been divorced.

personal affairs, that point has always to be remembered. In particular, Cicero's frame of mind during this period is not to be gauged from his correspondence with former Pompeians waiting more or less impatiently for Caesar's permission to come home. He had many friends among the dominant party, and was glad to use his influence with them in favour of these less fortunate ex-associates. One of them wrote to him in December 46:

... What am I to urge you to do for me? As you see, the time has arrived when a decision on my case must be made. There is no call, my dear Cicero, for you to wait for my son. Eagerness, youth, and anxiety make it impossible for him to think everything out. *You* must carry the whole affair. My entire hope lies in you. In your sagacity you know the kind of thing that gives Caesar pleasure and wins him over. The whole campaign must start with you, and be conducted by you to the finish. You have much influence with himself, and more with his whole circle. If only you make up your mind that it is not your business to do what is *asked* of you (though that is a great deal in all conscience), but that the whole load is yours to bear, you will succeed. Or do I act like a fool in my present sorry state, or presume too far on your friendship, when I saddle you so? You are so indefatigable on your friends' behalf that they have come not merely to hope for your help as I do, but to demand it as I am doing. ...

Five years earlier Caelius Rufus (one of the casualties of the civil war), *à propos* of his panthers, had paid Cicero a similar compliment.[1] By nature and by the habit of a career built on the accumulation of good will, Cicero was a serviceable man; his kind heart and established practice were now reinforced by the pleasure of displaying how much he could do with the powers in being and the hope that such good deeds would blunt the tongues of *boni* (themselves stay-at-homes in 49) who, as he put it to Marcus Marius, thought he had committed a crime by staying alive. These letters to exiles naturally tend to follow a pattern, and it is worth while to quote one specimen in full. The recipient was Nigidius Figulus, a former Praetor[2] and after Varro the most learned Roman of his day, though posterity remembered him chiefly as an astrologer and magician. The month of writing was probably August or September:

I have been asking myself this long while past just what to write to you, but nothing has come to mind—not any particular thing to say, nor even a *manner* of writing normally used in correspondence. The circumstances of

---

[1] See page 116.   [2] See page 60.

the time have taken away one element[1] customary in the letters we used to write in happier days. Fortune has made it impossible for me to write or even think in that vein. There remains a serious, doleful sort of letter-writing, suited to the times we live in. That too fails me. It should include either the pledge of some assistance or comfort for your distress. Now as for promises, I can make none, for myself I am in like case and support my misfortunes by others' help. I am more often inclined to complain of the life I lead than to be thankful for living at all.

True, I personally have suffered no injury outside the common, and I can think of nothing to wish for at such a time which Caesar has not spontaneously granted me. But my troubles are such that I feel guilty in continuing to live. I lack not only many personal intimates, snatched from me by death or scattered in exile, but all the friends whose good will I won when I defended the state with you at my side. I live among the wreckages of their fortunes, the plundering of their possessions. To hear of it would be sad enough, but I have actually before my eyes the heartrending spectacle of the dissipation of their estates—the men who were my helpers when I put out that fire[2] in days gone by. In the city where not long ago I stood high in influence, respect, and fame, I now have none of these things. I do enjoy the greatest consideration from Caesar himself, but that cannot counterbalance the violence, the total revolution of environment. Deprived therefore as I am of everything to which I had been accustomed by nature, inclination, and habit, I cut a sorry figure in other men's eyes, so at least I fancy, and in my own. Born as I was for action, incessant action worthy of a man, I now have no way to employ my energies or even my thoughts. I, who once had it in my power to help the obscure and even the guilty, now find myself unable even to make a kindly promise to Publius Nigidius, the most accomplished and the most stainless man of our time, once so influential, and so good a friend of mine.

This sort of letter writing is, therefore, ruled out. It remains for me to offer you comfort and to try by reasoned argument to divert you from your trouble. But you have in the highest degree, if ever any man had, the faculty of consoling yourself or another. Therefore I shall not touch that side of the subject which starts from recondite philosophical theory. *You* will see what is worthy of a man of sense and courage, what is demanded of you by dignity, elevation of mind, your past, your studies, the pursuits in which you have distinguished yourself from childhood upwards. I merely assure you of what my understanding and intuition tell me, being in Rome and keeping a close eye on the course of events: namely that you will not have to bear your present troubles much longer, but that those which you share with us may be with you always.

---

[1] i.e., joking.
[2] The Catilinarian conspiracy. Cicero is said to have relied much on Nigidius' advice during that episode.

To begin with the personage whose word is law, I think I see his mind and that it is favourable to your cause. These are not idle words. The less I have of his intimacy, the more curious I am to probe. It is only because he wants to make it easier for himself to give discouraging answers to people with whom he is more seriously annoyed that he has so far been slow to release you from your unpleasant predicament. But his friends, especially those he likes best, speak and feel about you with remarkable warmth. To that we can add the popular sentiment, or rather the universal consensus. Even the Republic, which counts for little enough at the moment, but must some day count for something, will exert whatever power she may have to win your pardon from those in whose hands she lies, and, believe me, it will not be long.

So I will now make you a promise, which earlier in this letter I refrained from doing. I shall both cultivate his intimates, who have no small regard for me and are much in my company, and find a way into familiar intercourse with himself, from which a sense of shame has deterred me hitherto. Assuredly I shall follow any path which I think likely to lead to our goal. In this whole sphere I shall do more than I venture to put on paper. Other kinds of service, I am sure, are at your disposal in many quarters; but from me they are most heartily at your command. Of my possessions there is nothing that I would not as soon were yours as mine. On this and all related points I say little, only because I would rather have you expect to enjoy your own, as I am confident you will.

It only remains for me to beg and implore you to be of excellent courage, and to remember, not only the lessons you have learned from other great men, but those of which you are yourself the author, the products of your intellect and study. If you bring them all together, you will hope for the best; and come what may, good or bad, you will bear it with philosophy. But all this you know better than I, or rather than any man. For my part I shall attend with all zeal and diligence to whatever I find to concern you, and shall treasure the memory of your kindness to me in the darkest days of my life.

Writing to people in Nigidius' position Cicero was bound to take a sombre tone about life in Rome and his own predicament. Cheerfulness would have been unfeeling, and from no angle could it have suited him to let them understand that his early defection had earned him a very tolerable existence under the new régime. About the same time he was writing to the apolitical Papirius Paetus, who had suffered nothing worse in the war than a loss on his investments, in a very different strain:

. . . So this is the way I live nowadays. In the morning I receive callers, both *boni* (numerous, but depressed) and these jubilant victors—who, I must say, are most obliging and friendly in their attentions to me. When the stream has ceased to flow, I immerse myself in literary work, writing or reading. Some of my visitors listen to me as a man of learning, because I know a little more than themselves. All the rest of the time is given to the claims of the body. As for my country, I have already mourned her longer and more deeply than any mother mourned her only son. . . .

And again:

You really are absurd! After a visit from our friend Balbus you ask *me* what I think is going to happen about those towns and lands! As though I know anything that he doesn't know! Or, as though, if ever I do know anything, I don't get my information from him! On the contrary, if you are a friend of mine, *you* tell *me* what is going to happen to us! After all, you had him in your power, you could have pumped him, drunk if not sober. But as for me, my dear Paetus, I am not inquisitive about such matters. For about four years past the fact that we are still alive is a bonus to which we are not entitled—that is, if to survive freedom can be called a bonus or a life. Moreover, I fancy I know the answer: what will happen will be what those who have the power want to happen. And power will always lie with armed force. So we ought to be content with whatever is allowed us. Anybody unable to put up with life on these terms should have taken leave of it.

They are surveying land at Veii and Capena. That is not so far from Tusculum. But I have no fears. I enjoy while I am able, I pray I may always be able. But if my prayer is not granted, well, as a man of courage and a philosopher, I exalted life above all else. Therefore I cannot but feel beholden to the man to whose favour I owe it. Even if he were to will that the state be such as he perhaps desires and as all of us ought to pray for, there is nothing he can do. He has too many associates to whom he has tied himself.

But I am going further than I meant—after all, I am writing to *you*. However, you may take my word for it that not only I, who am not in his counsels, but the great man himself does not know what will happen. We are his slaves, but he is the slave of circumstances. So he does not know what circumstances will demand, and we do not know what he has in his mind. . . .

Starved of social amenities for years, Cicero soon found himself in a mood to enjoy them. No doubt Caesarian 'friends,' Balbus, Hirtius, and the rest, had other than convivial reasons for liking him to be seen at their tables. His name still counted for something with respectable persons who looked askance at a somewhat raffish régime. But his company was valued for its own sake. 'Words can hardly convey the power of affability and charm of conversation to win men's hearts,' he told his son in his tract 'On Duties.' His wit had become legendary. The absent Dictator gave instructions that Cicero's latest *mots* were to be reported as part of his regular information service, and claimed as a connoisseur to be able to pick out any spurious ones, as an authority on Plautus' plays could detect a false line.

'And so I go dining out with our rulers,' wrote Cicero to Varro in May 46. 'What am I to do? One must move with the times.' One such occasion lives in a note scribbled to Paetus at table. The host was Volumnius Eutrapelus, a wit reputed second only to Cicero—hence his Greek surname, *eutrapelia* being defined by Aristotle as 'cultured insolence.' Volumnius' freedwoman, the actress Cytheris, mistress of his gambling-crony Mark Antony, was on the dining-couch beside him:

I am scribbling the lines of which you are reading a copy on my tablets after taking my place at dinner at three of the afternoon. If you wish to know where, my host is Volumnius Eutrapelus. Your friends Atticus and Verrius are on either side of me. Does it surprise you that we have become such a merry lot of slaves? Well, what am I to do? I ask *you*, since you are attending philosophy lectures. Am I to torture and torment myself? What should I gain? And how long should I keep it up? You may advise me to spend my life in literary work. Surely you realise that this *is* my only occupation, that if I did not spend my life in that way I could not live at all. But even this pursuit has—I won't say its saturation-point, but its due limit. When I leave it, little as I care about dinner (the one problem *you* put to philosopher Dio), I really do not see anything better to do with the time before I go to bed.

Well, to the rest of my tale. Cytheris lay down next to Eutrapelus. 'So?' I hear you say, '*Cicero* at such a party,

> "He the admired, upon whose countenance
> The Greeks all turned their eyes"?'[1]

I assure you I had no idea *she* was going to be there. But after all, even Aristippus the Socratic did not blush when someone twitted him with keeping Lais as his mistress. 'I keep Lais,' said he, 'but I am not in Lais' keeping!' (it's better in the Greek; make your own translation, if you care to). As for me, even in my young days I was never attracted by anything of the sort, much less now that I'm an old man. It's the party I enjoy. I talk about whatever comes uppermost, as they say, and transform my sighs into shouts of laughter.

So life passes. Every day a bit of reading or a bit of writing. Then, since something is due to my friends, I dine with them. We don't go beyond what the law[2] (if there is such a thing nowadays) allows, we even stop short of it, and that by a considerable margin. So you don't have to dread my arrival. You'll receive a guest with a small appetite for food, but a big one for mirth.

[1] From an unknown Latin tragedy.
[2] Passed by Caesar in the autumn of 46 to control expenditure on banquets.

The qualms of an Arpinate conscience at this high living ('What business has a man from Arpinum with the hot springs?' asked 'Pretty-Boy' Clodius in the old days) were seconded by a sexagenarian digestion. Fabius Gallus, art-expert and Epicurean, may have smiled as he read:

For the last ten days my stomach has been seriously out of order, but as I did not have a fever I could not convince folk who wanted my services that I was genuinely sick. So I have taken refuge here at Tusculum, after two days of strict fasting—not so much as a drop of water! Famished and exhausted, I was craving your good offices rather than expecting you to demand mine. I am terrified of all forms of illness; but dysentery—your master Epicurus gets a rough handling from the Stoics for complaining of trouble with his bladder and bowels, the latter being according to them a consequence of overeating and the former of an even more discreditable kind of indulgence —well, dysentery is my bugbear. However, I think I am better for the change, or maybe the mental relaxation; or perhaps the malady is simply wearing itself into abatement.

But in case you wonder how it happened or what I did to deserve it, the Sumptuary Law, which is supposed to bring plain living, has been my downfall. Our *bons vivants*, in their efforts to bring into fashion products of the soil exempted under the statute, make the most appetising dishes out of fungi, potherbs, and grasses of all sorts. Happening on some of these at Lentulus' Augural Dinner, I was seized with a violent diarrhoea, which has only today begun (I think) to check its flow. So: oysters and eels I used to resist well enough, but here I lie, caught in the toils of Mesdames Beet and Mallow. Well, I shall be more careful in future. . . .

But if Cicero was not solitary, neither was he idle—even though he had now formed the habit of a daily siesta. A letter to Eutrapelus refers to a 'concourse of important affairs,' which he implies were of a public nature; they seem to have been connected with Caesar's return from Africa at the end of July. That, however, must have been exceptional, for although he sometimes attended the Senate, he did not speak (before a celebrated occasion in September, presently to be noticed), and had not resumed practice in the courts. His main occupation was reading and writing. To Manius Curius in early August:

. . . After receiving my friends' morning calls, which are in even greater number than of yore because they seem to see a loyal citizen as a rare bird of good omen, I bury myself in my library. And so I produce books—of their importance you will perhaps judge. . . .

Within a few months of returning to Rome Cicero began work on his

'Brutus,' a history of Roman oratory in the form of a dialogue between himself, Atticus, and the dedicatee. His friendship with Marcus Brutus, now high in Caesar's favour and himself a notable speaker, had ripened during their sojourn in Pompey's camp. Back at the scene of his forensic triumphs, Cicero had found the courts 'a desert;' the never failing sequence of more or less politically motivated prosecutions was a thing of the past, and Cicero's voice was no more heard in the Forum than in the Senate-House. The 'Brutus' was partly the outcome of a nostalgia that reveals itself in the almost immediately following 'Stoic Paradoxes,' a rhetorical presentation of such dogmas as 'all wise men are free and all foolish men are slaves.' This trifling piece shows a notable tendency to dwell on the past, working off old grudges against Clodius, Crassus, Lucullus and his fellow 'fish-fanciers.' The end of a letter to Varro in April 46 suggests that Cicero had another political treatise in mind—perhaps he had resumed his work on his unfinished 'Laws:'

. . . Only let us be firm on one point—to live together in our literary studies. We used to go to them only for pleasure, now we go for salvation. If anybody cares to call us in as architects, or even as workmen, to help build a commonwealth, we shall not say no, rather we shall hasten cheerfully to the job. If our services are not required, we must still read and write 'Republics'. Like the learned men of old, we must guide the state in our libraries, if we cannot in Senate-House and Forum, and pursue our researches into custom and law. Such are my sentiments. You will oblige me greatly if you will write and tell me what *you* intend and what course you think best.

But this seems to have been put aside in favour of a laudation (now lost) of Brutus' uncle Cato, news of whose Stoic suicide in Africa reached Rome about the beginning of May. The book was undertaken at Brutus' prompting—both he and Cicero had consciences to ease. Cicero foresaw difficulties, as he told Atticus:

. . . Now about the 'Cato,' it's a problem for an Archimedes. I cannot work anything out which your boon companions would read with equanimity, let alone enjoyment. Even if I were to keep clear of his speeches in the Senate and his whole political outlook and opinions and choose simply to praise his seriousness of purpose and steadfastness, even this would grate upon their ears. But no genuine eulogy of that remarkable man is possible without paying tribute to the way he foresaw our present situation, and strove to avert it, and gave up his life rather than witness it in actuality. Can any of that be made palatable to Aledius?[1] . . .

---

[1] A Caesarian; see page 203.

However the result satisfied him. 'I'm pleased with my "Cato",' he writes in July or August, 'but then Lucilius Bassus[1] is pleased with his productions too.' Brutus seems to have been less satisfied, since in the following year he composed a 'Cato' of his own, with reference to which Cicero wrote acidly to Atticus in March 45:

I have read Brutus' letter and am returning it to you; not a very knowledgeable answer to your queries. However, that's his affair; though his ignorance on one point is really shocking. . . . And then he thinks he is giving me a fine tribute when he calls me 'an excellent Consul.' Why, which of my enemies has spoken fainter? And his answers to your other comments! He merely asks you to make a correction about the decree. He would have done that much if his attention had been drawn to it by a copyist. But again, it's his affair. . . .

There was a curious sequel. Hirtius rejoined with an 'Anti-Cato', and as this contained praise of himself, Cicero used Atticus' resources to get it into circulation:

From the pamphlet which Hirtius has sent me I perceive what Caesar's denunciation in answer to my eulogy is going to be like. Hirtius makes a collection of Cato's faults, but sings my praises loudly at the same time. So I have sent the piece to Musca for him to give your clerks. I want it to have a wide circulation, and to facilitate that please give instructions to your people. . . .

The tell-tale 'so' disposes of the writer's subsequent explanation: 'The reason I want the pamphlet Hirtius sent me about Cato disseminated by your staff is to let these people's abuse win *him* greater eulogy.' But Hirtius' piece was only 'a sort of rough-cast' for a more elaborate denigration by the Dictator himself. When this appeared, Cicero, after precautionary soundings, sent its author a letter of congratulation:

It slipped my mind to send you a copy of the letter I sent to Caesar. It was not what you suspect, that I was ashamed to let you see it in case you might think it ludicrously ''umble.' I assure you I did not write otherwise than as one author to another. I do think well of that book, as I told you when we were together. I wrote therefore *sans blague*, but at the same time in such terms as I think will please him enormously. . . .

That was on 24 August. The letter to Caesar was a *quid pro quo*, for about a fortnight earlier Balbus had conveyed a delicate compliment from Caesar to Cicero:

---

[1] An unknown author, presumably a bad one.

... I met Balbus. ... His first words were: 'I have just received a letter in which Caesar confirms emphatically that he will be back before the Roman Games.' I read the letter, which contained a good deal about my 'Cato.' He says that reading and rereading it has improved his powers of expression, whereas after reading Brutus' 'Cato' he began to fancy himself as a writer. ...

From the Sphere of the Moon[1] the occasion of these literary courtesies might have smiled ('What an amusing Consul we have!'). After all, there had never been much love lost between the two.

The 'Cato' was followed by another treatise (not a dialogue) on eloquence, likewise addressed to Brutus. Cicero writes of it to a friend in January 45:

I am greatly pleased that you think so well of my 'Orator'. I do flatter myself that I have put into that book whatever judgment I may possess on the subject of public speaking. If it is as you say you find it, then I too amount to something. If not, then I am content that my reputation for sound judgment and the book shall suffer in exactly the same proportion. ...

He had found another compensation for public silence in the practice of private declamation for the benefit of his juniors, notably Hirtius and Dolabella, his 'pupils in oratory, masters in gastronomy.' To Paetus in July 46:

While I was at a loose end at Tusculum, having sent my pupils to meet their friend[2] with the idea that they should at the same time put me in the best possible odour with him, I received your most charming letter. It appears then that my plan meets with your approbation. Like Dionysius the tyrant, who is said to have opened a school in Corinth after his expulsion from Syracuse, I have set up as a schoolmaster, as it were, now that the courts are abolished and my forensic kingdom lost.

Well, I too am pleased with my plan, which brings me many advantages. To begin with, I get some protection against the hazards of the times, which is what is most needed just now. What that amounts to I don't know; all I can see is that nobody else has yet produced a plan which I consider superior to mine. ...

That then to begin with. Next, I benefit directly, first in health, which I lost when I gave up my exercises. Then my oratorical faculty, if I had any, would have dried up had I not gone back to these exercises. There is a final point, which *you* might perhaps put first. I have polished off more peacocks than you young pigeons. While you enjoy Haterius' gravity in Naples, I

---

[1] The souls of good Stoics went to the Sphere of the Moon.
[2] Caesar.

regale myself with Hirtius' gravy[1] here. Be a man then and come along! Let me teach you the *principia* you want to learn—though it will be a case of the pig and Minerva.[2] But, as I see the situation, if you can't sell your valuations or fill a pot with sixpences, you have got to move back to Rome. Better die of stomach-ache here than of starvation down there. I see you have lost your money, and I expect it is the same with your friends in Naples. So if you don't look ahead, it's all up with you. You can get up on that mule, which you say you still have left after eating your pack-horse, and ride to Rome. There will be a chair for you in school next to mine as assistant master, and a cushion to go with it.

For a long time the shape of the political future under Caesar remained to be seen, for in 47 he had spent a mere couple of months in Rome before leaving to settle accounts with the republican revival in Africa, and did not get back until the end of July 46. Successive phases in Cicero's attitude and expectations are reflected in his letters. In one to Varro at the end of May Caesar figures as the proprietor of the Roman world who visits provinces like a great landowner touring his estates:

. . . Some think he may come by way of Sardinia. That is one of his properties that he has not yet inspected. It's the worst he owns, but he doesn't despise it. . . .

But the period immediately following Caesar's return brought a change of tone. The letters to republican exiles usually contain tributes to Caesar's merciful nature, regard for people of talent and culture, and personal amenity to Cicero; if Rome was a bad place to be in, that was the fault of circumstances rather than of Caesar. All this has to be taken with a due allowance of salt. It was what men hoping for pardon would like to read, and what it was prudent for Cicero to write to people who were friendly acquaintances rather than friends. But letters to comparative familiars, Paetus and Curius, show a similar trend, though little or no hope of political improvement. This one to Curius is usually assigned to August:

. . . But truth it is that in those days I mourned for the commonwealth, which for benefits conferred as well as received was dearer to me than life; and that now, though consoled not only by reflexion, which ought to be man's most efficacious comforter, but by time, which is wont to bring healing even to fools, I still grieve to see our common heritage so fallen to pieces that not

[1] A pun on two senses of the word *ius*, 'law' and 'sauce.' Hirtius was famous as an epicure, Haterius was presumably a jurist.
[2] i.e., of teaching one's grandmother to suck eggs.

even the hope of better things one day is left us. Nor does the fault, now at any rate, lie with our all-powerful governor (unless in the sense that there ought not to be any such person). No, events have so fallen out, part by chance but part also by *our* fault, that recrimination is idle. I see no hope remaining. So, to go back to my starting-point, if calculation made you leave Rome, you are a wise man; if chance, a lucky one.

We infer that Caesar had been personally gracious, and had let it be understood that sheer autocracy was not what he wanted. Cicero remained correctly pessimistic, but in the middle of September was temporarily encouraged by a scene in the Senate which he reported to Sulpicius Rufus, then governing Greece by Caesar's commission:

. . . On one point we had the advantage of you. We learned of your colleague Marcellus'[1] restitution a little sooner, and furthermore I will add that we saw *how* the matter was handled. For I do assure you that since the start of these calamities, that is to say since force of arms first came to be arbiter of constitutional right, no other piece of public business has been transacted with dignity. Caesar himself, after complaining of Marcellus' 'acerbity' and lauding *your* fair-mindedness and wisdom in the most complimentary terms, suddenly and unexpectedly declared that, if only for the omen's sake, he would not say no to the Senate's petition on Marcellus' behalf. This was after the House had risen and approached Caesar in supplication, which they did when Lucius Piso[2] had made mention of Marcellus in his speech and Gaius Marcellus[3] had fallen at Caesar's feet. All in all, it seemed to me a fine day's work; I thought I saw some semblance of reviving constitutional freedom.

Accordingly, after all those called upon to speak ahead of me had expressed thanks to Caesar, except Vulcatius (*he* said he would not have done it in Caesar's place), my name was called; and I changed my resolution. I had determined to hold my peace for ever, not, let me say, from sluggishness, but because I remembered the station that used to be mine and is mine no longer. This resolution of mine was overborne by Caesar's magnanimity and the Senate's solicitude. So I expressed gratitude to Caesar at considerable length, and I am afraid I may thus have forfeited in other contexts the decent retirement which was my only consolation in adversity. However, now that I have escaped his displeasure (he might have thought that I did not regard the present régime as constitutional if I never broke silence), I shall do this in moderation, so as to meet his wishes on the one hand and the claims of my literary pursuits on the other.

[1] Marcus Marcellus, Consul (with Sulpicius Rufus) in 51. After Pharsalia he settled in the Aegean island of Lesbos.
[2] Consul in 58, Cicero's one-time enemy and Caesar's father-in-law.
[3] Marcus Marcellus' cousin, Consul in 50.

When Cicero set out to eulogize or flatter he did not do it by halves. The speech (extant) is fulsome, like some of the less candid of his private letters; but his appreciation of Caesar's generosity can be considered genuine, and when he urged Caesar to his crowning task as healer and rebuilder of the commonwealth he was not simply playing the courtier. Writing, perhaps shortly afterwards, to two correspondents, admittedly both Caesarian partisans, he indicates some degree of faith in Caesar's intentions. To Servilius Isauricus:

... On my side, I shall not often be giving you my views on high politics because of the risk attached to such letters, but I shall write fairly often about what is going on. All the same, I think I see a hope that our colleague[1] will try, and is already trying, to get us some sort of a constitutional system. It would have been very desirable that you should have been present and party to his plans. ...

To Cornificius, orator and poet:

... Reports of disturbances have reached us from Syria. As you are nearer their source than we, I am more concerned on your account than on my own. Rome is profoundly quiet. One would prefer some action, of a wholesome and honourable sort. I hope there will be such—Caesar evidently has it in mind. ...

But within three months or so between the pardon of Marcellus and Caesar's departure for Spain (where Pompey's sons had rekindled the war) it became plain that nothing was to be hoped in this direction. The Dictator did not even see fit to have the normal offices filled for the coming year. He himself was elected Consul without a colleague in 45, and Rome in his absence was left in charge of his Master of the Horse (traditional title of a Dictator's second-in-command), Lepidus, assisted by some City Prefects. Although Cicero continued to appear in public, and delivered another speech on behalf of an exile whose case Caesar was reviewing, he had to put aside any idea of constructive political activity under the existing régime. He thought of retiring from Rome altogether and buying a house in Naples, home of Papirius Paetus, to whom he wrote shortly before Caesar left:

... In your second letter you excuse yourself. You say you were not dissuading me from buying a house in Naples, but encouraging me to spend my time in Rome. That was what I took you to mean; but I also understood (as I understand from this later letter) that you thought I do not have the right to abandon metropolitan life, as I conceive myself entitled to do, not

---

[1] Caesar, as Augur.

altogether indeed, but to a great extent. You talk to me of Catulus and those days. Where is the resemblance? At that time I did not myself care to be absent too long from the guardianship of the commonwealth. I was sitting in in the poop, you see, with my hands on the helm. But now I have scarcely so much as a place down in the hold. Do you suppose there will be any fewer senatorial decrees if I am in Naples? When I am in Rome, up and down the Forum, decrees are drawn up at the residence of your admirer, my very good friend.[1] What is more, when it happens to occur to him, I am put down as witness to drafting, and I hear of some decree, allegedly passed on my motion, reaching Armenia and Syria before I know that the matter concerned has been so much as mentioned. You must not suppose that I am joking. Let me tell you that letters have been brought to me before now from monarchs at the other end of the earth, thanking me for my motion to give them the royal title, when I for my part was unaware of their very existence, let alone of their elevation to royalty. . . .

In the winter of 46–45, with the issue of the war in Spain in the balance, the political outlook was darkness visible. Whichever side won, wrote Cicero to the exiled Aulus Torquatus, the effect would be the same; to die first would be no misfortune. A good conscience was the only comfort in such times; every imaginable evil seemed imminent. Compare a note to Cassius in December:

This letter would have been longer if I had not been asked for it just as your post was leaving—longer, anyhow, if I had had any *bavardage* to hand, since writing *au sérieux* is hardly possible without risk. Is joking possible, you will ask. Well, It certainly isn't very easy, but we have no other means of diversion from our troubles. Where then is philosophy? Yours[2] is in the kitchen, mine is a scold—to be a slave makes me ashamed of myself. So I make believe to be otherwise engaged, so as not to have Plato's reproaches in my ears.

Of Spain nothing yet for sure, no news at all in fact. I am sorry for my own sake that you are away, but glad for yours. But the courier is getting impatient. So keep well and fond of me, as you have been from a boy.

'Of politics' he wrote to the same correspondent about a fortnight later 'I write nothing, for I do not care to write what I feel.'

[1] Probably Balbus is meant.
[2] Cassius was an Epicurean. The Academics claimed to follow Plato.

CHAPTER TWENTY-ONE

Tullia Dead

'I reduced the outward show of grief. Grief itself I could not reduce, and would not if I could. . . .'

Cicero to Atticus

UNDER Caesar at least domestic life could continue. In the Cicero family the result was a long-foreshadowed series of divorces, beginning with Cicero's own. Neither date nor proximate circumstances are known precisely, but the business seems to have been done within a year of Cicero's return to Rome in October 47. Plutarch (probably following Tiro) lists as the 'most specious grounds put forward' on the husband's side: that Terentia had not visited him at Brundisium, had failed to provide Tullia with proper travelling equipment, had involved him in debts, and had made away with the contents of his town house during his absence. The first charge is answered by Cicero's own letter to her at the time. Terentia denied them all. But the economic character of the last three fits in with earlier indications. However, there appears to have been something worse. Among the ex-Pompeians awaiting repatriation was Gnaeus Plancius, whose kindness in his own exile was green in Cicero's memory. Toward the end of 46 Plancius' letter of congratulation on Cicero's remarriage produced a somewhat cryptic reply:

. . . As for your felicitations on the step I have taken, I am sure your good wishes are sincere. But I should not have taken any new decision at so sad a time, were it not that on my return I found my household affairs in as sorry a state as the country's. In my own house I knew no security, had no refuge from intrigue, because of the villainy of those to whom my welfare and estate should have been most precious in view of the signal kindnesses I had showered upon them. Therefore I thought it advisable to fortify myself by the loyalty of new connexions against the treachery of old ones. . . .

Cicero is evidently accusing his former wife of having plotted against him, but what was the nature of the plot? Perhaps a letter of May 45 contains a clue. He is explaining to Atticus why he cannot go ahead with a projected political tract in the form of a letter to the Dictator, and ends:

> ... Better let him want for what I don't write than disapprove of what I do. Lastly—let him feel as he pleases. The worry I had when I set you a 'problem for an Archimedes' has disappeared. I assure you I now pray for the fate I had in mind far more earnestly than I then feared it—or any he cares to inflict.

The 'problem for an Archimedes' brings us back to May 46, when Atticus was consulted about a subject for a literary work acceptable to Caesar.[1] At that time Cicero must have been afraid of some injurious action on Caesar's part. This can hardly have been anything but a financial penalty; there is reason to believe that he actually was mulcted in the form of a forced loan, but he may have feared something more drastic. The letter to Plancius suggests that he had discovered, or thought he had discovered, that Terentia was working against him in this matter, and that he hoped to find in his new marriage connexions a safeguard against her machinations. In a letter to Atticus which is usually assigned to the end of November (by the sun), but may well be considerably earlier, plans to replace Terentia are discernible:

> ... And, not to leave anything out, Caesonius has sent me a letter to say that Postumia, Sulpicius' wife, has been to see him at his house. I wrote to you in answer to your remark about Pompey the Great's daughter that I had no such thought at present. As for the other lady you mention,[2] I think you know her. She is phenomenally ugly. However I am coming, and we shall talk of it together. ...

The final choice was surprising, even mildly scandalous—a young girl called Publilia, whose large fortune Cicero is said to have been holding in trust under her father's will (rallied on his wedding day about marrying a virgin at sixty, he replied succinctly, 'she won't be one tomorrow'). There was more than one opinion as to his motives. Terentia, according to Plutarch, put it down as a plain case of an old man's infatuation, whereas Tiro wrote in his biography that Publilia was married for her money, which he seems to have considered a more respectable reason. But Cicero's language to Plancius indicates another —to improve his position with Caesar.

[1] See page 193.
[2] Perhaps Hirtius' sister. According to St. Jerome Cicero declined to marry this lady on the ground that nobody could devote himself equally to a wife and to philosophy.

This would imply that the 'new connexions' were *personae gratae* to the Dictator. Have we any independent evidence of that? Publilia's only known male relative (perhaps a brother) was one Publilius, whose name often crops up in letters of this period. One problem sometimes helps with another, and one of the many minor puzzles in the letters to Atticus is a certain Aledius (or Atedius) who is mentioned once in May 46 and four times in March 45. Cicero's question in a letter already quoted,[1] 'How can praise of Cato be made acceptable to Aledius?' implies that he was a partisan of Caesar's, a fact which is also clear from another reference in March 45. But it seems odd on the face of it that this obscure person rather than some well-known friend of Caesar's and Cicero's—Balbus, say, or Hirtius—should stand for the whole category, none the less odd because he so quickly disappears from view. Can Aledius, as one scholar suggested, be a nickname for somebody more notorious? But the name seems quite innocent. The truth becomes clear as soon as one notices that Aledius is twice mentioned in connexion with Publilius, as someone who would know (and in fact did know) Publilius' whereabouts. He may even have been a relative, one of the 'new connexions.' Hence his appearance just at this time, and his disappearance after the marriage had broken up.

In the same autumn or early winter of 46 Tullia and Dolabella were divorced. Cicero's relations with his ex-son-in-law remained friendly, though the problem of paying Tullia's dowry was replaced by the problem of getting it back.

Soon after Caesar set out for Spain Cicero made a short tour of his country estates, which he may not have seen since 49. His first visit was to a recent acquisition, at Astura, a few miles down the coast from Antium. His house stood on a promontory almost surrounded by the sea, backed by dense woods. Even nowadays it is a lonely, sombre place:

I should really like this place and like it better every day. . . . Nothing could be more agreeable than this solitude, apart from a temporary interruption by the son of Amyntas,[2] tiresome proser that he is! All else is truly quite charming—the house, the shore, the view of the sea, indeed everything here. But this is no matter for a long letter, and I have nothing to write about, and I am half asleep.

[1] See page 193.
[2] The man meant is Lucius Marcius Philippus, Consul in 56, husband of Caesar's niece and stepfather to the future Emperor Augustus. He is called 'son of Amyntas' because that was the name of the father of the famous King Philip of Macedonia.

Two pleasant notes, to Marcus Marius at Pompeii and Papirius Paetus at Naples, mark Cicero's arrival at Cumae. To Marius:

On 21 November I arrived at my place near Cumae with your, or rather our, friend Libo. I mean to go on to Pompeii straight away, but I shall send you word in advance. I always wish you to keep well, but particularly during my visit; for you can see how much we are likely to be together hereafter. So if you have an appointment with the gout, please put it off to another day. Take care of yourself then, and expect me in two or three days' time.

To Paetus:

I arrived at Cumae yesterday, and shall perhaps be with you tomorrow. But when I know for certain, I shall send you word a little beforehand. To be sure, when I met Marcus Caeparius in Poultry Wood and asked after you, he told me you were in bed with the gout. I was properly sorry, of course, but decided to come all the same—to see you, visit you, and even have dinner with you, for I don't suppose your cook is a fellow-sufferer. Expect a guest then—a small eater and a foe to sumptuous banquets.

He returned via Arpinum and Tusculum to Rome, where Tullia was again expecting a baby. After her son was born at Cicero's house in January (45), they moved to Tusculum; and there, in the middle of February, Tullia died. The child lived, but only for a few months.

The funeral probably took place in Rome. Cicero could not bear to stay on in his own house there, or to return to Tusculum. For a fortnight or so he stayed with Atticus, getting what comfort or distraction he might from reading 'Consolation-literature' in his host's library. But on 6 March he left for his secluded retreat at Astura, where he remained till the end of the month. Daily letters to Atticus illustrate his state of mind. 7 March:

I am much concerned about Attica,[1] though I agree with Craterus.[2] Brutus' letter, sensible and friendly though it was, cost me many tears. The loneliness here irks me less than the bustle of the city. You are the only one I miss. But my studies go on as easily as if I were at home. None the less, the old agony goads me as before and persists, not with my indulgence, I do assure you, but despite all efforts to resist. . . .

8 March:

. . . It is like you to want me to recover from my grief, but you are my witness that I have not been remiss on my own behalf. Nothing has been

[1] Atticus' six-year-old daughter.
[2] A celebrated doctor, mentioned also by Horace and Galen.

written by any author on the alleviation of grief which I did not read in your house. But my sorrow is stronger than any consolation. I have even done something which I imagine no one has ever done before, consoled myself in a literary composition. I shall send you the piece as soon as the copyists have finished it. I can assure you there is no consolation so effective as this. I write all day long, not that I do myself any real good, but just for the time being it distracts me—not indeed enough, for grief is powerful and importunate; still it brings a respite. And I try all I know to bring my face if not my heart back to composure, if I can. While I do this I sometimes feel I am committing a sin, at others that I should be sinning if I failed to do it. Solitude helps, but it would be far more efficacious, paradoxically, if you were here to share it; that is my only reason for leaving this spot, which is well enough in the circumstances. And yet this too is a source of distress, for you will not be able to feel toward me as in the past. The things you liked in me are gone for good.

I have already written to you about Brutus' letter. There was much good sense in it, but nothing that could help me. I wish he were here himself, as he wrote to you he would be. He would certainly have done me some good, so fond of me as he is . . .

9 March:

. . . In this lonely place I do not talk to a soul. Early in the day I hide myself in a thick, thorny wood, and don't emerge till evening. Next to yourself, solitude is my best friend. When I am alone, all my conversation is with books, but it is interrupted by fits of weeping, against which I struggle as best I can. But so far it is an unequal fight. . . .

10 March:

I wouldn't have you leave your own affairs to visit me; better for me to come to you, if you are going to be held up for some considerable time. I should never have gone out of your sight if it had not been that nothing, *nothing* was any use to me. But if any relief were possible, it would be in you and you only; and as soon as anyone can give it, that one will be you. And yet at this moment I cannot bear to be away from you. But we agreed that your house was not suitable, and I cannot stay in mine; and even if I were somewhere closer by, I should still not be in your company. The same thing that is holding you up now would still hold you up and prevent you from spending much time with me. Thus far the loneliness here suits me as well as anything. I am afraid Philippus may break it. He arrived yesterday evening. Reading and writing bring me, not solace indeed, but distraction.

15 March:

. . . You urge me to disguise the intensity of my grief and say that others think I do not do so sufficiently. Can I do it more effectively than by spending my entire time in literary work? True, I do this not for the sake of disguise but rather to ease and heal my mind; but even if I myself get little good out of it, at least I cannot be accused of failing to disguise my feelings. . . .

16 March:

. . . I have nothing to write to you, but I have started the practice of sending a daily letter to evoke yours, not that I expect anything from them—and yet somehow or other I do expect something. So whether you have anything to say or nothing, write something all the same, and take good care of yourself.

17 March:

. . . You summon me to the Forum. That is a place I avoided even in my happy days. What is the Forum to me without the courts and the Senate-House, with people crossing my path whom I can't see without discomposure? You say that people demand of me that I be present in Rome and are not willing to let me be absent, or only to allow it up to a certain point. I can assure you that for long enough I have thought more of your single self than of them all. Nor do I despise *myself*; I had much rather stand by my own judgment than by that of all the rest of the world. Still I go no further than the best philosophical authorities allow me. Not content with reading all their writings to that purpose (which was itself the behaviour of a brave invalid—taking one's medicine), I have conveyed them into my own, which at any rate was not like a despondent, broken mind. Don't call me away from these remedies back to your city hurly-burly, or I may relapse.

19 March:

. . . Atticus, everything is over with me, everything, and has been for long enough, but now I admit it, having lost the one link that held me. So I seek the lonely places; though if anything happens to bring me back to Rome, I shall do my utmost, if it lies in my power (and it will), to make my grief imperceptible to everyone but you, and if by any means possible, even to you. . . .

22 March:

. . . With regard to what you say about Nicias, if I were in any state to enjoy his agreeable society, there are few people I should so much like to have with me. But solitude and retirement are my concern. I miss Sicca the more because he did not mind this. Besides, you know how delicate and easily upset our friend Nicias is. Why should I wish to give him trouble when he can give me no pleasure? . . .

24 March:

... You tell me to go back to my old ways. For a long time it has been my part to mourn our liberties and I did so, but not so intensely, because I had a source of comfort. Now I simply cannot follow that course of life, and on this matter I do not feel obliged to pay any attention to other folk's opinions. My own conscience counts for more with me than all the world's talk. As for my literary consolation, I am not dissatisfied with what it achieved. I reduced the outward show of grief; grief itself I could not reduce, and would not if I could. ...

It was fortunate that before the bereavement he had already made a start with the literary programme which was to absorb his energies for nearly two years. Cicero's attachment to Greek philosophy is usually represented, not without warrant in certain expressions of his own, as a life-long passion. No doubt he had been a keen student of the subject in his young days, but in middle life neither his publications nor his correspondence show him as much concerned with it, except on the political side. References in his letters to ethical or metaphysical philosophy are very scarce—as when in 51 he writes from Athens that philosophy there is in a poor way (the sort of observation that a Classics graduate might make on a visit to his old College), or when soon afterwards he appeals to Cato in the name of their common love and practice of the 'true old philosophy.' Especially significant is the absence, already noticed, of any mention of philosophical comfort in the letters of his two most unhappy periods, in 58 and 48–47. But after his homecoming there are signs that his mind was turning this way, though he continued to write on other themes. In a note to Varro (a great authority) in June 46 he makes play with a philosophical technicality. That was after spending a few days in Varro's company at Tusculum. They seem to have made a strong impression:

... I always thought you a great man, because in this stormy weather you almost alone are safe in harbour. You reap the most precious fruits of learning, devoting your thoughts and energies to pursuits which yield a profit and a delight far transcending the exploits and pleasures of these worldlings. These days you are now spending down at Tusculum are worth a lifetime by my reckoning. Gladly would I leave all earthly wealth and power to others, and take in exchange license to live thus, free from interruption by any outside force. ...

After the completion of the 'Orator,' philosophy became Cicero's main intellectual business, as he writes to Sulpicius about the beginning of October (contemporary calendar):

... From my childhood I have taken pleasure in every liberal art, most of all in philosophy; but my devotion to it grows upon me every day. I suppose I have reached an age for wisdom; and the evils of the times are such that nothing else can relieve one's mind of its burdens. I see from your letter that business is distracting *you* from this pursuit, but the lengthening nights will be some help. ...

According to his own published statement it was Brutus who propelled Cicero into this field of authorship; whereas in a private letter to Gaius Matius *he* is given the same credit. However conceived, the idea of presenting the Greek systems to Roman readers in their own language could hardly fail to grip. Politics and advocacy virtually abandoned, literary distinction remained, and here was an ideal area for Cicero. He had it pretty much to himself, but with the widespread contemporary interest in these matters, public response was certain. At the same time he would be arming his own spirit against tricks of fortune and rendering a national service.

The series began with an 'exhortation to philosophical study' called 'Hortensius,' of which only fragments now remain, but which was one day to turn St. Augustine's mind away from worldly things. Both this and the 'Academic Questions' seem to have made some progress when Tullia's death caused a diversion. The consolatory tract addressed to himself of which he wrote to Atticus also became famous in antiquity and is now lost except for fragments. After finishing it Cicero turned back to less personal themes, and the flow of composition went on almost without interruption until politics reclaimed him.

He also looked for comfort in another direction. A letter to Atticus of 11 March begins:

In trying to escape the memories which pain me like fangs in my flesh, I have recourse to sending you a reminder. Please forgive my doing so, whatever you think of the project. I can indeed cite several of the authors whom I am constantly reading just now as recommending the plan about which I have often talked to you and for which I want to gain your approval. I refer to that shrine. Please give it an amount of thought proportionate to the affection in which you hold me. I myself have no hesitation about the form of shrine (I like Cluatius'[1] proposal), nor about the idea itself (my mind is made up); about the site I do sometimes waver. So please think it over. As far as practicable in this age of culture, I shall naturally hallow her with every kind of memorial which Greek and Latin genius can supply. Perhaps that will gall my wound. But I consider myself as virtually bound by a vow and pledge,

[1] An architect, apparently.

and the long expanse of time after I shall cease to be is of more account to me than this little span, which yet seems to me too long. I have tried everything and found no comfort. While I was engaged on the work of which I wrote to you in an earlier letter,[1] I was as it were laying a fomentation on my pains. Now I reject all aids, and find nothing easier to bear than solitude—Philippus did not intrude as I feared he might. After paying me a call yesterday he left immediately for Rome. . . .

Which of the (Greek) authors on Cicero's reading list prescribed apotheosis of the loved and lost we are not told; as he never cites a Roman precedent he probably knew of none. Even in the Hellenic world such a proceeding seems to have been most unusual, though we do hear of a rascally minister of Alexander the Great who put up a shrine in Babylon to his dead mistress—and was censured for it by a contemporary historian. Cicero's 'Consolation' contained a rationale, based on the acknowledged promotion to deity of former heroes and benefactors of the human race. A passage from it survives in quotation by the 'Christian Cicero,' Lactantius:

So we see that many former human beings of either sex are among the Gods, and we worship at their hallowed temples in town and countryside. Let us then yield assent to the wisdom of those to whose genius and discoveries we owe our entire way of life based upon and embellished by laws and institutions. And if any living creature ever deserved such consecration it was surely she. If it was right for the children of Cadmus or Amphitryon or Tyndareus to be raised by glory to the skies, assuredly *she* deserves the same honour and dedication. This I shall effect. Best and most accomplished of women, with the blessing of the Immortal Gods themselves I shall set you in your consecrated place among them, for all mortals to approve.

Cicero had no firm faith in a life after death, and can hardly have hoped even vaguely to better Tullia's condition in another world. Deification might perhaps help to keep her memory alive in *this* world, something to which he would attach importance. But his principal motive was no doubt to emphasize and advertise the greatness of his loss—much as a modern parent might more conventionally do by endowing a charity named after the deceased.

The question of where to build the shrine, or 'fane' (*fanum*), obsessed Cicero's mind and letters for months to come. His own estates at Astura, Arpinum, and Tusculum were considered and rejected in turn. He wanted something more in the public way, and proposed to buy a house and grounds in the suburbs of Rome on the north bank of the

---

[1] The 'Consolation'.

Tiber—the kind of estate which the Romans called *horti* (generally, but misleadingly, translated 'gardens'). A number of such properties came under review, and Atticus, who was not enthusiastic about the project, conducted the negotiations, which were complex, protracted, and ultimately abortive.[1] As time passed and sorrow abated, a change of view makes itself apparent: the 'fane' becomes secondary, and the proposed purchase is rather thought of as a 'place to grow old in' (*engerama*). But in July Cicero came by information that the property in the Campus Vaticanus which he then had in mind to buy was menaced by city planners:

We were speaking of Varro. Talk of the devil! He called, and at such an hour that I had to ask him to stay. But I took care not to tear his coat (I remember your phrase 'they were many, and we were unprepared'). No use! Soon after along came Gaius Capito and Titus Carrinas. *Their* coats I hardly touched. However they stayed, and it turned out pleasantly enough. But Capito happened to be talking of the enlargement of the city, saying that the Tiber is being diverted at the Milvian Bridge to run alongside the Vatican Hills, that the Campus Martius is being built over, and the other Campus, the Vaticanus, is becoming a new Campus Martius. 'What's that?' said I, 'I was going to the auction to buy the Scapula estate if I could get it at a reasonable figure!' 'Better not,' said he. 'This law will go through. Caesar wants it.' But what do *you* say?—though I don't know why I ask. You know Capito's assiduity in ferreting out news. He rivals Camillus. So you will let me know about the Ides. It was that which was bringing me to Rome. I had combined my other business with it, but that can easily wait two or three days. However, the last thing I want is for you to wear yourself out travelling. I even excuse Dionysius. As to what you say about Brutus, I have left him a free choice so far as I am concerned. I wrote to him yesterday that I did not need his services on the Ides.

That seems to have been the end of the whole project. A year later a casual reference to money 'put aside for that fane' shows that it never materialized. Cicero's hankering for a suburban residence may have been diverted by his acquisition in August of a handsome property on the outskirts of Puteoli under the will of a wealthy banker.

At the end of March the solitude of Astura was threatened with an incursion from the outer world. Cicero writes on the 28th:

I write this in my own hand. Pray see what is to be done. Publilia wrote to me that her mother had talked to Publilius and would be coming over for a talk with me, and that she would accompany them if I would allow it. She

[1] See Appendix III to Volume V of my edition.

begs me beseechingly and at some length to permit this and to send her a reply. You see what a tiresome business it is. I wrote back that I was in an even poorer way than when I told her I wanted to be alone, so I should prefer her not to come at present. I thought that if I did not reply at all she would come with her mama. Now I don't think she will, as the letter was obviously not her own composition. But I also want to avoid what clearly *is* impending, a visit from the other two; and the only way to avoid it is to make myself scarce. A nuisance, but it has to be. Now I want you to find out just how long I can stay here without getting caught. You'll go about it, to use your own word, gently. . . .

His second marriage had crashed almost immediately after takeoff. According to Plutarch he had sent Publilia packing 'because she seemed pleased at Tullia's death.' A divorce, which was followed by some financial unpleasantness with Publilius, was arranged soon afterwards. In so far as the motives for the marriage had been economic, whether precautionary or directly acquisitive, they had lost their relevance. As Cicero often told Atticus, he had ceased to care about money (for the time being) now that Tullia was no longer to be provided for; and he probably knew that he had no longer anything to fear from Caesar.

Dislodged from Astura, Cicero again took refuge with Atticus, this time in a country house a few miles out of Rome. There he spent the month of April, and wrote two letters which make interesting reading. Sulpicius Rufus in Athens had sent a long letter of condolence. It contains a passage which has become as well known as anything in the correspondence, thanks perhaps to Byron's reference in 'Childe Harold:'[1]

. . . I want to tell you of something which has brought *me* no slight consolation, in the hope that it may have some power to lighten your sorrow too. As I was on my way back from Asia, sailing from Aegina toward Megara, I began to gaze at the panorama around me. There behind me was Aegina, in front of me Megara, to the right Piraeus, to the left Corinth; once flourishing towns, now lying low in ruins before my eyes. I began to think to myself: 'Ah! How can we manikins wax indignant if one of us dies or is killed, ephemeral creatures as we are, when the corpses of so many towns lie abandoned in a single spot? Check yourself, Servius, and remember that you were born a mortal man.' That thought, I do assure you, strengthened me not a little. . . .

'The Roman friend of Rome's least mortal mind' ended as follows:

I am ashamed to write to you at greater length on this subject, lest I seem

[1] Canto II, stanza 3.

to doubt your good sense, and so I shall end my letter with one final observation. We have seen more than once how nobly you sustain prosperity, and how great the glory you gain thereby. Let us recognise at last that you can bear adversity too with equanimity, and that you count it no heavier load than you should, lest of all fine qualities you may seem to lack this only.

As for me, I shall inform you of what is going on here and of the state of the province, when I hear that your mood is calmer. Good-bye.

He received this reply:

Yes, my friend, I wish you had been with me, as you say, in my most grievous affliction. How much your presence would have helped me by consolation and by sorrow well-nigh equal to my own, I readily recognise from the measure of easement I felt when I read your letter. You have written the words that could alleviate my misery, and your own no small distress has given you the means of comforting mine. But your son Servius has shown how much he thinks of me, and how welcome he believes such a disposition on his part will be to you. His attentions have often made me happier than they make me now (as you may imagine), but never more grateful.

Not only am I comforted by your words and (I might almost say) your fellowship in sorrow, but by your counsel as well. I feel it unseemly in me not to bear my bereavement as so wise a man as you considers it should be borne. But sometimes I am overwhelmed, and scarcely offer any resistance to grief, because I have no such solaces as others in similar plight, whose examples I set before my mind, did not lack. Quintus Maximus lost a son of consular rank, high reputation, and splendid record. Lucius Paulus lost two in a single week. Then there was Gallus in your own family, and Marcus Cato, who lost a son of the highest intellectual and moral qualities. But they lived in periods when the honourable standing they gained in public life assuaged their mourning. *I* had already lost the distinctions which you yourself mention and which I had gained by great exertions. The one comfort still left to me was that which has now been snatched away. Neither my friends' concerns nor the administration of the commonwealth detained my thoughts. I had no wish to appear in the courts, I could not endure the sight of the Senate-House. I considered, as was the fact, that I had lost all the fruits of my work and prosperity. However, I reflected that I shared this situation with yourself and certain others; I conquered my feelings and forced myself to bear it all with fortitude. But while I did so, I had a haven of refuge and repose, one in whose conversation and sweet ways I put aside all cares and sorrows.

Now this grievous blow has again inflamed the wounds I thought healed. When in the past I withdrew in sadness from public affairs, my home received and soothed me; but I cannot now take refuge from domestic grief in public life, or find relief in what it offers. My house and the Forum are alike strange to me, for neither public nor private life can any longer comfort the distress which either occasions me.

All the more then do I look forward to your return and desire to see you as soon as possible. No abstract reflexion can give me greater comfort than our fellowship in daily life and talk. However, from what I hear, I hope your arrival is imminent. One reason among many why I am anxious to see you as soon as may be is that I should like us to ponder together how we should best pass this present time, all of which must be accommodated to the wishes of one individual.[1] He is a man of sense and generosity, and I think I have seen cause to believe him no enemy of mine and a very good friend of yours. Even so, what line we are to take needs careful consideration. I am not thinking of any positive action, but of retirement by his leave and favour. Good-bye.

The other letter is to Dolabella in Spain. In the circumstances its warmth is remarkable, and this is maintained in later letters and allusions. Perhaps Tullia, who was so anxious that her father should not offend Clodius in 54,[2] had wished it so for his sake. Moreover Dolabella was the father of her child, and for all we know to the contrary they had parted friends:

I wish my failure to write had been due to my own death rather than to the grievous calamity which has come upon me. Your wise words and signal affection for me would be a real solace. However, I shall soon be seeing you, so we think here. You will find me in a state that offers plenty of scope for assistance. Not that I am so far broken down as to forget the conditions of our mortal lot, or to think it right to sink beneath fortune's blows. But the gaiety and charm which people saw in me, and you in particular used to find agreeable, is all swept away. My fortitude and resolution, however, if I ever possessed those qualities, you will recognize as no whit diminished.

You tell me that you have to fight my battles. I am less concerned that you should rebut my detractors than anxious that your affection for me should be recognized, as it surely is. Let me earnestly request you to act accordingly, and to forgive the brevity of this letter. I expect we shall shortly be together, and I have not yet sufficiently regained my strength for writing.

At the end of the month Cicero felt able to return to Astura, where, as he told Atticus, he went on writing all day long, which brought no comfort, but still gave him something else to think about. His abjection had come under some criticism, to which he reacted sharply in a letter of 7 May:

You say you think it time that my strength of mind should be made clearly apparent, and that certain people are talking about me in more censorious terms than either you or Brutus use in your letters. Well, if those

[1] Caesar.   [2] See page 87.

who think me broken-spirited or enfeebled only knew the amount and character of my literary output, I believe that in common decency they would either spare their criticisms or even admit that I am entitled to some praise; for they would have to allow either that I have so far recovered as to bring an untrammelled mind to writing on these difficult subjects or else that I have chosen the most elevated means of distraction from my sorrow and the most fitting for a man of culture. . .

Again, two days later:

. . . You say you are afraid my popularity and prestige may suffer by my present mourning. I don't know what people find to criticize or what they expect. Do they want me to stop grieving? How can I? Or not to be prostrated with grief? Was any one ever less so? While I had the comfort of staying in your house in Rome, whom did I keep out? What visitor had cause to complain? From there I went to Astura. These happy folks who take me to task cannot read as many pages as I have written—how well is immaterial; but the kind of composition was such as no mind sunk in dejection could have managed. I spent a month at the 'homestead.'[1] Did anyone complain that I refused to meet him or to converse with him easily? At this very time I am reading and writing; and my companions find it harder to do nothing than I to work. . . . When I come back to Rome neither my looks nor my words will give any occasion for censure. The gaiety with which I used to season the sadness of these times of ours is gone for ever, but resolution and fortitude in mind and word will not be wanting. . . .

But the paroxysmal stage was over, and by the middle of May he was able to face a return to the scene of Tullia's death:

. . . As things stand with me, I could be as comfortable at Astura as anywhere else I have to stay. But my companions are in a hurry to get home, finding my mourning irksome I suppose, so although I could well stay on I shall leave here as I wrote to you for fear of appearing forsaken. But where to? My *endeavour* is to go from Lanuvium to my house at Tusculum. But I shall inform you straight away. . . .

The next day:

I think I shall conquer my feelings and go from Lanuvium to Tusculum. Either I must keep away from my place there for ever and a day (for my grief will remain unchanged, only less on the surface) or I don't know what difference it makes whether I go there now or in ten years' time. And in truth the reminders will be no more poignant than those which harass me day and night. Is literature no use, you may ask. In this case I'm afraid it actually

---

[1] Atticus' country house near Rome.

makes the other way, for without it I should perhaps be made of harder stuff. In a cultivated mind there is nothing coarse or callous. . . .

He arrived at Tusculum on the 17th:

Excellent news about Attica. I am concerned to hear about your languor, though you say it is nothing. Tusculum will be more convenient for me in that I shall get letters from you more often and see yourself from time to time. Otherwise life was more tolerable at Astura, and the things that chafe the wound do pain me more here; and yet, wherever I am, they are with me. . . .

From this point on the bereavement is seldom mentioned. Emerson's saying that our moods are strangers to one another was more than ordinarily true of Cicero. Tullia lost, he thought the taste had gone out of his life forever. A few months would show that this was not altogether so. Obsessive while it lasted, his grief was also demonstrative and in a sense wilful. The bizarre gesture of the 'fane,' his feeling that grieving was a kind of duty, his behaviour to his new wife, suggest interior motives of discontent and guilt, not necessarily related to Tullia herself. Beyond the flow of Cicero's self-regarding laments lay a broad, bitter hinterland of thwarted ambition and domestic failure.

CHAPTER TWENTY-TWO

Under Caesar (11)

'What a lot you have to do! You deal with items like these, you put my affairs straight, and you take almost as much trouble with your own business as you do with mine!'

Cicero to Atticus

A STREAM of letters or notes to Atticus in the spring and summer of 45 keep Cicero's movements under observation. Back in Tusculum on 17 May, he stayed there until 21 June, apart from a brief visit to Rome shortly before he left. Thence to Arpinum:

... I must go to Arpinum. My little properties there need my attention, and I am afraid I may not be able to get away once Caesar comes home. ...

On arrival there (22 June) he felt forlorn:

'Other the aspect.'[1] I thought it was easy. All is changed now that I am more cut off from you. But it had to be done, both in order to fix the trifles of rent on my properties and not to place too heavy a burden of civility on our friend Brutus. ...

28 June:

You see the virtue of propinquity. Well, let us secure a property in the suburbs. When I was at Tusculum it was as though we talked to one another, letters passed to and fro so rapidly. But it will soon be so again. ...

Moreover, the weather was unkind:

Seeking streams and solitude to make life more endurable, I have so far not stirred a foot out of doors because of heavy and incessant rain. ...

He stayed at Arpinum until 3 July. Then followed another long spell at Tusculum, punctuated by another visit to Rome later that month. On 25 August he was back in Astura, but only for a few days. An invitation to Atticus and his wife to dine at Cicero's house in Rome on the 31st ends the series.

[1] From Euripides' 'Ion:' 'Other the aspect of events appears / when far away and when seen close at hand.'

This part of the correspondence reflects the interest which Cicero was again able to take in a variety of concerns, though the project of the suburban purchase continues prominent until its sudden disappearance. Literary matters are to the fore, especially the ticklish question of a dedication of the 'Academic Questions' to Varro, of whom Cicero always stood somewhat in awe. 12 July:

... Now why, I wonder, do you shake in your shoes when I tell you that the book is to be given to Varro at your risk? If you really have any misgivings even at this stage, let me know, for it's a really choice piece of work. I want Varro, especially as he desires it. But as you know, he's 'One to be fear'd. E'en blameless folk he'd blame.'[1] ...

Assisted by a freedman or slave called Eros, Atticus had apparently taken full charge of his friend's affairs, and his services were never more multifarious. They include negotiations with Terentia (after Tullia's death new testamentary arrangements had to be made, generating further friction) and Publilius. 26 August:

I arrived at Astura at sunset on the 25th, having rested three hours at Lanuvium to avoid the heat. If it is not too much trouble, I should be grateful if you would arrange so that I need not come to Rome before the 5th (you can do that through Egnatius Maximus), and in particular if you would settle with Publilius in my absence. Let me know what people are saying about it. 'As though the public troubled about that.'[2] No, I dare say not. It was a nine days' wonder. But I wanted to fill the page. I won't write more, since I shall be with you presently, unless you grant an extension. I wrote to you about the place in the suburbs.

Marcus junior had to be financially equipped for a journey to Athens and residence there. The decision to give him this ancient counterpart of a university career had been taken the previous autumn. His own wish had been to go soldiering again in Caesar's Spanish war, along with his cousin Quintus. A discussion between father and son, probably in October (by the sun) 46, was reported to Atticus:

I have put down all the items you desire on tablets and given them to Eros —briefly, but more in fact than you ask, including something about Marcus. You started me thinking about this. I spoke to him in a very liberal way—you might ask the boy himself about this, that is if you conveniently can. Still, why put it off? I explained that you had brought to my notice both his wishes and his wants: that he wished to go to Spain and wanted a handsome

---

[1] From the Iliad.
[2] Quoted from Terence's play, 'The Girl from Andros'.

allowance. As to the latter, I said I would give him as much as Publius Lentulus or Flamen Lentulus gave their sons. On Spain I made two comments. The first I had already made to you, that I was afraid of public censure. People might ask whether it was not enough that we had abandoned the struggle, without enlisting on the other side. Then I urged that it would be mortifying for him to find himself outdone by his cousin in friendly contacts and general consideration. I would rather he availed himself even to excess of my liberality than of his own liberty. However, I gave my leave, as I had gathered that you were not too much opposed. I shall think about it further, and should be glad if you would do the same. It is no light matter, and the straightforward thing is for him to stay; the other has both pros and cons. However, we shall see. . . .

But ultimately the decision was for Athens, and to Athens in the spring Marcus went. His father was not pleased with him—perhaps the young man had reacted badly to the rejection of his Spanish plan—but was none the less determined that he should have as handsome an allowance as any aristocrat ('It is against my credit to let him run short this year, no matter what he is. Afterwards I shall exercise more careful control.'). Atticus saw to the details and supplied good advice as well. 23 May:

Your letter to Marcus is exactly right, grave and gentle at the same time— just what I should have wished. Your letters to the Tullii[1] too are most judicious. Well then, either these will work or we shall have to stop worrying. . . .

A different aspect of Atticus' usefulness appears in an embroilment between Cicero and one of the Dictator's hangers-on, a musical adept called Tigellius. A letter of 22 August gives the details:

First my love to Attica. I suppose she is in the country. Much love then, and to Pilia.

Any news about Tigellius? As Fabius Gallus has written to me, he is airing a most unreasonable grievance against me, namely that I let Phamea[2] down after undertaking his case. I *had* undertaken it, contrary to my inclination, it being against the Octavius boys, Gnaeus' sons. But I was well disposed to Phamea too, for, if you remember, he had offered me his services through you when I was standing for the Consulship, and the fact that I made no use of them did not lessen my sense of obligation. Well, he came and told me that his judge had appointed for the hearing the very day that our friend Sestius'

---

[1] Montanus and Marcianus, perhaps poor relations or clients of the family, who accompanied Marcus to Athens.
[2] Tigellius' uncle or grandfather.

case was due to come up under the Lex Pompeia—you know the days for those trials were determined in advance. I answered that he was aware of my obligations to Sestius. Let him fix any other day and I should not fail him. So he left in a huff. I think I told you the story. Naturally I did not concern myself or feel any need to trouble about the ill-humour, entirely unwarranted as it was, of a mere acquaintance. When I was last in Rome I told Gallus what I had heard, without mentioning Balbus junior by name. Gallus, as he says in his letter, made it his business. He says that Tigellius is giving out that my suspicions of himself spring from my bad conscience on account of my desertion of Phamea. So all I ask of you is to find out anything you can about that relation[1] of ours, but not to worry about me. It's nice to hate someone with a will and not to be everybody's slave . . . though for that matter, as you are aware, these people are more my slaves than I theirs, if courtesies count as servility.

In fact, Cicero was more concerned than he chose to admit, as 'follow-ups' in letters of the next two days sufficiently indicate:

. . . I wonder you have not yet had any talk with Tigellius. I am just dying to know, e.g., how much he actually got—and I don't care a rap. . . .

. . . send me all about Tigellius, and don't waste time, for I'm all agog. . . .

Another literary project, an open 'Letter of Advice' to Caesar, had been undertaken at Atticus' prompting. It did not go smoothly. 9 May:

. . . I make repeated attempts at a 'Letter of Advice.' I can think of nothing, though I have Aristotle's and Theopompus' letters to Alexander beside me. But where is the analogy? What *they* wrote was calculated both to do credit to the writers and to please Alexander. Can you think of anything of that sort? *I* can't.

Finally a draft emerged and was submitted to Balbus and Oppius for approval. But they suggested so many alterations that the author, not without pique, gave up the idea and resisted attempts to persuade him to resume it. 26 May:

. . . As regards the letter to Caesar, I give you my solemn word, I *cannot*. It is not shame that deters me, though it most assuredly ought—servility is shameful indeed when to be alive at all is a disgrace for me. But as I was saying, it isn't this unseemliness that deters me (I wish it were, for then I should be the man I ought to be), but nothing comes to mind. As for Alexander, you see the themes. A young man, fired by a passion for true glory and desiring some advice which would tend to his immortal fame, is exhorted to honourable distinction. Plenty to say there! What can *I* say? However, I did

---

[1] Apparently Quintus junior, but the translation is not certain.

hew some semblance of a shape out of the tough timber. It contained a few
things on a somewhat higher level than suits the present and past goings on,
so they are disapproved; and I am far from sorry. . . .

Two days later:

. . . As for the letter to Caesar, that's a *chose jugée*. And yet the very point
which your friends say he makes in his letter, that he will not go to fight the
Parthians until he has settled affairs here, was recommended in my epistle. He
might do whichever he pleased on my authority—that's what he's waiting for
of course, and won't do anything except on my advice! For pity's sake let's
chuck all this nonsense, and be half free at any rate! That we shall manage by
holding our tongues and lying low. . . .

The acerbity of these passages is matched by other references to the
Dictator. In a letter of 17 May he is, in effect, wished dead. On the
18th Atticus came over to Tusculum for the night—a note followed
him back to Rome:

Your departure has depressed me as much as your coming cheered me up.
So pay us another visit when you can, i.e., when you have attended Sextus'
auction. Even a single day will be beneficial to me—that it will be agreeable I
need not say. . . .

On the 20th:

I felt at the time how much good your presence was doing me, but I feel it
much more now that you have gone. Therefore, as I wrote to you earlier,
either I must stay with you all the time or you with me as much as you can.

Not long after you left me yesterday, certain slaves (?), of the town to
judge by their looks, brought me a verbal message and a letter of considerable
length from 'Gaius Marius, son of Gaius, grandson of Gaius.'[1] It amounted
to a plea in the name of my family connexion with the writer, of the 'Marius'[2]
composed by me, and of the eloquence of his grandfather Lucius Crassus, to
undertake his defence; a full statement of the case accompanied. I replied that
he had no need of an advocate, since his excellent and generous kinsman[3]
Caesar was all-powerful; but that he could count on my good wishes. What
days we live in! To think that a time was to come when Curtius[4] would
'have doubts' about standing for the Consulship! But enough. . . .

[1] Cicero repeats the formal superscription of the letter. The man was an impos-
tor, claiming to be the son of Gaius Marius the Younger and Licinia, daughter of
the orator Crassus. He was executed by Mark Antony a year later.

[2] Cicero's poem so entitled.

[3] Caesar's aunt Julia was the wife of Marius the Elder.

[4] Curtius Postumus, whose call so annoyed Cicero in 49; see page 156.

18 (?) June:

. . . not, of course, that this is of any importance, especially to me, to whom the dead seem no worse off than the living. What are we[1] after all, or what can we be, at home or abroad? If it had not occurred to me to write these books of mine, such as they are, I should not know what to do with myself. . . .

17 August:

Indeed? Brutus reports that Caesar has joined the *boni*? Good news! But where is he going to find them—unless he hangs himself? As for Brutus, he knows which side his bread is buttered.[2] . . .

The prospect of Caesar's return from Spain, where he had won a final hard-fought campaign, was a source of disquiet at this time.
13 August:

. . . It really would not have done for me to go to Puteoli both for the reason I gave you and because Caesar is close at hand. Dolabella says *he* will be with me on the 14th. A tiresome schoolmaster!

With Caesar returned young Quintus, who in Spain had been at his old game of traducing his uncle. A letter of 6 May ends:

. . . Asinius Pollio has written to me about our blackguard of a nephew. He puts in the plainest possible language what Balbus junior recently intimated with sufficient clarity and Dolabella hinted at. I should be upset, if there were any room in my heart for a new vexation. All the same could anything be more blackguardly? A fellow to beware of! Though to me— but I must not let myself go. Send me a line, but only if you have the time, since there's no necessity.

17 (?) June:

You had just left yesterday when Trebatius arrived, and Curtius a little later—the latter only to pay his respects, but he stayed on invitation. Trebatius is my guest here. Dolabella came this morning. Much talk till late in the day. I must say he could not have been more forthcoming or affectionate. However, we got on to Quintus. I heard of much that is too bad for utterance or narration, and one thing of such a kind that if the whole army did not know of it I should not dare to put it on paper myself, let alone dictate it to Tiro * * *.[3] But enough.

---

[1] i.e., 'we Consulars.'
[2] The text and meaning are doubtful.
[3] The anecdote was apparently deleted, probably by Atticus himself in later days, when he used to let friends like Cornelius Nepos read the correspondence.

In mid-August a letter arrived from Quintus. Three letters of Cicero's pursue the question, how to receive him on his return from Spain:

As I was writing against the Epicureans before daybreak I went straight on to scribble something to you by the same lamp and dispatched it before dawn. Then I went back to sleep and awoke with the sun to be handed a letter from your nephew of which I am sending you the original. It starts offensively enough, but perhaps he did not stop to think—anyway it reads thus: 'For my part, whatever ugly things can be said against you—.' He implies that many ugly things *can* be said, but says he does not agree with them. Could anything be more outrageous? You will read the rest—I am sending you the letter—and judge. I suppose the constant eulogies of myself in which our friend Brutus, as a great many people have reported to me, daily indulges have provoked him to write something to me at long last, and to you also, I imagine—please let me know. What he has written about me to his father I don't know, but isn't this a dutiful way to write about his mother? 'I desired,' he says, 'in order to be with you as much as possible, that a house should be rented for me, and wrote to you accordingly. You took no notice. So we shall see less of one another, for I cannot stand the sight of *your* house. The reason you know.' This reason, according to his father, is his dislike of his mother.

Now, my dear fellow, help me with your advice, 'whether by honesty the loftier tower,' i.e., whether I should openly rebuff the fellow and spurn him off, or 'by crooked wiles.' Like Pindar's, 'my mind's in twain; which way declare the truth?'[1] The former best suits my character to be sure, but perhaps the latter best fits the times. . . .

Next day:

Incredible falseness! To his father he makes out that he can't be at home because of his mother: to his mother—all affection! But *he* is now weakening and says the young man has a right to be angry with him. But I shall follow your advice—you evidently favour 'wiles'. . . .

Two days later:

Yes, I have sent Quintus your letter to your sister. When he complained that a state of war existed between son and mother and said he would give up his house to his son for that reason, I told him that the young man had written a proper enough letter to his mother and none to you. The former piece of information took him aback, but as regards you he said the fault was his own

---

[1] The quotation from Pindar runs: 'Whether by honesty or by crooked wiles the race of men on earth mounts a loftier tower, my mind is divided which way to declare the truth.'

for having written more than once to his son in strong terms regarding your ill-treatment of him. As for what he says about my having weakened, after I had read your letter I told him 'with crooked wiles' that I should not be inexorable—that was when Cana's[1] name was mentioned. To be sure, if that scheme found favour there would be no choice. But as you say, dignity has to be considered, and we ought both to take the same line, though his offences against *me* are graver, or at any rate more widely known. But if Brutus adds a contribution, we cannot hesitate. However, when we meet. It's an important matter and needs very careful handling. Tomorrow then, unless I get some leave of absence from you.

Further cause for indignation a few days later:

. . . Balbus junior is with me. He brings no news really, except that Hirtius has been taking up the cudgels vigorously on my behalf. He says Quintus is at it constantly, especially at dinner-parties. When he finishes with me he comes back to his father, his most plausible line being that we are thoroughly hostile to Caesar and are not to be trusted. *I* am said to be actually dangerous. It would be alarming if I were not well aware that H.M. knows me for a coward. Quintus also alleges that my son is being bullied—but he is welcome to say that to his heart's content. . . .

However 'crooked wiles' prevailed—young Quintus' popularity in the dominant clique had to be taken into the reckoning. At the end of the year uncle and nephew were at any rate on speaking terms. From Tusculum:

He came to see me, 'right down in the mouth.'[2] I greeted him with ' "You there, why so pensive?" ' 'Need you ask,' was the answer, 'considering that I have a journey in front of me, and a journey to war,[3] a dishonourable journey too as well as a dangerous one?' 'What's the compulsion?' I enquired. 'Debt,' he answered, 'and yet I haven't so much as my travelling expenses.' At that I borrowed some of your eloquence—I held my tongue. He went on: 'What distresses me most is my uncle.'[4] 'How so?' 'Because he's annoyed with me.' 'Why do you let him be annoyed?—I prefer to say "let" rather than "make".' 'I shan't any more,' he answered. 'I shall do away with the reason.' 'Admirable!' said I. 'But if you don't mind my asking I should be interested to know what the reason is.' 'It's because I couldn't make up my mind whom to marry. My mother was displeased with me, and so consequently was he. Now I don't care what I do to put things right. I'll do what

---

[1] Prospective wife for Quintus junior.

[2] This, and Cicero's opening question, are citations from Greek New Comedy, probably Menander.

[3] Caesar's projected Parthian campaign—dishonourable for Quintus because he was escaping from his debts.

[4] Atticus.

they want.' 'Good luck then,' said I, 'and congratulations on your decision. But when is it to be?' 'The time makes no odds to me,' said he, 'now that I accept the thing itself.' 'Well,' I said, 'I should get it done before I left if I were you. That way you will please your father too.' 'I shall take your advice,' he replied. Thus ended our dialogue. . . .

Cicero seems to have spent the autumn and winter of 45–44 mainly in the capital, and only a few letters from that period have survived. He took some part in public life, more or less under compulsion, attending meetings of the Senate at which new and ever more extravagant honours were voted to the Dictator; and, probably in November, made another speech before Caesar's judgment-seat, this time at Caesar's residence. His client was an old friend, King Deiotarus of Galatia, accused in absence of an attempt on Caesar's life over two years previously. In so far as it touched on public matters the speech was naturally far from reflecting the real sentiments of the speaker, and he himself was not proud of it. To Dolabella in December:

. . . Contrary to what I thought, I find I have the little speech in defence of Deiotarus with me, and so I am sending it to you. Please bear in mind when you read it that the case was a meagre, paltry affair, hardly worth writing up. But I wanted to send my old friend and host a little present—on the light, coarse-spun side, as his own presents are apt to be.

Disgust with affairs in Rome, where Caesar (preparing for a new war against the Parthians) was at no pains to soften the contours of autocracy, comes out in a letter of January 44 to Manius Curius at Patrae:

Not so. I no longer urge or ask you to come home. On the contrary, I am anxious to take wing myself and go to some place 'where nevermore of Pelops' line I'll hear the name or fame.'[1] You cannot imagine the sense of personal dishonour I feel at living in the Rome of today. Farsighted indeed you turn out to have been when you fled this country. Although the happenings here are painful enough in the report, yet it is more tolerable to hear of them than to see them. At least you were not in the Campus when the Quaestorship elections began at nine o'clock in the morning. A chair of state had been placed for Quintus Maximus, whom these people used to call Consul. His death was announced and the chair removed. Whereupon he,[2] having taken auspices for an assembly of the Tribes, held an assembly of the Centuries,[3] and at one o'clock of the afternoon declared a Consul elected, to remain in office until the Kalends of January, that very next morning that was

[1] One of Cicero's favourite quotations, from an unknown Latin tragedy.
[2] Caesar.
[3] Quaestors were elected by the Tribes, Consuls by the Centuries.

to be. So in the Consulship of Caninius you may take it that nobody had breakfast! However, at any rate no crime was committed during the same period—the Consul's vigilance was extraordinary! Throughout his entire term of office he never closed an eye! You find this laughable, for you are not on the spot; if you were here to witness, you could not help but weep. What if I were to tell you the rest? Incidents of the same character are innumerable. I could not bear them if I had not brought my boat into the harbour of philosophy, and if I did not have our dear Atticus to share my avocations. . . .

With all this, Cicero not only retained Caesar's personal good will ('for some reason he was extraordinarily tolerant where I was concerned,' wrote the former soon after the latter's death), but was even recognized as a man of influence at court. At dinner with Caesar and on other occasions he repeatedly took up the case of Atticus' neighbours in Epirus, the town of Buthrotum, which was in danger of losing its land for assignment to veterans (Atticus had an important financial interest). In December an old foe and friend, Vatinius, now governing Illyricum and grumbling at Caesar's failure to give due recognition to his military successes, enlisted Cicero's support. Another letter shortly after Caesar's murder gives a glimpse of another intercession:

. . . Matius also told me (I may as well put things down as they occur to me) that recently, when I called on Caesar at Sestius' behest and was sitting waiting to be summoned, Caesar remarked 'I must be a most unpopular man. There's Marcus Cicero waiting and can't get to see me at his own convenience. He's the most easy-going of mankind, but I don't doubt he detests me.' . . .

But the most graphic picture of Caesar and Cicero together at this time is the latter's account to Atticus of what may have been his last social contact with the man he privately called 'the King.' It happened in December at his villa near Cumae, or perhaps in his newly acquired suburban estate at Puteoli. Caesar was in the neighbourhood and came to dinner:

Strange that so onerous a guest should leave a memory not disagreeable! It was really very pleasant. But when he arrived at Philippus' place on the evening of 18 December, the house was so thronged by the soldiers that there was hardly a spare room for Caesar himself to dine in. Two thousand men, no less! I was a good deal perturbed about what would happen next day, but Cassius Barba came to the rescue and posted sentries. Camp was pitched in the open and a guard placed on the house. On the 19th Caesar stayed at Philippus' until one o'clock, admitting nobody—at accounts, I believe, with Balbus. Then he took a walk on the shore. Towards two he went to his bath.

That was when he heard about Mamurra;[1] his expression did not change. After anointing, he took his place at table. He was following a course of emetics, and so ate and drank with uninhibited enjoyment. It was really a fine, well-appointed meal, and not only that but

'cooked and garnished well,
good talking too—in fact, a pleasant meal.'[2]

His entourage, moreover, were lavishly entertained in three other dining-rooms. The humbler freedmen and slaves had all they wanted—the smarter ones I entertained in style. In a word, I showed I knew how to live. But my guest was not the kind of person to whom one says 'Do come again when you are next in the neighbourhood!' Once is enough. We talked of nothing serious, but a good deal on literary matters. All in all, he was pleased and enjoyed himself. He said he would spend a day at Puteoli and another at Baiae.

There you are—a visit, or should I call it a billeting, which, as I said, was troublesome to me but not disagreeable. I shall stay here for a short while, then to Tusculum. . . .

---

[1] Caesar's former adjutant in Gaul. Perhaps he had just died.
[2] From the satirist Lucilius.

CHAPTER TWENTY-THREE

After the Ides

'Let us be satisfied, as you recommend, with the Ides of March.'
Cicero to Atticus

THE shortest letter in Cicero's extant correspondence is addressed to one Minucius Basilus:

Congratulations! I am delighted on my account. Be sure of my affection and active concern for your interests. I hope I have *your* affection, and want to hear what you are doing and what is going on.

Basilus had been a lieutenant of Caesar's in Gaul and, allegedly for personal reasons, had joined the conspiracy against his life which took effect in the Senate-House on the Ides (15th) of March, 44. Cicero's note has generally (not universally) been read as a reaction to the event, but this is far from likely. It seems to be implied that Basilus was out of town; but he certainly took part in the murder (Cicero himself was an eye-witness), wounding one of his fellow assassins in the scuffle. Moreover, he is congratulated in the first person singular, not as one of a group. But the note does assuredly correspond to Cicero's sentiments about Caesar's killing.

The plotters had not taken him into their confidence, though some of them were his friends, notably their leader, Marcus Brutus. Plutarch plausibly explains that he was considered too timid and too old—he was now sixty-two, and the conspirators were all, or nearly all, men in their thirties and forties. But when Brutus brandished the dagger he had just plunged into Caesar's body and shouted congratulations to Cicero by name, he knew he could count on a wholehearted response. Cicero saw the murder as a splendid feat of patriotic heroism, and the victim as a public enemy over whose fate all good citizens should rejoice and be glad. For Caesar had made himself a despot, and in the ethics of the ancient city-state such a man put himself outside the community and had no more right to live than a mad dog. It was symbolically fitting that he should have been struck down at the feet of a statue of Pompey which had been replaced by his orders, for some of the strikers were former Pompeians whom he had pardoned or even (like Marcus Brutus and Cassius) promoted; others were old friends and officers of his own. His clemency had destroyed him: so his followers were to complain, as well they might. Sulla had died in his bed after liquidating his enemies by the thousand; but Sulla had also abdicated his Dictatorship and restored a free constitution. Caesar, who had been heard to call Sulla's abdication the act of a politician who did not know his A B C, could not buy immunity with pardons.

If Cicero had simply approved of the killing as an act of supreme justice and necessity, he would merely have been conforming to his code. But certain terms in his letters, as when he writes to Atticus of having 'feasted his eyes on the just death of a tyrant!', or to Cassius of the late Dictator as a 'blackguard,'[1] point to warped emotions. Cicero had solicited and accepted generous treatment from the man he now vilified—and resented it. Was it not Caesar, as he had written to Atticus in 49, who had robbed him not only of what he had, but of what he was? It was Caesar, not Cicero, who had lived Achilles' slogan 'Far to excel, out-topping all the rest', and whose success in wicked courses had reduced the premier Consular of 62 to something like a sycophant —not only of Caesar but of Caesar's creatures. 'You must be polite to him,' he wrote to Atticus anent Caesar's secretary Faberius, from whom he needed a financial accommodation, 'though these fawnings are little less than criminal.' Even so, a happier man might have resisted the temptation to gloat. The desert of Cicero's domestic life did not engender the flower of magnanimity. He could not be expected to feel about Caesar and Caesar's assassins as Gaius Matius did:

. . . I am well aware of the criticisms which people have levelled at me since Caesar's death. They make it a point against me that I bear the death of a friend hard and am indignant that the man I loved should have been destroyed. They say that country should come before friendship—as though they have already proved that his death was to the public advantage. But I shall not make debating points. I acknowledge that I have not yet arrived at that philosophical level. It was not Caesar I followed in the civil conflict, but a friend whom I would not desert, even though I did not like what he was doing. . . . Well then, can I, who desired every man's preservation, help feeling indignant at the slaughter of the man who granted it—all the more

[1] Literally 'foul fellow'. The only other persons to whom Cicero applies the adjective *impurus* in his letters are the tutor Dionysius, his nephew Quintus, and Mark Antony.

when the very persons who brought him unpopularity were responsible for his destruction? 'Very well,' they say, 'you shall be punished for daring to disapprove of our act.' What unheard-of arrogance! Some may glory in the deed, while others cannot even grieve with impunity! Even slaves have always had liberty to feel fear or joy of their own impulse, not someone else's. That freedom the 'authors of our liberty', as these persons like to style themselves, are trying to snatch from us by intimidation. But they are wasting their breath. No threats of danger shall ever make me false to obligation and good feeling. I never thought an honourable death a thing to shun, indeed I should often have welcomed it. . . .

Noble words, to which, however, Cicero had his answers. But Caesar's magnificent qualities, to which Cicero was far from blind, his past consideration, even partiality, for Cicero himself, and the compliments which Cicero had addressed to him publicly and privately during his supremacy, make some of Cicero's words ignoble.

No letter of his illuminates the eventful weeks following; though one from Decimus Brutus (formerly Caesar's close friend, now his assassin) to Marcus Brutus (only very distantly related) and Cassius survives to show how little the chief plotters knew what to do with their achievement. Marcus Brutus had yet to prove (and never did prove) himself as a practical politician; the others were an ill-assorted crew, most of whom apparently 'did what they did in envy of great Caesar,' or out of private discontents. They had planned no further than the act, and they made the momentous mistake of underrating the surviving Consul (Caesar himself had again borne the title in 44), Mark Antony. Austere intellectuals like Brutus and Cassius despised a man who seemed to live only for fighting and wassail. Cicero later claimed that if only *he* had been consulted, Antony would have gone the same way as Caesar. 11 May, to Atticus:

. . . That affair was handled with the courage of brave men and the policy of children. Any one could see that an heir to the throne was left behind. The folly of it! 'Strange *this* to fear and *that* to set at naught!'[1] . . .

More picturesquely, he told two of the conspirators in February 43 that if *he* had been invited to their dinner-party on the Ides of March, there would have been no left-overs. That was probably hindsight, for in less than a month after the murder he wrote to Atticus that he thought Antony was thinking more about his next feast than any political mischief. But on the night of the Ides he did urge Brutus and Cassius

[1] From an unknown Latin play.

(both Praetors in 44) to summon the Senate and seize control of events. Instead, they negotiated privately with Antony. Meeting on the 17th the Senate voted a general amnesty for the benefit of the assassins, but at the same time recognized the validity of all Caesar's ordinances (*acta*). Cicero spoke eloquently in favour of this compromise, though he afterwards wrote of it as a deplorable concession forced by fear. Next day a public funeral for Caesar was decreed.

Unmistakably the initiative had passed to Antony. The funeral produced rioting and attacks upon the houses of the conspirators, who fled from Rome; and though they came back after a few days, it was only to withdraw again after further outbreaks. Antony remained in full control. Caesar's wife Calpurnia had given him her husband's papers, so that any order he chose to make could be fathered on Caesar. Faberius attended to any necessary forgeries. Cicero had left for Campania in disgust on 5 April, and wrote from Puteoli on the 22nd:

Atticus, I fear the Ides of March have brought us nothing except joy and a satisfaction for our hatred and pain. The things I hear from Rome! And the things I see here! 'Twas a fine deed, but half done!'[1] You know how warm a feeling I have for the Sicilians and what an honour I consider it to have them as my clients. Caesar was generous to them, and I was not sorry that he should be—though the Latin franchise[2] was intolerable. Well, here is Antony posting up (in return for a massive bribe) a law allegedly carried by the Dictator in the Assembly under which Sicilians become Roman citizens, a thing never mentioned in his lifetime! Then there is Deiotarus' case. Isn't it much the same? No doubt he deserves any kingdom we give him, but not through Fulvia.[3] There are any number of such things. . . .

'We could not bear to own Caesar as master, but we bow down before his notebooks,' he wrote a week later.

His personal relations with Antony had had their ups and downs, but were now outwardly quite cordial. In late April an interchange of letters took place. Antony (not the best of stylists) wrote:

Pressure of business on my side and your sudden departure have prevented me from taking this matter up with you in person. On that account I fear that my absence may carry less weight with you than my presence would.

I petitioned Caesar to recall Sextus Cloelius[4] from exile, and gained my

[1] A Greek quotation, perhaps from a play.

[2] An inferior form of Roman citizenship, apparently granted to Sicily (or at any rate to some Sicilian communities) by Caesar.

[3] Wife of Antony, previously married to Clodius and then to Curio.

[4] A former satellite of Clodius, who had been exiled in 52 for his share in the riots after Clodius' murder. Until recently his name was supposed to be Sextus Clodius, after an error in certain manuscripts.

point. I had intended even then to take advantage of the favour only if you gave your consent. So I am all the more anxious to gain your sanction to my doing it through my own agency now. If, however, you show yourself unsympathetic toward his sad, unhappy case, I shall not persist in opposition to your wish, although I feel I have a duty to uphold Caesar's memorandum. But I must say that if you wish to take a view in accordance with humanity, wisdom, and a regard for myself, you will surely show yourself indulgent, and you will be willing for Publius Claudius,[1] a lad of the highest promise, to think that you refrained from bearing hard upon his father's friends when it lay in your power. Allow it, I beg you, to appear that you were his father's enemy for patriotic reasons, not because you despised the family. We lay aside feuds started on public grounds with greater credit and more readiness than those of stubbornness. Further, give me the opportunity to influence the boy here and now, and to persuade his impressionable mind to the opinion that quarrels should not be hereditary. Although I am sure that your position, dear Sir, is beyond all danger, I imagine none the less that you would rather pass your declining years in tranquillity and honour than amid anxieties. Finally I have some right to ask this favour of you, for I have done all I could on your behalf. But if I fail to obtain it, I shall not make the concession to Cloelius on my own. I hope you will see from this how much your approval means to me, and show yourself the more placable on that account.

Cicero to Antony:

For one reason and one only I would rather you had raised this matter with me in person than by letter. You could then have seen my affection for you not only in my words but in my eyes, written, as the saying goes, all over my face. That affection I have always felt, prompted by your own friendly disposition in the first instance and later by obligation actually conferred; and at the present time the national interest has commended you to my regard, so much so that no one is dearer to me. And now your affectionate and flattering letter has made me feel that I am not conferring a favour upon you, but receiving one at your hands, when you put your request in the form that you do not wish to rescue my enemy and your friend against my will, although you would have no difficulty in doing so.

Yes, my dear Antony, I yield to your wishes in this matter, and not without a lively sense of your generosity and the honour you do me by writing in such terms. In any circumstances I should feel bound to make you this concession unreservedly; and I am also making it to my natural humanity. Sternness and severity in any degree, let alone harshness, have never been part of my disposition except in so far as necessities of state have required it. Let me add that toward Cloelius personally I have never felt any special

[1] Or 'Clodius:' son of Cicero's enemy and Fulvia, therefore Antony's step-son.

hostility, and have always taken the view that we ought not to bear too hardly upon the friends of our enemies, especially those of humble station, and thus deprive ourselves of such support.

As for young Clodius, I think it is for you to imbue his impressionable mind, as you say in your letter, with such sentiments as may persuade him that there is no residue of family feud between us. I clashed with Publius Clodius when I was championing the public cause and he his own. The commonwealth stood umpire upon our disputes. If he were alive today, there would no longer be any strife between us. So since in making this request of me you say that you will not use your power in the matter against my wish, you may, if you think proper, present the concession to the boy also as coming from me; not that in view of our respective ages I could reasonably envisage any danger from his quarter, nor that a man of my standing need greatly fear any conflict, but in order that we ourselves may be on closer terms than we have been on hitherto. For in the past, with these feuds standing between us, your heart has been more open to me than your house. But I need say no more.

One thing in conclusion: I shall always, without hesitation and with my whole heart, do anything that I think accords with your wishes and interests. Of that I hope you will feel fully assured.

Cicero sent copies of the correspondence to Atticus with some covering remarks, which make further comment needless:

. . . I return to our unhappy, or rather non-existent, commonwealth. Mark Antony has written to me about the recall of Sextus Cloelius, in how complimentary a style so far as concerns me personally you will see from his own letter, of which I enclose a copy; how unscrupulously, disgracefully, mischievously, so that one is sometimes tempted to wish Caesar back, you will readily appreciate. Things that Caesar neither did nor ever would have done or permitted to be done are now brought out from his forged memoranda. As for me, I have shown myself all compliance to Antony. After all, having once made up his mind that he had a right to do what he pleased, he would have done it just the same if I had opposed. So I enclose a copy of my letter too.

Moreover, Antony had to be conciliated in the private interest of Atticus and his Buthrotans. 17 May:

. . . With Antony I shall go to work so as to convey to him that if he obliges us in this business, I shall be entirely at his disposal. . . .

Cicero spent April, May, and June moving restlessly from one country estate to another, writing to Atticus most days. This came from Puteoli on 26 April:

Your letter of the 19th has at last reached me, a week later. In it you ask (and you suppose that I myself don't know) whether I get more pleasure from the hills and the view or from the walk *au bord de la mer*.[1] Indeed it is as you say; both places are so agreeable that I hesitate which to prefer.

> 'But not of table-joys our thoughts.
> Great bane, O King, we see and are afraid.
> 'Tis life or death with us, I know not which.'[2]

This, probably, from Astura in mid-June:

This district, let me tell you, is charming; at any rate it's secluded and free from observers if one wants to do some writing. And yet, somehow or other, 'there's no place like home;' so my feet are carrying me back to Tusculum. After all, I think one would soon get tired of the nature-painting of this scrap of wooded coast. What is more, I am afraid of rain, if my 'Prognostics'[3] are to be trusted, for the frogs are speechifying. Would you please let me know where and what day I can see Brutus?

At times he thought of returning to Rome, but political conditions determined him to keep away. He wrote from Tusculum about the end of May:

. . . Both Balbus and Oppius write as you do about Brutus' and Cassius' provinces being settled by a senatorial decree. Hirtius says he won't be present (indeed he is already in his place at Tusculum), and strongly advises me to keep away. His advice is on the score of danger, which he says applied to himself too; but for my own part, even if there were no such danger, I am so far from sedulous to avoid arousing Antony's suspicions (it may look as though I don't find his successes agreeable) that my reason for not wanting to go to Rome is precisely that I don't want to set eyes on him. Our friend Varro, however, has sent me a letter from I don't know who (he had crossed out the name) stating that the most pernicious talk is rife among the veterans who are being put off (a certain number having got their discharge), so that Rome will be highly dangerous for any persons who may seem to be on the other side. Furthermore, how am I to manage my comings and goings, looks and bearing, among these people? And if, as you write, Decimus Brutus is to be attacked by Lucius Antonius[4] and the rest, what should I do and how should I behave? I am resolved, as things now stand, to stay away from the city in which my name stood high in the days of my greatness and was not wholly unrespected even in those of my servitude. I am not, however, so

---

[1] The comparison is between Cicero's estate at Cumae and the newly acquired one at Puteoli not far away.

[2] From the Iliad.

[3] Cicero's poem on weather-signs, translated from a Greek original.

[4] Mark Antony's younger brother.

definite about leaving Italy, on which I shall consult with you, as about not returning to Rome.

A letter from Puteoli of 17 April fairly represents the general tone of the correspondence at this period:

I have learned a variety of political news from your letters, of which I received several in a batch from Vestorius' freedman. Let me briefly answer your enquiries. First I am quite delighted with the Cluvius property.[1] But you ask me why I have sent for Chrysippus:[2] two of my shops have collapsed and the others are showing cracks, so that even the mice have moved elsewhere, to say nothing of the tenants. Other people call this a disaster, I don't call it even a nuisance. Ah, Socrates, Socratics, I can never repay you! Heavens above, how utterly trivial such things appear to me! However, there is a building scheme under way, Vestorius advising and instigating, which should turn this loss into a source of profit.

There's a great crowd here, and will be, as I hear, a greater, including the two so-called Consul-Designates.[3] Gods above! The tyranny lives on, the tyrant is dead! We rejoice at his slaughter—and defend his ordinances! So *[4] takes us pretty sternly to task, enough to make one ashamed of being alive, and right he is! It would have been better to die a thousand deaths than put up with such things—and they look to me like lasting a long, long time.

Balbus is here and I see a lot of him. He has had a letter from Vetus dated 31 December to the effect that when Caecilius[5] was besieged by him and on the point of capture Pacorus of Parthia came up with a very large force. Thus Caecilius was snatched from his clutches with the loss of many of his own men. He blames Vulcatius[6] in the matter. So it looks to me as though war in that quarter is imminent. But let Dolabella and Nicias worry.[7] Balbus also gives better news of Gaul. He has a letter three weeks old announcing that the Germans and the tribes there, hearing what had happened to Caesar, had sent envoys to Hirtius' deputy Aurelius promising to obey orders. All redolent of peace in fact, contrary to what Baldy[8] had said to me.

The following day's letter contained news of greater moment to Cicero and his world than he could then imagine:

[1] At Puteoli, inherited by Cicero from the banker Cluvius.

[2] An architect.

[3] Hirtius and Pansa, Caesar's nominees for the Consulship in 43 (hence 'so-called').

[4] The manuscripts have corrupted a proper name, possibly (Manius) Curius.

[5] Ex-Pompeian who had raised a revolt against Caesar in Syria with Parthian backing.

[6] Son of the Consular, now probably governor of Cilicia.

[7] Dolabella had succeeded to the Consulship left vacant by Caesar's death, and had been assigned the governorship of Syria. His protégé the scholar Nicias (see page 206) was going with him.

[8] Calvenna, a nickname for Gaius Matius.

. . . Octavius arrived in Naples on the 18th. Balbus met him there early on the next day and was with me later the same day at my house near Cumae; tells me that Octavius is going to accept the inheritance. But as you say, he fears a mighty tussle with Antony. . . .

Caesar's great-nephew Gaius Octavius was eighteen years old. When he heard in Greece that he had been named adoptive son and heir in Caesar's will, he came at once to claim the inheritance. Cicero met him a few days later:

. . . Octavius is with me here—most respectful and friendly. His followers call him Caesar,[1] but Philippus[2] doesn't, so neither do I. My judgment is that he cannot be a good citizen. There are too many folk around him. . . .

Staple political and private topics are sometimes supplemented by interesting miscellanea, such as an account of Cicero's relations with Queen Cleopatra of Egypt, who had been living for two years in Rome as Caesar's mistress:

. . . I dislike Her Majesty. Ammonius, who guaranteed her promises, knows I have the right to do so. These were of a literary kind, not unbecoming to my position—I should not mind telling them to a public meeting. As for Sara, over and above his general rascality, I found him personally insolent as well. Once and once only I saw him at my house. When I asked him in a friendly way what I could do for him, he replied that he was looking for Atticus! The arrogance of the Queen herself when she was living on the estate across the Tiber makes my blood boil to recall. So I want nothing to do with them. They must think I have no spirit, or rather that I hardly have a spleen. . . .

Or a response to a suggestion from Atticus about an imaginary speech to be composed on the theme of Caesar's death:

. . . You urge me to write a speech and send it to Brutus. My dear fellow, let me give you a general rule on matters in which I have a fair amount of experience. There was never a poet or orator yet who thought anyone better than himself. This applies even to the bad ones. How much more to one so gifted and erudite as Brutus! I actually made the experiment the other day in connexion with the manifesto. I composed a draft at your request. I liked mine, he preferred his own. Indeed, when at his own entreaty I might almost say, I addressed to him an essay on the best style of oratory, he wrote not only to me but to you that he could not agree with my preference. So pray let

---

[1] As Caesar's adopted son Gaius Octavius changed his name to Gaius Julius Caesar Octavianus.

[2] Octavian's stepfather; see page 203, note 2.

every man write as best suits himself. 'Every man his own bride, mine for me. Every man his own love, mine for me.' Not a very elegant distich. Atilius[1] wrote it, a most clumsy versifier. . . .

Or the hint of matrimonial snares:

. . . As for the lady you say is pestering you, I am surprised that you should have so much as given her a hearing. If I praised her in front of friends, with her three sons and your daughter listening, what of it? And why should I go about in a mask? Isn't old age itself a sufficiently ugly one? . . .

It seems to have been early in 44 that Quintus Cicero was finally divorced from Pomponia. In the current state of their relations his brother will scarcely have cared. As for Quintus:

. . . As for Quintus, he is not worrying about buying property just now. He has trouble enough over the repayment of the dowry, in which connexion he says he is infinitely grateful to Egnatius. As for marriage, he has so little inclination for it that he says a bachelor's bed is the most agreeable thing in the world. . . .

Quintus' marriage-bed of his brother's making had surely been a bed of thorns.

[1] Writer of Latin Comedy in the second century B.C.

CHAPTER TWENTY-FOUR

The First Philippic

'They say that men of my age should not go far away from their graves.'
Cicero to Atticus

ONLY too plainly inherent in the situation which followed Caesar's death were the possibilities of a new civil war. Indeed the old one had not been extinguished, for in Spain Pompey's younger son Sextus had managed to survive and resurge, while in the East an ex-Pompeian called Caecilius Bassus was in arms with Parthian support against Caesar's lieutenants. Once again Cicero felt a personal dilemma, which he outlined to Atticus in his letter of 26 April:

... All the same, if there is to be civil war (and there is bound to be if Sextus stays under arms, as I am certain he will), I cannot tell what we ought to do. Neutrality, which was possible in Caesar's war, will not be possible now. Anyone who in the opinion of this party of desperados was glad at Caesar's death (and we all showed our delight without the faintest concealment) will be considered by them as an enemy. This points to large-scale massacre. The alternative is to betake ourselves to Sextus' camp, or maybe Brutus';[1] a weary business and unbefitting our age, with no certainty as to the issue of the war—and somehow I might say to you and you to me

'My child, the works of war are not for thee.
Be thy concern the works of *worded* joy.'[2]

But this must be left to chance, which counts for more than calculation in such matters. Let us look to what ought to rest with ourselves, namely to bear whatever comes with fortitude and philosophy, and to remember that we are but men. And let us take much comfort in study, and not a little too in the Ides of March. ...

Again on 8 May:

Brutus says he is contemplating exile. I see a different harbour[3] ahead,

[1] i.e., Decimus Brutus, who had gone to Cisalpine Gaul as Proconsul by Caesar's appointment.
[2] From the Iliad (Zeus to Aphrodite). But Cicero adapts the quotation, writing *logoio* ('word') for *gamoio* ('marriage'—'wedded joy') in the original.
[3] Death is meant.

easier to reach at my time of life, though I would rather not have been carried in before I had seen Brutus flourishing and the constitution established. But this time, as you say, we are not free to choose—you agree with me that soldiering, especially in a civil war, is not for people of our age. . . .

And on 14 May:

. . . It occurs to me that if Pompey comes this way with a strong army, as the evidence suggests he will, there will be war for a certainty. This picture as I think of it disturbs me deeply. What was possible for you *then*[1] will not be possible for me now, for I have made no secret of my rejoicing. Also they talk much of my ingratitude. Definitely, what was possible then for you and many others won't be possible. Am I then to come into the open and go to the wars? Better a thousand deaths, especially at my age. So the Ides of March don't give me as much consolation as they did. They have one glaring defect, though to be sure the young men 'wipe off by other doughty deeds this slur.'[2] But if you have any better hopes, since you hear more than I and are party to their plans, please write to me, and also consider what I ought to do about a Votive Commission.[3] I receive many warnings hereabouts not to go to the Senate on the Kalends. Soldiers are said to have been collected secretly for the occasion, against your friends. It looks to me as if they will be safer anywhere than in the Senate.

Even in Caesar's lifetime he had thought of travelling on a 'Votive Commission' to Athens, where a parental visit would, he believed, do much to steady Marcus junior. On 15 April:

. . . I have had a letter from Marcus, really classically phrased and pretty long. Other things can be assumed, but the style of the letter shows he has learned something. Now I earnestly request you (we were talking of it the other day) to see that he wants for nothing. That is for me a matter both of duty and of reputation and prestige. I know you feel the same. Of course if I get off to Greece in July, everything is more straightforward; but since the times are such that we cannot foresee with any certainty what will be honourable for me or practicable or expedient, pray make sure that we maintain him in really handsome and liberal style. . . .

Progress reports were still not altogether reassuring. 21 April:

. . . What you write about Marcus is pleasant for me to read; I hope it augurs well. I am most grateful to you for your trouble in seeing that he gets plenty to live on in good style, and I beg you once more to do this. . . .

---

[1] i.e., in 'Caesar's war.'
[2] A Greek verse, probably from a lost play. The 'defect' (or 'slur') lay in letting Antony survive.
[3] See page 57, note 1.

On 2 May:

. . . Now, my dear fellow, do come to my rescue. When I have given our Brutus his full due, I am anxious to run over to Greece. It is very important for Marcus' sake, or rather for mine, or indeed for both our sakes, that I should look in on his studies. As for that letter of Leonides'[1] you sent me, pray, what is so very satisfactory about it? I shall never be content with a good report of him which is qualified 'on present showing.' That isn't the language of confidence, rather of apprehension. I had charged Herodes to write to me in full detail, but there has not been a line from him so far. I fear he has had nothing to tell which he thought would be agreeable for me to know. . . .

On 11 June:

At last a courier from Marcus! But upon my word the letter is classically written, which in itself would argue some progress, and others too send excellent reports. Leonides, however, sticks to his 'so far;' but Herodes is enthusiastic. Truth to tell, I am not unwilling to be deceived in this case and gladly swallow all I'm told. If there is anything in letters from your people which concerns me, please let me know.

Cicero was still anxious that his son should lack for nothing. 13 June:

. . . The more modest my boy is in his requests, the more concerned I am to meet him. He said nothing to me about this matter (of course I was the proper person to approach), but wrote to Tiro that nothing had come to him after the 1st of April, that being the end of his first year. Naturally generous as you are, I know that you have always favoured my treating him very liberally, indeed more than liberally—lavishly, and further that you considered I owed it to my position to do so. So please (I should not be troubling you if I could manage it through anyone else) arrange a bill of exchange to Athens for enough to cover his expenses for the year. Eros of course will pay. I have sent Tiro for the purpose. So please see to it and let me know if you have any further views on the subject.

And the following day:

. . . It is most kind of you to promise that Marcus will not go short. Messalla, who is on his way back and came over from Lanuvium from them[2] to me, brought a splendid report of him. And really his own letter is so

[1] Leonides and Herodes were Athenian friends of Atticus.
[2] Brutus and Cassius. Messalla (Corvinus) was a young patrician who later became the patron of the poet Tibullus and (if St. Jerome could be believed) Terentia's third husband.

affectionately and classically written that I should not mind reading it before an audience. This makes me the more inclined to indulge him. . . .

About this time Cicero received a letter from an old friend, Gaius Trebonius, dated Athens, 25 May. Trebonius had been one of those Caesarian partisans and officers who had joined in the assassination. He was now on his way to govern the province of Asia, and prefaced a proposal that young Marcus should make a trip there with some golden opinions:

I arrived in Athens on 22 May, and there saw what I most desired to see, your son devoting himself to liberal studies and bearing an exemplary character. How much pleasure this gave me you can appreciate even without my telling you. You are not unaware how much I think of you and how warmly I welcome any gratification that comes your way, even the most trifling, let alone such a blessing as this. Such is the long-standing and sincere affection between us. Do not suppose, my dear Cicero, that I tell you this because it is what you want to hear. This young man of yours (or rather ours, for you can have nothing I do not share) could not be more popular with everybody in Athens, nor more enthusiastically attached to the studies for which you care most, that is to say, the highest. And so I am happy to congratulate you, as I can sincerely do, and myself no less, upon the fact that in him we have a young man for whom it is a delight to care, since care for him we were bound to, however he had turned out. . . .

But the chief monument of Marcus Cicero junior's academic career is a letter of his own to Tiro. The exact date is uncertain; perhaps about the end of August:

I am eagerly expecting couriers every day, and at last they have come, forty-five days after leaving home. I had been longing for their arrival. My kindest and dearest father's letter gave me great pleasure, and then your own most agreeable letter put the finishing touch to my happiness. I am no longer sorry to have made a break in our correspondence, rather the contrary, since as a result of my letters falling silent I am repaid by this example of your good nature. I am truly delighted that you have accepted my excuses without question.

I don't doubt that you are pleased with the reports you are hearing of me, dearest Tiro, and that they are such as you wished to hear. I shall take good care and work hard to see that this tiny new image of mine gets larger and larger, twice as large, as the days go by. So you can carry out your promise to be my publicity agent with every confidence. Young men make mistakes, and mine have brought me so much unhappiness and torment that I hate to think of what I did, or even to hear it mentioned. Very well, I know that you shared my worry and unhappiness, as well you might, for you wanted all to go right for me, not for my sake only, but for your own too, because I have always wanted you to have a part in any good things that come my way. Well, since I gave you unhappiness then, I shall make sure to give you twice as much happiness now.

You will like to know that Cratippus[1] and I are very close, more like father and son than teacher and pupil. I enjoy hearing him lecture, and quite delight in his pleasant company. I spend all day with him and often part of the night, for I coax him into dining with me as frequently as possible. Now that he has got into the habit, he often drops in on us at dinner unawares, and then he puts off the grave philosopher and jokes with us in the most genial way. So you must try to meet him as soon as possible—he is such a pleasant, excellent man.

As for Bruttius,[2] what can I say? I never let him out of my sight. He lives simply and strictly, and he is the best of company too. Fun goes hand in hand with literary study and daily discussion of problems. I have rented a lodging for him near mine, and as he is a poor man, I help him as best I can out of my own meagre funds. Also I have started regular declamation in Greek with Cassius, and I want to practise in Latin with Bruttius. Some people whom Cratippus brought over from Mytilene, scholars whom he entirely approves of, are my friends and daily associates. I see a lot of Epicrates too (a leading man in Athenian society), and Leonides, and people of that sort. So as to myself—*voilà*!

As for what you say about Gorgias,[3] he *was* useful to me in declamation practice, but I have put obedience to my father's directions above all other considerations. He had written telling me *sans phrase* to get rid of Gorgias at once. I thought I had better not boggle over it—if I made too much fuss, he might think it suspicious. Also it came to my mind that I should be taking a lot upon myself in judging my father's judgment. All the same I am very grateful for your concern and advice.

I quite accept your excuse about shortage of time. I know how busy you generally are. I'm really delighted to hear that you have bought a property, and I hope it turns out a successful investment. Don't be surprised at my congratulations coming at this stage in my letter—that was about the point where *you* put news of your purchase. Well, you are a landed proprietor! You must shed your townbred ways—you are now a Roman squire! How amusing to picture the delightful sight of you now! I imagine you buying farming tackle, talking to the bailiff, hoarding pips at dessert in your jacket pocket! But seriously, I am as sorry as you that I was not there to lend you a

[1] Cratippus of Pergamum, eminent philosopher and friend of Cicero, who had got him made a Roman citizen by Caesar.
[2] Otherwise unknown. The name is Italian.
[3] A rhetorician, later at least of some celebrity, whom Cicero accused of leading his son astray ('into pleasures and winebibbing' Plutarch).

hand. However, my dear Tiro, I *shall* help you, provided luck helps me, especially as I know you have bought the place to share with us.

Thank for you attending to my commissions. But do please get a clerk sent out to me, preferably a Greek. I waste a lot of time copying out my notes.

Take care of your health first and foremost, so that we can be students together. I commend Anteros[1] to you.

Cicero's proposed journey to Greece had another motive besides his son's welfare. After Caesar's death he wanted to escape from a political situation which only intermittently seemed to offer any hope for the future. But there were counter-considerations, and his mind wavered. On 26 April he wrote to Atticus:

. . . Now put your mind to the personal question which exercises me; so many points occur to me on either side. If, as I had decided, I go to Greece on a Commissionership, I feel I am to some extent avoiding the danger of impending massacre, but am likely to incur some censure for failing the state at so serious a time. If on the other hand I stay in Italy, I shall clearly be in danger, but I have a notion that in certain contingencies I might be able to do service to the state.

On 3 June Dolabella, who had succeeded to Caesar's Consulship and was looking forward to the governorship of Syria, gave Cicero an appointment on his staff, which left him free to travel where he pleased. On hearing of it Cicero paid a visit to Antium, where Brutus was staying *en famille*:

I arrived at Antium before midday. Brutus was glad to see me. Then before a large company, including Servilia, Tertulla, and Porcia,[2] he asked me what I thought he ought to do. Favonius too was present. I gave the advice I had prepared on the way, to accept the Asiatic corn commission.[3] I said his safety was all that concerned us now; it was the bulwark of the Republic itself. I was fairly launched on this theme when Cassius walked in. I repeated what I had already said, whereupon Cassius, looking most valorous I assure you, the picture of a warrior, announced that he had no intention of going to Sicily. 'Should I have taken an insult as though it had been a favour?' 'What do you mean to do then?' I enquired. He replied that he would go to Greece. 'How about you, Brutus?' said I. 'To Rome,' he answered, 'if you agree.' 'But I don't agree at all. You won't be safe there.' 'Well, supposing I

---

[1] The bearer of the letter.

[2] Brutus' mother, half-sister (married to Cassius), and wife respectively.

[3] The Senate had just given Brutus and Cassius permission to go abroad, and charged them with the purchase of grain in Asia and Sicily respectively. Cicero writes of this in his next letter as 'Antony's contumelious favour,' such a function being far from prestigious ('the meanest duty known in public service').

could be safe, would you approve?' 'Of course, and what is more, I should be against your leaving for a province either now or after your Praetorship. But I cannot advise you to risk your life in Rome.' I went on to give reasons, which no doubt occur to you, why he would not be safe.

A deal of talk followed, in which they complained, Cassius especially, about the opportunities that had been let slip, and Decimus came in for some severe criticism. To that I said it was no use crying over spilt milk, but I agreed all the same. And when I began to give my views on what should have been done (nothing original, only what everyone is saying all the time), not however touching on the point that someone else[1] should have been dealt with, only that they should have summoned the Senate, urged the popular enthusiasm to action with greater vigour, assumed leadership of the whole commonwealth, your lady friend[2] exclaimed 'Well, upon my word! I never heard the like!' I held my tongue. Anyway it looked to me as though Cassius would go (Servilia undertook to get the corn commission removed from the decree), and our friend Brutus was soon persuaded to drop his empty talk about wanting to be in Rome. He therefore decided that the Games[3] should be held in his absence under his name. It looked to me as though he wanted to go to Asia direct from Antium.

In short, nothing in my visit gave me any satisfaction except the consciousness of having made it. It would not have been right to let him leave Italy without seeing me. Apart from this obligation of affection and duty I could only say to myself 'Prophet, what signifies your journey now?'[4] I found the ship going to pieces, or rather its scattered fragments. No plan, no thought, no method. Hence, though I had no doubts even before, I am all the more determined to fly from here, and as soon as I possibly can, 'where never more of Pelops' line I'll hear the deeds or fame.'[5] . . .

And look here! In case you don't know, Dolabella appointed me to his staff on the 3rd. I was informed of this yesterday evening. You too did not like the idea of a Votive Commission. It would really have been absurd for me to pay vows after the overthrow of the Republic which I made for its safety. Besides, Free Commissions have a time limit under the Lex Julia, or so I believe, and it is not easy to add to that type of commission a license to come and go as one pleases. This additional advantage I now have. Also it's agreeable to have the privilege to use as one pleases for five years—though why should I be thinking of five years? I have the feeling that the sands are running out. But *absit omen*.

After some further hesitations Cicero said good-bye to Atticus (who

---

[1] Antony.

[2] Servilia, who seems to have bridled at Cicero's criticism of her son.

[3] As City Praetor Brutus should have been in charge of the Apollinarian 'Games', held annually in July (6–13).

[4] From an unknown Greek play.

[5] See page 224, note 1.

wept) at Tusculum, and reached Arpinum on 1 July; from there, via Formiae and Puteoli, to Pompeii. The land route to Brundisium being too dangerous because of Antony's soldiers, he went on by sea down the coast of Italy, writing to Atticus from Vibo on 25 July:

So far (I have now reached Sicca's place at Vibo) my voyage has been comfortable rather than strenuous, by oar in large part. No sign of the seasonable northerly gales. We were in luck to cross both the two bays we had to cross (of Paestum and of Vibo) with sheets level. So I arrived at Sicca's a week after leaving Pompeii, having stopped for one day at Velia, where I had a very pleasant time at our friend Talna's house. My reception, particularly as he was away, could not have been more handsome. So to Sicca's on the 24th. Here, of course, it is like being in my own home, so I am swallowing up the next day as well. But when I reach Regium I suppose I shall there have to consider, 'pondering a lengthy voyage,'[1] whether to make for Patrae by cargo boat or for Tarentine Leucopetra and thence Corcyra by rowing-boats; and if by freighter, whether direct from the Straits or from Syracuse. I shall write to you on the subject from Regium.

But upon my soul, my dear Atticus, I often say to myself 'what signifies your journey?' Why am I not with you? Why am I not gazing at those pearls of Italy, my little houses in the country? But it's enough and more than enough that I am not with you. What am I running away from? Danger? At present, unless I am mistaken, there is none. It is just the danger period to which you counsel me to return. You say that my going abroad is enthusiastically approved, but on the understanding that I get back before the Kalends of January, which I shall certainly make every effort to do. I would rather be frightened at home than secure in your Athens. However, watch the way things tend in Rome and write to me, or else, as I should prefer, bring your news in person. So much for that. . . .

The 28th found him at Regium (Reggio), from where he sent Trebatius Testa an abstruse little work on the Sources of Arguments ('Topica'), with legal examples, composed during the voyage. On 1 August he was at Syracuse and left next day, only to be driven back by contrary winds to Leucopetra (Capo dell'Armi) at the toe of Italy. On the 6th he tried again with the same result. While waiting at Leucopetra in a friend's villa for the weather to change he met some leading citizens of Regium who had just arrived from Rome with news of a favourable turn there. For the moment it had looked as though Antony was about to come to terms with the 'liberators,' and a meeting of the Senate had been convoked for 1 August. 'On hearing this,'

---

[1] From the Odyssey.

wrote Cicero on 19 August as his returning ship was approaching
Pompeii, 'I unhesitatingly threw up my plan to go abroad, with which
to tell the truth I had already been feeling none too happy.' On the 17th
at Velia he had met Brutus, who was sailing with a flotilla for the East,
for the last time. The hoped-for compromise had not materialized.
Instead, Antony had issued a violent manifesto and threatened the
'liberators' with armed force. In the Senate, however, Lucius Piso, once
Cicero's enemy and Caesar's father-in-law, had protested against
Antony's high-handedness. But he got no support, and Cicero saw
little hope:

> ... I have read Antony's edict, sent to me by Brutus and Cassius, and their
> admirable reply. But what practical effect these edicts have or what they aim
> to achieve I frankly fail to see. Nor am I now returning to Rome in order to
> take part in politics, as Brutus recommends. Did anybody support Piso? Did
> he come back himself the next day? However, they say that men of my age
> should not go far away from their graves. . . .

There are no more letters to Atticus for two months. On the last day
of August Cicero re-entered Rome to an enthusiastic welcome described by Plutarch: 'So great a throng poured out to meet him in joy
and eagerness to have him back. The handshakes and embraces at the
gates as he entered lasted almost half a day.' On 1 September the Senate
met at Antony's summons to pass a decree honouring Caesar's
memory. Cicero sent his excuses (fatigue after his journey), which
provoked Antony to threats. On the 2nd, in Antony's absence, Cicero
delivered the first of the series of speeches which he himself jestingly
christened 'Philippics,' after Demosthenes' denunciations of Philip II
of Macedon. The name became standard.

After an explanation of his reasons for going abroad and returning
he presented an indictment of Antony's record during the summer,
urging him to mend his ways and be warned by Caesar's example. By
Roman standards the tone is moderate, and the friendly relations
between Antony and the speaker are explicitly, if somewhat ironically,
acknowledged. Antony retired to his house at Alba (formerly Pompey's) to compose a counterblast with the help of a Sicilian rhetorician
—and the bottle. On 19 September he delivered it, 'vomiting, as usual,
rather than speaking,' as Cicero wrote to Cassius. It contained a
repudiation of Cicero's friendship and a comprehensive attack on his
career. For the challenge had been one which Antony could not over-
look. Cicero, as both he and Antony knew, was the one obvious

rallying-point for republican sentiment in Italy. That made him a menace, as Piso or the Caesarian Servilius Isauricus (who had supported Cicero on the 2nd) could not be. The first Philippic was a deliberate public intimation of his readiness to take the key role. According to his own statement[1] in the speech he had come home expressly to deliver it: 'in order that, if anything were to happen to me (and many dangers seem to loom, over and above what is natural and appointed), I might leave the words I speak today in testimony to our country of my undying loyalty to her.' Friends of Antony, he said, had told him he would be risking his life, but 'I am pretty well content with my span, be it measured in years or in glory.'

The risks were indeed evident, even though Antony was not at the moment in a position to go to extremes. For the Caesarian party was split. Octavian had emerged as a rival for the loyalty of Caesar's veterans, and the Consuls-Designate, Hirtius and Pansa, did not want another dictatorship. Shortly after Antony's rejoinder Cicero wrote to the governor of Africa, Cornificius:

Here I have a fight on my hands with a most rascally sort of gladiator, our colleague[2] Antony. But it is no fair match—words against weapons. However, he also makes speeches to public meetings—about you! Not with impunity—he shall find to his cost what sort of people he has provoked! However, I suppose you get details of all that has happened from other correspondents; it is my business to inform you of what is going to happen, and that is hard to forecast just now.

The whole country is under heel. The *boni* have no leader, our tyrannicides are at the other end of the earth. Pansa's sentiments are sound, and he talks boldly. Our friend Hirtius is making a slow recovery from his illness. What will come of it I simply don't know, but the only hope is that the People of Rome will at last show themselves like their ancestors. I at any rate shall not fail the commonwealth, and shall bear with courage whatever may befall, provided that I am not to blame for it. Of one thing you may be sure—I shall protect your reputation and prestige to the best of my ability.

We shall never know after what private hesitations Cicero set foot on the fatal ladder. Perhaps this time he did not hesitate at all. The mortifications and disappointments of his later career and the calamities of his private life had only sharpened his urge for primacy—not power such as Caesar had had and Pompey had been suspected of wanting, but, in the words of his speech, 'equality in freedom, primacy in

---

[1] Discountenanced, however, by the letter just quoted.
[2] As Augur.

esteem.' Much in his record that looked like timidity was really an incapacity or reluctance to seize the essential in a complex moral problem. But the case of the Republic against Antony in 44 held no complexities for Cicero. Conscience chimed with ambition, striking his hour.

CHAPTER TWENTY-FIVE

The New Caesar

'I was never in a greater quandary.'
Cicero to Atticus

THE exchange in the Senate had no immediate dramatic consequences.
Cicero and the other two Consulars who had spoken out thought it
unsafe to reappear in the House. Antony on his side was waiting for the
arrival in Italy of an army which had been stationed in Greece to take
part in Caesar's projected eastern war. Meanwhile he went on bidding
for military support by further demonstrations of loyalty to Caesar's
memory and hostility to his murderers, among whom he chose to
include Cicero. A *rapprochement* with Octavian, forced upon both by
the soldiery, did not last, and early in October Antony accused his
young rival of attempting to get him assassinated. Cicero chose to
believe him, and wrote to Cornificius in Africa:

. . . I feel quite sure that the city gazettes are sent to you. If I thought
otherwise, I should give you the particulars myself, especially about Caesar
Octavian's attempt. The general public thinks Antony has trumped up the
charge because he wants to lay hands on the young man's money; but wise
and honest folk both believe in the fact and approve. In a word, high hopes
are set on him. He will do anything, it is thought, for honour and glory. As
for our friend Antony, he is so conscious of his unpopularity that after
catching his would-be murderers in his house he does not dare to make the
matter public. So on 9 October he set off for Brundisium to meet the four
Macedonian legions. He intends to buy their good will, and then to march
them to Rome and set them on our necks. . . .

Such is the political situation in outline, if a political situation can exist in
an armed camp. I often feel sorry for you because you are too young to have
sampled any part of a free state in sound working order. Formerly it was at
least possible to hope, but now even that has been wrested from us. What
hope is left when Antony dares to say in a public meeting that Cannutius[1] is

[1] A Tribune.

trying to make a place for himself with people[1] who can have no place in the community so long as he, Antony, is a member of it?

For my part, I take all this, and whatever else can happen to mortal man, with profound thankfulness to philosophy, which not only diverts me from anxiety, but arms me against all assaults of fortune. I recommend you to do the same, and not to reckon as an evil anything devoid of culpability. But you know all this better than I. . . .

In fact, Cicero's current literary occupation was not philosophical. He was busy composing a riposte to Antony in the form of a speech— the Second Philippic, his most celebrated invective. It was never delivered, perhaps never published in the author's lifetime. But arrived in Puteoli (after Antony's departure he saw no point in staying on in Rome), he absorbed himself in writing the last and most famous of his *philosophica*, the treatise 'On Duties' addressed to his son.

On 25 October he wrote to Atticus expressing agreement with the characteristic advice 'neither to lead the van nor to bring up the rear.' But eight days later sensational news intruded:

When I know what day I shall get back I shall send you word. I have to wait for the baggage which is coming from *[2] and there is sickness among my people.

On the evening of the Kalends a letter for me arrived from Octavian. He has great schemes afoot. He has won the veterans at Casilinum and Galatia over to his views, and no wonder, since he gives them 500 denarii[3] apiece. He plans to make a round of the other colonies. His object is plain: war with Antony, and himself as commander-in-chief. So it looks to me as if in a few days' time we shall be in arms. But whom are we to follow? Consider his name; consider his age. And now he asks me, in the first instance, for a secret interview in Capua or somewhere in the vicinity—childish, if he thinks it could be done secretly. I wrote pointing out that this was neither needful nor possible. He sent me one Caecina of Volaterrae, a friend of his, with intelligence that Antony is advancing on Rome with the Larks,[4] levying money on the towns and marching the legion under colours. He wanted my advice on whether he should proceed to Rome with 3,000 veterans, or hold Capua and block Antony's route, or go to join the three Macedonian legions now marching along the Adriatic coast, which he hopes to have on his side. They refused to take a bounty from Antony, so *he* says, booed him savagely, and left him standing as he tried to harangue them. In short, he proffers himself as

[1] i.e., the 'liberators.'
[2] The place-name is corrupt in the manuscripts.
[3] 2,000 sesterces (about £60).
[4] Alaudae. The word is Celtic, the legion having been recruited by Julius Caesar from the native population in Gaul.

our leader and expects me to back him up. For my part I have recommended him to go to Rome. I imagine he will have the city rabble behind him, and the *boni* too, if he convinces them of his sincerity. Ah, Brutus, where are you? What a golden opportunity you are losing! I could not foretell *this*, but I thought something of the kind would happen.

Now I ask your advice. Do I return to Rome, or stay here, or should I flee to Arpinum, which offers security? ∗∗[1] Rome, for fear I may be missed if people come to think that something has been achieved. So solve this problem. I was never in a greater quandary.

Never indeed! The fate of the Republic might ultimately depend on what happened in far-flung provinces—in Spain, where Sextus Pompey had laid down his arms under an agreement reached with the Caesarian governor, Aemilius Lepidus;[2] in Gaul, divided between the same Lepidus and Cicero's friend Munatius Plancus (also a Caesarian, but credited with republican sympathies); above all in the East, where Brutus and Cassius were about to seize control. But in Italy the soldiers of the Republic were commanded by the Consul Antony, except for Decimus Brutus' small force in the north. In raising a private army in Campania from among Caesar's veterans who had been given farms there, Octavian was of course acting outside the constitution; but the constitution had already in effect been suspended by Antony's intimidation. As Cicero later wrote to Decimus Brutus, 'the will of the Senate should be accepted in lieu of authority, when its authority is trammelled by fear.'

His attitude to the new Caesar had remained much what it was when the latter first arrived. On 18 May he wrote to Atticus:

> . . . About Octavian's speech I feel as you do, and I don't like the preparations for his show or the choice of Matius and Postumus as his agents. . . .

About 10 June:

> . . . Octavian, as I perceived, does not lack intelligence or spirit, and he gave the impression that his attitude toward our heroes would be such as I could wish. But how much faith to put in one of his years and name and heredity and education—that's a great question. His step-father[3] thinks none at all—I saw him at Astura. Still he is to be encouraged and, if nothing else, kept apart from Antony. If Marcellus[4] is recommending my writings, that's

---

[1] Something has fallen out of the text: e.g., 'I should prefer the last, but am thinking of Rome. . . .'

[2] In the north. The south was under another Caesarian, Asinius Pollio.

[3] Philippus.

[4] Gaius Marcellus (Consul 50) was Octavian's brother-in-law.

fine. Octavian seemed to me much attached to him. He was not over-much inclined to trust Pansa and Hirtius. A good disposition, if it lasts.

To Cornificius in October he expressed himself more positively, as has been seen.[1] But Cornificius had been a Caesarian, and Cicero did not open his mind to such. Plutarch's picture of an elder statesman blinded in one eye by hatred of Antony and in the other by a young man's flatteries is demonstrably untrue of these earlier stages, and it was probably never essentially true. But to reject Octavian's advances would be to lose a possibly heaven-sent opportunity of rehabilitating the Senate's authority under his own leadership.

He continued to hesitate. 4 November:

Two letters to me from Octavian in one day! Now wants me to return to Rome at once, says he wants to work through the Senate. I replied that the Senate could not meet before the Kalends of January, which I believe is the case. He adds 'with your advice.' In short, he presses and I play for time. I don't trust his age and I don't know what he's after. I'm nervous of Antony's power and don't want to leave the coast. But I'm afraid of some star performance during my absence. Varro doesn't think much of the boy's plan. I take a different view. He has a strong force at his back, and *can* have Brutus.[2] And he's going to work quite openly, forming companies at Capua and paying out bounties. War is evidently coming any minute now. Let me have an answer to all this. I am surprised that my courier left Rome on the Kalends without a letter from you.

The following day:

. . . I have not buried myself down at Pompeii as I wrote that I should, partly because the weather is abominable, partly because I get letters every day from Octavian urging me to put my shoulder to the wheel, come to Capua, save the Republic a second time, and at all events return to Rome at once. 'Durst not for shame refuse, for fear accept.'[3] He has certainly shown, and continues to show, plenty of energy, and he will go to Rome with a large following; but he is very much a boy. Thinks the Senate will meet at once. Who will come? On the Kalends of January he may be some protection: or perhaps the issue will be fought out before then. The boy is remarkably popular in the towns. On his way to Samnium he passed through Cales and stayed the night at Teanum. Amazing receptions and demonstrations of encouragement. Would you have thought it? For this reason I shall return to Rome sooner than I had intended. I shall write as soon as I decide definitely.[4] . . .

---

[1] See page 248.   [2] Decimus.   [3] From the Iliad.
[4] The letter ends with a domestic touch: 'Please give Attica a kiss from me for being a merry little thing. It is what one likes to see in children.'

On 8 November Cicero set out from Puteoli for Rome, but changed his plans *en route*. To Atticus from Sinuessa (near modern Mandragona):

I arrived at my place[1] near Sinuessa on the 8th. It was common talk that Antony would be stopping that night at Casilinum. So I changed my plan—had intended travelling direct to Rome by the Appian Way. He would easily have caught me up, for they say he moves with Caesarian speed. Accordingly I am turning off at Minturnae towards Arpinum, and have decided to stay the night of the 9th either at Aquinum or Arcanum. And now, my dear fellow, do bring your whole mind to bear on this problem, which is really of great importance. There are three courses open: shall I stay at Arpinum, shall I come closer, or shall I return to Rome? I shall do what you advise. But don't put it off. I am eagerly awaiting a letter.

The 9th (early morning), near Sinuessa.

The next day:

What an extraordinary coincidence! I got up before daybreak on the 9th, off from Sinuessa, and had reached Tuscan Bridge at Minturnae, where there is a turning on to the road to Arpinum, just as it was getting light, when the courier met me 'pondering a lengthy voyage.'[2] My first words: 'Anything from Atticus? Let me have it.' We could not read as yet because we had sent our flambeaux away and there was not enough daylight. When it grew brighter I had the earlier of your two letters read to me. It is the most elegant of compositions—what I say I think, hang me if I don't! I have never read anything in better taste. Yes, I'll follow where you beckon,[3] provided only that you help. But at first sight it all seemed quite remarkably *mal à propos* as a reply to the letter in which I sought your advice. Then, lo and behold, the second letter, in which you encourage me to proceed 'by windy Mimas, to Psyria's isle,'[4] with the Appian Way 'on our left hand' of course. So I stayed that night at Aquinum—a longish journey and a bad road.

He arrived at Arpinum on the 11th. Probably on the next day he canvassed the problem yet again:

I have really nothing to write about. It was a different story at Puteoli, when every day brought something fresh about Octavian and much (some of it untrue) about Antony. In answer to what you write (I got three letters

---

[1] Not another country house, but a lodge, such as wealthy Romans acquired for overnight accommodation on journeys.

[2] See page 244, note 1.

[3] Atticus had been urging Cicero to write history.

[4] From the Odyssey. 'Mimas' represents the Appennines, 'Psyria's isle' an island in the river on Cicero's property at Arpinum.

from you on the 11th), I strongly agree with you that if Octavian were to
have much power the tyrant's measures would be far more solidly approved
than in the temple of Mother Earth,[1] and that this will be bad for Brutus. On
the other hand, if he is beaten, you can see that Antony will be intolerable, so
one can't tell which to prefer.

That courier of Sestius' is a rascal. He said he would reach Rome from
Puteoli the next day. You advise me to go one step at a time and I agree,
though I had other ideas. Nor am I impressed by Philippus or Marcellus.
Their position is different; and if it isn't it appears to be. But that young man,
though he has spirit enough, lacks weight. Consider all the same whether it
might not be better for me to be at Tusculum, if I can stay there safely. I shall
be happier so, for I shall get all the news. Or shall we decide this when
Antony comes? . . .

The last extant letter to Atticus, written perhaps a day or two later,
shows Cicero still in no hurry to commit himself:

. . . To come to public affairs, many indeed are the wise words I have
heard from you on matters of politics, but nothing wiser than this letter. This
boy is taking the steam out of Antony, but we had best wait and see the issue.
But what a speech!—a copy was sent to me. Swears 'by his hopes of rising to
his father's honours,' stretching his hand out towards the statue! Sooner
destruction for me than a rescuer such as this! But as you say, the clearest test
will be our friend Casca's Tribunate.[2] I told Oppius on that very subject,
when he was pressing me to join the young man and his whole movement and
band of veterans to boot, that I could do nothing of the kind unless I was sure
that he would be not only no enemy but a friend to the tyrannicides. When he
replied that this would be the case, 'What's our hurry then?' said I. 'He needs
no help from me before the Kalends of January and we shall plainly see his
disposition before the Ides of December over Casca.' He quite agreed. So
much for this then. . . .

After sealing up his letter Cicero received another from Atticus,
counselling him to stay at Arpinum 'until we see the outcome of these
disturbances.' The advice, wrote Cicero in a postscript, was wise and
kind,

but my dear fellow, it is not really the commonwealth that is on my mind
just now; not that anything in the world is or ought to be dearer to me, but
even Hippocrates forbids medical treatment in hopeless cases. So good-bye to
all that. It is my finances that are on my mind. . . . So come I must, even if it

---

[1] Tellus, in whose temple the Senate had held its meeting after Caesar's murder,
and ratified his 'acts.'

[2] Casca was one of Caesar's assassins, due to take office as Tribune on 10
December. Cicero thought Octavian might oppose this; in fact he did not.

means moving straight into the furnace. Private bankruptcy is more dis-honourable than public. I am too much worried on this account to reply in my usual fashion to the other matters of which you write so agreeably. Join me in this anxiety I am in to be clear of debt—as to how, I have ideas, but can decide nothing definitely till I see you. And why should I not be as safe in Rome as Marcellus? But that is not the question, and I am not over-much concerned about it. What I *am* concerned about you see. So I am coming.

Perhaps Cicero was not being quite frank with his friend whose advice he was rejecting. At any rate the outcome lends his final words, *adsum igitur*, a significance he did not intend. For *adsum* also meant 'present!,' the self-announcement of a Roman, soldier or civilian, reporting for duty.

CHAPTER TWENTY-SIX

'Our Blackguard of a Nephew'

'A comic scene in this serious drama was enacted by young Quintus.'
Tyrrell and Purser, 'The Correspondence of Cicero'

WHILE young Marcus improved or amused himself at Athens, his cousin was once again making himself objectionable to his elders at home.

After the dialogue of December 45, the younger Quintus reappears in a letter to Atticus of 19 April:

... Quintus senior writes to me in severe terms about his son, the chief complaint being that he is now complaisant to his mother, whereas formerly, when she was behaving well, he was against her. He denounces him to me in a fiery epistle. If you know what the young man is doing and have not yet left Rome, please send me word—and any other news to be sure. Your letters give me lively pleasure.

Quintus senior had taken umbrage at his son's attitude to his own divorce and possible remarriage. Marcus was irritated by political posturing, as when young Quintus advertised his Caesarian sympathies at a festival commemorating Caesar's victory at Munda:

'Now tell me once again your tale.' Our Quintus wearing a wreath on Shepherds' Day![1] All by himself?—though you mention Lamia too, which amazes me. But I should very much like to know who the others were, though I need no telling that they were rascals one and all. ...

3 May:

... Quintus junior has written his father a most bitter letter, which was delivered to him after our arrival at Pompeii. The main point was that he could not stand Aquilia as a step-mother. That perhaps one might tolerate, but when he says he owes everything to Caesar and nothing to his father, and for the future looks to Antony—what a blackguard! But *on s'en occupera*. ...

---

[1] 21 April was also the Shepherds' Festival (*Parilia* or *Palilia*).

Five days later:

> . . . As for the wearers of wreaths, when your nephew was taxed by his father, he wrote back that he had worn one in Caesar's honour and laid it aside in mourning; he finishes by saying that he is glad to bear censure for loving Caesar even after his death. . . .

Not content with honouring Caesar dead, the young man had attached himself to Caesar's successor. In his uncle Atticus' sarcastic phrase, he was now 'Antony's right-hand boy.'[1] But Quintus was nothing if not volatile. About June 18:

> . . . Statius has written to me to say that young Quintus has told him very emphatically that he cannot put up with the present régime and has made up his mind to go over to Brutus and Cassius. I am now fairly longing to learn more about this—I can't make out what it means. He may have said something in a fit of temper with Antony, he may be looking for a new feather to put in his cap, or the whole thing may be just a *boutade*—and no doubt that's what it is. Still I am apprehensive, and his father is upset. . . . What he is up to I really don't know. . . .

A day or two later a letter from Quintus himself gave Statius' report a new twist:

> What do you think? Father Quintus is jumping for joy. His son writes giving as his reason for wanting to take refuge with Brutus that when Antony gave him the job of making him Dictator and seizing a strong point he had refused, the reason for the refusal being that he did not want to vex his father. On that account Antony had become his enemy. 'Then' says he 'I pulled myself up, for fear that in his anger against me he might do you some injury. So I appeased him. What is more, I have got 400,000 for sure, with prospect of more to come.' Moreover Statius writes that he wants to live with his father (surprise indeed!), and that delights Quintus. Was there ever a more out and out good-for-nothing than that young man? . . .

Quintus may possibly have been Quaestor-Designate at this time by Caesar's appointment, though he was only 22 years old; but there was no legal way for him to make a Dictator of Antony, one of whose laws had just abolished the title for all time. Apparently he meant some sort of *coup de main*, but Cicero was probably right to pooh-pooh the whole story.

About 22 June Quintus left town. 'We can congratulate ourselves on young Quintus' departure,' noted his uncle. A week or so later

---

[1] Literally 'little right hand' (*dextella*).

Quintus senior was bothered about some financial transaction in which his son had made unauthorized use of his name. By 6 July Quintus junior really had broken with Antony:

> . . . I have replied to all your points; now let me give you mine. Quintus junior is going as far as Puteoli (a fine patriot—Favonius[1] is not in the same class with him!) for two reasons: to bear me company and because he wants to make his peace with Brutus and Cassius. But what do you say to this latest?— I know you are a friend of the Othos. He says that Tutia is making him proposals, the divorce having been settled. His father asked me what sort of a reputation she has. I said, not knowing why he asked, that I had heard nothing in particular against her except about her oral habits and her father. 'But why?' He answered that his son wanted to marry her. On that, disgusted as I was, I said I did not believe the stories. His aim in view is to avoid having to give our young man a penny; as to the lady, she is not worried. However, I suspect he's romancing as usual. But you might make enquiries, as you easily can, and let me know.

His political conversion posed a problem: should his two uncles take the prodigal back into favour? Cicero again resorted to 'crooked wiles.' On 9 July he gave young Quintus a letter to take to Atticus:

> . . . Now let me tell you something of prime importance. Quintus junior has been with me for several days, and would have stayed even longer if I had desired. But as long as his visit lasted you will scarcely believe how pleased I was with him in all respects, and especially on the point as to which I formerly felt least satisfied. So complete has been the change in him produced by certain writings of mine which I have in hand and by constant talk and advice that his political sentiments are likely in future to be just what we desire. After he had not only promised but persuaded me of this, he requested me, deliberately and at some length, to stand guarantor with you that he will in future be a credit to us both. He added that he did not ask you to believe this straight away, but to give him your affection only when you had seen for yourself. If I had not been convinced, if I had not formed the opinion that this frame of mind would last, I should not have done what I am about to tell. I took the young man along to Brutus. He so fully accepted what I have just told you that he took Quintus' word without more ado and declined my offices as guarantor; and in commending him he referred to you in the most affectionate terms, and dismissed him with an embrace and a kiss. I have therefore more reason to congratulate you than to plead. And yet I do also request you, if in the past, through the instability of his age, his conduct has at some points appeared somewhat deficient in settled principle, to conclude that he has put all that aside, and to believe my assurance that your influence

---

[1] 'Cato's Sancho' (Mommsen).

will contribute much, or rather more than anything, to confirm his good intentions. . . .

But the previous day Cicero had sent another letter by special messenger to make sure that Atticus was not misled:

. . . Now let me tell you why I have sent a courier. Quintus junior assures me that he will be a Cato in the future. Both father and son have asked me to be his guarantor with you, on the understanding that you will believe it only after you have proved it for yourself. I shall give him a letter in any terms he likes. Don't let it impress you. I write this so that you may not think that *I* have been impressed. I devoutly hope that he lives up to his promises—we should all be delighted. But for my part—I say no more. He leaves on the 9th, for he says he has a transfer of claim on the 15th and is hard pressed. You will be guided in your reply by what I write. More when I have seen Brutus and send back Eros. I accept my Attica's apology and am very fond of her indeed. Give her and Pilia my love.

This letter arrived as planned in advance of the other. 17 July:

. . . About Quintus junior, I am glad to know that my courier delivered my letter to you before the young man himself, though you would not have been misled. Still, it's as well. But I am waiting to hear what he said to you, and how you answered—no doubt you both spoke in character. . . .

An ironical reference in November implies that nothing had really changed:—'I send you Quintus (senior's) letter to show you the warmth of his affection toward a certain person for whom the coolness of yours distresses him.' Later in the month:

. . . Your grandfather's great-grandson writes to my father's grandson that he intends to clear up the Temple of Ops as from the Nones on which I did great deeds, and to do so moreover before the Assembly. . . .

That was to say that when the new City Quaestors, custodians of the state treasury, entered office on 5 December, Quintus (so he wrote to his cousin) proposed to investigate Antony's peculations. If he was one of the Quaestors himself, this could have been more than another flight of self-importance. Whether or not anything came of it, Antony thought him worth an onslaught in one of his official manifestos. In the Senate, on 20 December, Cicero was all righteous indignation.

He also rebukes my nephew Quintus Cicero in a manifesto, not having the sense to realise that a rebuke from him is a recommendation. Could this young man have hoped for anything better than to be universally recognised as a partner in Caesar's counsels and an enemy of Antony's madness? The ruffian has even dared to allege that he planned to murder his father and uncle. The reckless, audacious impudence of it! To put such a thing in writing about a young man for whom my brother and I vie in our affection, which his personal charm and outstanding talents so well deserve—who is constantly in our sight, in our hearing, in our very arms!

So Quintus had found yet another patron—Caesar Octavian. No good was to come of that either. But for lack of letters to Atticus we cannot follow the comedy further, down to its tragic epilogue.

CHAPTER TWENTY-SEVEN

False Dawn

'He was, in fact, Prime Minister of Rome.'
Strachan-Davidson, 'Cicero'

IF a date in the manuscript of one of his letters is to be trusted, Cicero returned to Rome several weeks later than he had intended, on 9 December. Much had been happening. In Brundisium Antony found himself with something like a mutiny on his hands among the newly arrived troops, and suppressed it drastically; according to Cicero 300 Centurions and private soldiers were executed. Hurrying back with a single legion (the famous 'Larks,' recruited by Julius Caesar in Gaul) and leaving the Fourth and Martian legions to follow, he was in Rome again by mid-November, fulminating against Octavian (who had retired to Arretium) in another manifesto. On the 24th the Senate was convened to pronounce Octavian a public enemy; but the sitting had to be cancelled when a report came in that the Martian legion in Central Italy had declared for Caesar's heir. Antony dashed off to their camp, but failed to get the men to change their minds. On the 28th the Senate met under his presidency, but only after news that the Fourth legion had followed the Martians' example. Antony dropped his motion against Octavian, and after putting through some reallocations of provincial governorships, again left the city. With the troops still loyal to him he marched north to dispossess Decimus Brutus of Cisalpine Gaul, which had been reassigned to himself by a law passed earlier in the year.

On 20 December Cicero again addressed the Senate. His speech, the Third Philippic, hammered home a logical alternative: either Antony was still to be regarded as a Consul, in which case those in arms against him without public authority were traitors; or, if they were to be applauded, then the traitor and public enemy was Antony. The orator's own view was expressed in lavish encomia of Decimus, Octavian (whom he claimed to have inspired and encouraged), and the two deserting legions. In conclusion he called upon the Senate to adopt a

motion approving their actions. It was passed. That same evening
Cicero addressed a public meeting, making the same points.

In the First Philippic he had announced himself against Antony at a
time when it was doubtful whether any effective opposition could be
mounted from within Italy. In the Third he asserted leadership of the
opposition that had taken shape:

Waiting for this day I evaded the criminal violence of Marcus Antonius
when he assailed me in my absence, little understanding that I was reserving
myself and my strength for a time to come. If I had chosen to answer him
then, just when he was looking for a chance to start a massacre with myself as
the first victim, I should be in no position to work for our country now. But
the opportunity has arrived. Gentlemen, from now on my days and nights
shall be dedicated to giving thought where thought is needed on behalf of the
freedom of the Roman People and the dignity of this House; and as to necessary *action*, I shall not hang back, in fact I shall seek and demand it.

Cicero was well aware that the speech began a new era; that day, as
he afterwards put it more than once, he 'laid the foundations of the
Republic.' In the following February he wrote to Trebonius:

. . . Ever since the Senate was able to meet in freedom after Antony's
ignominious departure, my old spirit has returned to me, the spirit which you
and that ardent loyalist, your father, always praised and admired.
The Tribunes had summoned a meeting on 20 December and put another
matter to the House. I then entered upon a comprehensive survey of the
whole political situation. I did not mince my words, and, more by will-
power than by oratorical skill, I recalled the weak and weary Senate to its old,
traditional vigour. That day, and the energy of my address, brought to the
Roman People the first hope of recovering their freedom. And from that
time forward I have used every possible moment, not only in thought but in
action, on behalf of the commonwealth. . . .

The rest of Cicero's life (except its last three months) belonged to
the state. The same is true of his letters. From the first seven months of
43 just over a hundred survive, of which not far short of half were
written by others. Apart from a few of recommendation and suchlike,
all are on public affairs, with one exception. That is a letter addressed to
Papirius Paetus in early February; and even here cares of state intrude.
After a paragraph about a common friend, the letter continues:

. . . I am sorry to hear that you have given up dining out. You have
deprived yourself of a great deal of amusement and pleasure. Furthermore
(you will not mind my being candid), I am afraid you will unlearn what you

knew, and forget how to give little dinner-parties. For if you made such small progress in the art while you had models to imitate, what am I to expect of you now? When I laid the facts before Spurinna[1] and explained to him your former mode of life, he pronounced a grave danger to the supreme interests of the state unless you resume your old habits when Favonius[2] starts blowing; at the present time of year he thought it might be borne, if *you* could not bear the cold.

But really, my dear Paetus, I advise you in all seriousness, as something which I regard as relevant to happiness, to spend time in honest, pleasant, and friendly company. Nothing becomes life better, or is more in harmony with happy living. I am not thinking of physical pleasure, but of community life and habit and of mental recreation, of which familiar conversation is the most effective agent; and conversation is at its most agreeable at dinner-parties. In this respect our countrymen are wiser than the Greeks. *They* use words meaning literally 'co-drinkings' or 'co-dinings,' but *we* say '*co-livings*,'[3] because at dinner-parties more than anywhere else life is lived in company. You see how I try to bring you back to dinners by philosophizing! Take care of your health—which you will most easily manage by constantly dining abroad.

Do not suppose, if you love me, that because I write rather flippantly I have put aside my concern for the commonwealth. You may be sure, my dear Paetus, that my days and nights are passed in one sole care and occupation— the safety and freedom of my countrymen. I lose no opportunity of admonition, or action, or precaution. Finally it is my feeling that, if I must lay down my life in my present care and direction of public affairs, I shall consider myself fortunate in such a destiny. Once again, good-bye.

The other addressees and writers are governors and army commanders (and their lieutenants) throughout the empire; Marcus Brutus and Cassius in Greece and the East, Cornificius in Africa, Decimus Brutus in North Italy and (later) Gaul, Lepidus and Plancus in Gaul, Asinius Pollio in Spain. Whatever might happen in Italy, these men were important. If Antony won, he would still have to reckon (and did) with the 'liberators' in the East; if he lost, he might find succour (and did) in the West, ruled by former Caesarians of various shades. Cicero's function was to keep in active being a constitutional centre—the Senate in Rome—to focus more or less doubtful loyalties on the periphery. His own letters are therefore mainly informative and hortatory, with few enlivening personal touches. Taken together with

[1] The Etruscan soothsayer (*haruspex*) who had warned Caesar to 'beware the Ides of March.' Cicero is determined to be jocular, as usual in writing to Paetus; but the effort is apparent.

[2] The West Wind, harbinger of spring.

[3] *convivia*. Cicero compares the Greek words *symposia* and *syndeipna*.

the ten remaining Philippics, delivered between 1 January and 21 April, they present a new Cicero, laden but not overwhelmed with responsibility, dedicated to the job in hand.

This was not easy. Antony had many supporters in Rome, ready to exploit any turn in his favour; others only wanted peace. In the Senate their leader was a man whom Cicero had never liked, Fufius Calenus, father-in-law of the new Consul Pansa. Nearly all the other Consulars were either suspect of disloyalty or elderly ineffectives; the best of them from Cicero's point of view was Sulpicius Rufus, but he died in January on a peace mission to Antony. This mission of three senior Consulars, was authorized by the Senate against Cicero's advice, and its failure will have strengthened his hand. He wrote to Cassius about the end of the month:

A pity you did not invite me to dinner on the Ides of March! There would have been no leavings! As it is, your leavings are giving me plenty to do— yes, me in particular. True, we have an excellent pair of Consuls, but the Consulars are a shocking collection. The Senate is firm, but firmest in its lowest ranks. As for the people, they are magnificently firm and loyal, so is the whole of Italy. The envoys Philippus and Piso have played a disgusting, scandalous role. They were sent to convey definite instructions to Antony according to the will of the Senate. After he had refused to obey any of these, they took it upon themselves to bring back a set of intolerable demands from him to us. Accordingly there is a rally to me, and I have now become a popular favourite in a good cause. . . .

And a few days later:

. . . The Senate is thoroughly resolute, except for the Consulars, of whom only Lucius Caesar[1] is resolute and straight. With Sulpicius' death we have lost a tower of strength. The rest are without energy or without principle. Some are jealous of the credit of those whom they see high in public esteem. But the unanimity of the people of Rome and of all Italy is quite remarkable.

That is about all I wanted you to know. My prayer now is that from those lands of the sunrise the light of your valour may shine.

While Cicero galvanized and fortified the Senate, though not without occasional setbacks, a military decision was in the making around the town of Mutina (Modena), where the forces of both sides had converged. Decimus Brutus had shut himself up inside the place to stand Antony's siege. Outside, Antony himself was threatened by three republican armies under the two Consuls and Octavian. A letter to Cassius about the beginning of April reports the anxiety in Rome:

[1] A very distant relative of the Dictator who had been Consul in 64, the year before Cicero. He was Mark Antony's uncle.

... Of one thing I hope you are thoroughly convinced, that honest men look for refuge solely to yourself and Brutus, should any reverse unfortunately take place. As I write, the ultimate crisis is upon us. Brutus is hard put to it to hold out any longer at Mutina. If he is saved, we have won. If not, which heaven forfend, there is only one road for us all—to you. Your courage and preparations must be on the scale needed for the recovery of the whole commonwealth.

About the same time Cicero wrote to Marcus Brutus:

As I write, the ultimate crisis is thought to be upon us. Letters and messages come in from our friend Brutus breathing gloom. They do not greatly disturb *me*, for I cannot possibly lack confidence in our armies and generals, nor do I subscribe to the majority opinion—I do not doubt the loyalty of the Consuls, which is under strong suspicion; though in certain respects I could have wished for greater wisdom and promptitude. Had that been forthcoming, we should have had public order restored this while past. I need not remind you of the importance of the right moment in political affairs, and what a vast difference it makes whether the same decree, or enterprise, or course of action be adopted before or after. If only all the strong measures decreed during this turmoil had been accepted the day I proposed them, and not put off from one day to the next or dragged out and procrastinated *after* action upon them had been taken in hand, we should now have no war. My dear Brutus, I have done all that lies with one who stands where I, by judgment of Senate and People, stand today. I have not only given all that can fairly be demanded of an ordinary man—good faith, vigilance, patriotism; these, after all, it is everybody's duty to render. But I conceive that something more is required of one whose voice is heard among leading statesmen, namely wisdom. And having presumed to take the helm of state, I should hold myself no less to blame if any counsel I gave the Senate were inexpedient than I should if it were dishonest.

I know you receive full and careful reports of events both past and current. As coming from myself, I should like you to be well aware that my own mind is in the fighting line—I am not looking over my shoulder, unless it so happen that the interests of the community make me turn my head; but the minds of the majority are looking backwards, to you and Cassius. So, my friend, I would have you adjust yourself to the realisation that either it will be your duty to improve our body politic, should the present conflict go well, or to restore it, should we meet with a reverse.

About 17 April a report of an Antonian victory in the north threw loyalists into panic. The truth followed on the 20th. Antony had been defeated, but the Consul Pansa was seriously wounded (fatally, as it turned out). That night or the following morning Cicero wrote again to Marcus Brutus:

Our affairs are in better shape. I am sure your correspondents have informed you of what has occurred. The Consuls have proved such as I have often described them to you. As for the boy Caesar, his natural worth and manliness is extraordinary. I only pray we may succeed in guiding and holding him as easily as we have done hitherto. That will be more difficult, it is true, but still I do not despair. The young man is persuaded (chiefly through my agency) that our survival is his work; and sure it is that if he had not turned Antony back from Rome, all would have been lost.

Three or four days before this splendid victory the whole community fell into a panic, and poured out with wives and children to join you; but on 20 April they recovered, and would now like you to come over here instead. That day I reaped the richest possible reward for my many days of labour and nights of wakefulness—if there is any reward in true, genuine glory. The whole population of Rome thronged to my house and escorted me up to the Capitol, then set me on the rostrum amid tumultuous applause. I am not a vain man, I do not need to be; but the unison of all classes in thanks and congratulations does move me, for to be popular in serving the people's welfare is a fine thing. But I would rather you heard all this from others. . . .

On the 21st the Fourteenth Philippic, last of Cicero's extant orations, was delivered in the Senate. The conclusion of the speech proper, an eulogy of the republican soldiers killed in the battle, reaches a Demosthenic level; for once the speaker's whole heart was in his words. Then he recited his motion to the House; the Latin language has no statelier monument:

Forasmuch as Gaius Pansa, Consul and Imperator, did commence battle with the enemy, in which battle the Martian legion defended the freedom of the Roman People with exemplary valour, as did also the legion newly recruited; and Gaius Pansa, Consul and Imperator, did himself receive wounds in the thick of combat; and forasmuch as Aulus Hirtius, Consul and Imperator, on report of the engagement and cognizance of the situation, did with notable gallantry and presence of mind lead out his army from camp and attack Marcus Antonius and his army and cut them to pieces without the loss of a single man from his own ranks; and forasmuch as Gaius Caesar, Propraetor and Imperator, by skilful and prudent generalship did successfully defend his camp, putting to rout and slaughter such enemy forces as approached the position; therefore let this House judge and pronounce that by the courage, ordinance, skill, steadfastness, resolution, devotion, and fortune of the three said commanders the Roman people has been freed from most cruel and degrading servitude. And forasmuch, further, as in combat and hazard of their lives they have preserved the Republic, the City of Rome, the temples of the Immortal Gods, and the property, estate, and children of us all; in honour of the said successful operations let Gaius Pansa and Aulus

Hirtius, Consuls and Imperators, either one or both, or in their absence Marcus Cornutus, City Praetor, institute services of public thanksgiving for the period of fifty days in every place of worship. And forasmuch, further, as the legions have shown valour worthy of their illustrious commanders; let the Senate on the restoration of public order discharge with all zeal the promises previously made to our legions and armies. And forasmuch as the Martian legion took the lead in engaging the enemy, and, fighting against odds, lost certain of their own number while inflicting heavy losses on their adversaries, sacrificing their lives for their country with no backward thought; and forasmuch as soldiers of the remaining legions died no less gallantly for the safety and liberty of the Roman people: let it please this House that Gaius Pansa and Aulus Hirtius, Consuls and Imperators, either one or both, if they see fit, do make provision and contract for the erection of a monument on the grandest scale to those who have shed their blood for the life, liberty, and estate of the Roman People, for the City of Rome, and for the temples of the Immortal Gods; and that they do direct the City Quaestors to give, assign, and pay monies for the said monument, to the end that it bear eternal testimony before posterity both to the wickedness of our savage foes and to the noble valour of our own men. Further, let the gratuities which this House has previously authorized to the soldiers of the Republic be paid to the parents, wives, or brothers of those who died for their country in this war; and let these receive what the men themselves should have received, had they lived victorious who for victory died.

As Cicero was speaking, it may be, a second battle at Mutina was in progress. It ended in another victory for the Republic and the death of the remaining Consul Hirtius. Antony had to raise the siege and retire with the remnants of his forces in the direction of Gaul. On the 26th, the day after the news reached Rome, the Senate took the final step which Cicero had been urging for months, of branding Antony and his followers as public enemies.

Freedom, as Cicero later wrote to Decimus Brutus, seemed assured for centuries to come.

CHAPTER TWENTY-EIGHT

End of an Old Song

'I hope better things are in store. But if it turns out otherwise (may the Gods avert the omen!). I shall grieve for the Republic, which ought to be immortal. As for me, how little time remains!'

Cicero to Marcus Brutus

CICERO had never thought much of his good friends Hirtius and Pansa. 'Those fellows think of nothing but drinking and sleeping,' he wrote to Atticus in July 44. Quintus senior, writing to Tiro in the following December, was even more scathing:

. . . I know them through and through. They are riddled with lusts and languors, utter effeminates at heart. Unless they retire from the helm, there is every risk of universal shipwreck. You would not believe the things they did to my knowledge on active service, with the Gauls encamped right opposite. Unless a firm line is taken, that bandit[1] will win them over by comradeship in vice. The position must be fortified by the Tribunes or by private initiative. As for those two worthies, you would hardly trust one to be mayor of Caesena, or the other as cellarman in Cossutius' tavern[2]. . . .

In office Cicero had to admit that they had not turned out badly—not wise or energetic, but at least well-intentioned. 'We have lost the two Consuls—patriotic Consuls, but that is all one can say,' he told Marcus Brutus on receiving the news from Mutina. Their sudden removal left his own leadership in Rome all the more conspicuous, but for his cause and himself it spelled disaster. The armies they had commanded refused to serve under Decimus Brutus and passed over to Octavian, now the only natural focus for that section of the Caesarian party which had broken with Antony. One immediate and fatal consequence was that Antony got away unpursued. Of all the 'liberators' Decimus had stood closest to the man they killed, and so was especially odious to Caesar's former followers. Collaboration between him and Caesar's adopted son was hardly to be expected. An interview

---

[1] Antony.

[2] Caesena was a small town in Cisalpine Gaul. But the exact point of these doubtless devastating judgments is obscure.

after the battle produced nothing but acrimony. 'If Caesar had listened to me,' wrote Decimus on 3 May, 'and crossed the Apennines, I should have driven Antony into so tight a corner that lack of supplies rather than cold steel would have finished him. But Caesar is not biddable, neither can Caesar bid his army—both very bad things.' His own 'apology for an army' was 'most sadly reduced and in very bad shape through lack of all things needful.'

So Antony was able to join up with a strong force commanded by one of his lieutenants and cross the Maritime Alps into southern Gaul. The Roman army there was commanded by Aemilius Lepidus, Shakespeare's 'slight, unmeritable man,' but the bearer of an ancient name who had held the highest posts under Caesar. Though connected by marriage with both Brutus and Cassius, he was rightly suspected of Antonian leanings. In March he had irritated Cicero by addressing an appeal for peace to the Senate. Cicero's letter will not have pleased him:

The great good will I bear you makes me very anxious for you to enjoy the highest measure of public esteem. For that reason I was pained by your omission to thank the Senate after having been signally honoured by that body. I am glad that you are desirous of restoring peace between your fellow-countrymen. If you draw a line between peace and slavery, you will do a service both to the state and your own reputation. But if the peace you have in view is one which will put unbridled autocratic power back into the hands of a desperado, then you should understand that all sane men are of a mind to prefer death to slavery. You will therefore, in my opinion at least, be wiser not to involve yourself in a kind of peace-making which is unacceptable to the Senate, the People, and every honest man.

However, you will be hearing all this from others, or will be informed by your correspondents. Your own good sense will tell you what is best to do.

To Lepidus' brother-in-law Marcus Brutus Cicero wrote in April:

. . . I suppose that the levity, fickleness, and unpatriotic disposition of your connexion Lepidus (who hates his relations by marriage worse than anybody in the world except his brother) has already been made quite clear to you in letters from your family. . . .

After Mutina Decimus Brutus wrote of Lepidus as a 'weathercock:' he was 'utterly certain that Lepidus would never behave well;' and Lepidus' army was thoroughly disloyal. Yet Decimus and others hoped against hope that he would not join forces with Antony, as in fact he did on 27 May. In a dispatch to the Senate he represented that his troops had forced his hand:

Marcus Lepidus, twice Imperator, Pontifex Maximus, to the Praetors, Tribunes of the Plebs, Senate, People and Plebs of Rome, greetings.

I trust you and your children are well. I and my army are well.[1]

I call Gods and men to witness, Conscript Fathers, how my heart and mind have ever been disposed toward the commonwealth, how in my eyes nothing has taken precedence of the general welfare and freedom. Of this I should shortly have given you proof, had not fortune snatched my decision out of my own hands. My entire army, faithful to its inveterate tendency to conserve Roman lives and the general peace, has mutinied; and, truth to tell, has compelled me to champion the preservation in life and estate of so vast a number of Roman citizens.

Herein, Conscript Fathers, I beg and implore you to put private quarrels aside and consult the supreme interests of the state. Do not treat the compassion shown by myself and my army in a conflict between fellow-countrymen as a crime. If you take account of the welfare and dignity of all, you will better consult your own interests and those of the state.

Dispatched 30 May from Pons Argenteus.[2]

Lepidus was declared a public enemy a month later. On 1 July Marcus Brutus wrote in anticipation to plead for his children:

Other people's fears make me apprehensive about Marcus Lepidus. If he tears himself away from us (I hope the general suspicion that he may do this is hasty and unjust), let me beg and entreat you, Cicero, in the name of our close friendship and your good will toward me, to forget that my sister's children are Lepidus' sons and to regard me as having replaced him as their father. If you grant so much, I am sure there is nothing you will hesitate to do on their behalf. Others may stand on different terms with their kith and kin, but nothing I can do in the case of my sister's children can satisfy my desire or my duty. . . .

Cicero had already written on the subject: that children should suffer for their fathers' sins might seem hard, but it was sanctioned by precedent and analogy. But in the last paragraph of his letter he assures his friend that he is in fact doing his best for the children, even at some sacrifice of consistency. Probably they were allowed to keep some of their father's forfeited property.

In charge of Gaul to the north of Lepidus' province was Lucius Munatius Plancus—he and Decimus Brutus were Consuls-Designate

---

[1] A conventional formula. (See page 38, note 3.)

[2] A bridge on the river Argens between Fréjus and Aix-en-Provence.

for 42 by Caesar's appointment. Cicero had known his father and been
in friendly relations with Plancus himself since the latter's childhood,
despite the fact that one of his brothers, Plancus Bursa, was one of his
own *bêtes noires*. Having little love for Antony, Plancus would no
doubt have preferred to stand by Cicero and the Republic if fortune
had done the same; and after Mutina he made a strong effort to hold
Lepidus. But his earlier conduct had been ambiguous, and time was to
reveal him as an opportunist of the first water. The style of Cicero's
letters to him betrays his mistrust. On none of his correspondents (not
even Crassus, Dolabella, and Antony) does he shower compliments
and affectionate protestations more lavishly; the falser the note, the
more Cicero was always apt to force it. But some of his preachments do
not lack eloquence:

. . . Continue then in your present courses and hand down your name to
eternity. Despise the semblances of glory, made up of vain badges of distinction; hold them for brief, unreal, perishable things. True dignity lies in
virtue; and virtue is most conspicuously displayed in eminent services to the
state. Such you have a splendid opportunity to render. You have grasped it;
do not let it slip. Make your country's debt to you no less than yours to
her. . . .

Plancus replied in kind. Generally reckoned the best stylist among
Cicero's correspondents, he is certainly the most Ciceronian, in what
for some of us is Cicero's least endearing manner.

About the middle of June Plancus was joined by his prospective
colleague Decimus Brutus. The armies remained inactive until some-
time in August or September, when Plancus, with Asinius Pollio as
intermediary, joined the opposition, handing over his five legions to
Antony and Lepidus. Decimus' men deserted and he fled into the
mountains, hoping to make his way east disguised as a native. He was
captured by brigands, whose chief killed him by Antony's orders.

Meanwhile events had taken an even more disastrous turn in Italy.
After brief days of triumph and security the republicans had to face the
demoralizing knowledge that the war they had believed won might be
only just beginning. Cicero wrote to Decimus about 13 May:

. . . From what you write and from what Graeceius says, the flames of war,
so far from having been extinguished, seem to be blazing higher. Knowing
your exceptional perspicacity, I do not doubt you realise that if Antony
acquires a position of any strength all your splendid services to the state will
come to nothing. According to reports reaching Rome and to the universal
persuasion here, Antony had fled in despair with a few unarmed and terrified

followers. If in fact his condition is such that, as I hear from Graeceius, a clash with him will be a dangerous matter, I do not regard him as having fled from Mutina, but as having shifted the war to another theatre. Accordingly the public mood has changed. There are even those who criticize you men in the field for having failed to pursue Antony. They think that with prompt action he might have been overwhelmed. No doubt it is a characteristic of the masses, those of Rome in particular, to exercise their liberties upon the one person of all others through whose agency they have gained them. Even so, care must be taken not to give just grounds for complaint. The case stands thus; the man who crushes Antony will have won the war. What this means I would rather leave you to consider than put it in plainer words myself.

Cicero himself was weary, as he told Cornificius about a week after the second battle of Mutina:

. . . We have lost our colleagues Hirtius and Pansa at a very unfortunate moment. In their Consulship they gave good service to the state, which is now rid of Antony's brigandage, but not yet completely out of the wood. If permitted, I shall fight the good fight as ever, though I am very tired. But no weariness should stand in the way of duty and loyalty. Well, enough of that. I would rather you heard about me from others than from myself. . . .

The Senate, he felt, was no longer behind him. To Decimus, 29 May:

. . . And yet, what is the use? Believe me, Brutus, as one not given to self-depreciation, I am a spent force. The Senate was my right hand, and it has lost its cunning. Your splendid break-out from Mutina and Antony's flight with his army cut to pieces had brought such high hopes of assured victory that there has been a universal relaxing of energy, and those vehement harangues of mine look like so much shadow-boxing. . . .

Pressing appeals to Marcus Brutus and Cassius to come to the rescue went unanswered. They were busy consolidating their hold over the eastern half of the empire, and Cicero and the Senate must shift for themselves.

The main problem, of course, was Octavian. In his Fifth Philippic on 1 January Cicero had avowed his confidence in the young Caesar's good intentions, ending with a solemn personal guarantee to Senate and People 'that Gaius Caesar will always be such a citizen as he is today, such as we must most wish and pray for him to be.'

Less hostile than Cicero to Antony, Marcus Brutus had no faith in Octavian. He disapproved of certain honours which the Senate had voted the young man, writing to Cicero about 5 May:

... In this connexion, my excellent and gallant friend, whom I love so well for your own sake and the country's, I feel you are trusting your hopes too fondly. The moment somebody makes a patriotic move you seem to set no bounds to your favours and concessions, as though a mind corrupted by largesse could not possibly be swayed to bad courses. I know your heart is too good to take offence at a warning, especially where the common welfare is at stake. But you will do as you think best. ...

In the new situation after Mutina difficulties soon arose. The Senate, whether against Cicero's advice we do not know, behaved tactlessly, both in appointing Decimus Brutus Commander-in-Chief in the war against Antony and in lesser matters. On 24 May Decimus wrote to Cicero:

My affection for you and your services to me make me feel on your account what I do not feel on my own—fear. Here is something I have often been told and have not thought negligible—my latest informant is Segulius Labeo (he never acts out of character), who tells me that he has been with Caesar and that a good deal of talk about you took place. Caesar he says, made no complaints about you, to be sure, except for a remark which he attributed to you: 'The young man must get praises, honours—and the push.'[1] He added that he had no intention of letting himself get the push. I believe the remark was repeated to him (or invented) by Labeo, not produced by the young man. ...

Cicero replied in obvious agitation:

Confound that Segulius, the most arrant scoundrel alive or dead or yet to be! Do you really suppose he talks only to you or to Caesar? He has told the same tale to every person he could find to listen to him. But I am properly grateful to you, my dear Brutus, for wanting me to know this piece of tittle-tattle, such as it is—a notable mark of your affection. ...

By not denying Segulius' story he virtually admitted that it was true, though Octavian would have been wrong to attach importance to it. Most witty men sometimes say more than they mean for the sake of a joke at someone else's expense; and sometimes it is the joker who pays.

It was time for the young tiger to flesh his claws. Cicero wrote to Marcus Brutus in June:

... But Caesar, who has so far been guided by my counsels and is a fine young fellow in himself, remarkably steady, has been prodded by certain persons with rascally letters and shifty go-betweens and messengers into a very confident expectation of the Consulship. As soon as I had an inkling of

[1] *Laudandum, ornandum, tollendum.* The last word has a double meaning— 'to be elevated' and 'to be got rid of'.

it, I wrote him letter after letter, and taxed those friends of his who seem to be backing his ambition to their faces, and I did not scruple to expose the origins of these criminal designs in open Senate. The Senate and magistrates behaved as well as I can remember in any context. In the case of an extraordinary office for a powerful individual—or let us say a *very* powerful individual, since power now resides in armed force—it is unheard of that *nobody*, no Tribune or other magistrate or private person, should appear as sponsor. But with all this steadiness and courage, the community is anxious. The fact is, my dear Brutus, we are made a mockery by the caprices of the soldiers and the insolence of generals. Everybody demands as much political power as there is force behind him. Reason, moderation, law, tradition, duty count for nothing—likewise the judgment and views of the citizen body and respect for the opinion of those who come after us. . . .

The Consulship at nineteen! An indecent proposal, which showed that Caesar Octavianus (so unlike Caesar Augustus!) cared as little as his great-uncle for constitutional forms, or even less. According to later accounts Octavian originally suggested that Cicero should take the other Consulship and promised to be his obedient instrument. However that may have been, the Senate said no. At the end of July 400 Centurions and private soldiers from Octavian's army appeared before the House with these demands: the Consulship for their general, money for the troops as promised, and the lifting of the ban against Antony. One of them (the story may be apocryphal) left the House and came back with his sword in his hand: 'If you gentlemen don't give Caesar the Consulship, then *this* shall give it him,' he told the Conscript Fathers. 'Well,' replied Cicero, 'if that's the way you ask—he'll get it.' The last of his extant letters (to Marcus Brutus of 27 July) expresses the fear that his pledge to the Republic in respect of Octavian might be impossible to fulfill.

When his soldiers returned with a second rejection, the new Caesar crossed the Rubicon, and for the second time marched on Rome. The Senate enjoined him to halt, but his troops occupied the city without bloodshed and he was elected Consul along with another relative of the Dictator, a respectable nonentity called Quintus Pedius, on 19 August. So died the Roman Republic.

Octavian received the man he had called 'father' with ironic courtesy and excused him from attendance in the Senate. A fragment from Cicero's letter of thanks survives: 'I am doubly happy at your giving myself and Philippus leave of absence—it means forgiveness for the past and dispensation for the future.'

Cicero's hour was over, but he had used it well. It is hard to see how any man in his position could have done better. Given his political premises, the policy of no compromise with Antony was justified, for Antony had sufficiently demonstrated his incompatability with a restored constitution. What has been called Cicero's fanaticism, his ferocity against the 'bandits' in speeches and letters, may have been rooted in private bitterness as well as in patriotic policy. But it helped to define realities, where gentler or more generous language might have encouraged dangerous illusions. Ancient and modern criticisms of his dealings with Octavian ignore the exigencies. The risk had to be taken, and would only have been aggravated by any show of mistrust in the outcome. Ancient historical accounts of events after Mutina may reflect Augustan apologetics, but if the Senate did give Octavian legitimate grievance, it may not have been Cicero's fault, and it made no difference. Sentiment and self-interest urged Octavian to break the unnatural alliance with his adoptive father's killers and seize the reins. After all, the débâcle was due primarily to sheer bad luck. The death of the Consuls saved Antony and gave Octavian his chance.

For Cicero's memory it was probably better so. He and his 'liberator' friends were not the statesmen to save the Republic victorious. They would surely have bungled that intractable task. Honourable and atoning defeat dispensed him from such a future.

CHAPTER TWENTY-NINE

Last Lap

'On a fair estimate, indignation at his death could be modified by the reflection that he had to suffer nothing worse at the hands of a victorious enemy than he would have inflicted on that same enemy if he himself had been the victor.'

Livy

IN October Octavian marched north again, ostensibly against Antony. But the cancellation by the Senate of the decrees under which Antony and Lepidus had been proclaimed public enemies showed the way of the wind. At the end of the month a comprehensive settlement was hammered out between the three at a conference on an island in the river Reno, north of Bologna. The despotic office of Dictator had been legally abolished for ever, and besides had never been held by a consortium. So the dynasts became 'Triumvirs for the Constitution of the Republic' for three years, and the western provinces which they controlled were parcelled out between them. Other decisions included the liquidation of enemies by the Sullan technique of 'Proscription;' lists were published, with rewards for the killing of the persons named. In 49 Julius Caesar had written to Oppius and Balbus:

I am indeed glad that you express in your letter such hearty approval of the proceedings at Corfinium. I shall willingly follow your advice, all the more willingly because I had of my own accord decided to show all possible clemency and to do my best to reconcile Pompey. Let us try whether by this means we can win back the good will of all and enjoy a lasting victory, seeing that others have not managed by cruelty to escape hatred or to make their victories endure, except only Lucius Sulla, whom I do not propose to imitate. Let this be the new style of conquest, to make mercy and generosity our shield. . . .

But Caesar had been assassinated. Moreover, the Triumvirs needed money, which the confiscated estates of the victims helped to supply. According to one account a preliminary short list containing Cicero's name was sent to Rome at once, but in that case his survival for another month or more is hard to explain.

Cicero died on 7 December, nearly at the end of his 64th year. After his dismissal by Octavian a curtain falls, only to rise for the final scenes. Why no more letters to Atticus? Did Atticus suppress them because they contained reflexions upon Octavian? But Cicero would hardly have risked writing such letters. Or because they revealed a state of moral collapse? But Atticus did not suppress the correspondence of 58 and 48—47. Probably there were no letters. According to Livy Cicero did not leave Rome until shortly before the arrival of the Triumvirs about the middle of November, and in the few dark weeks before the end either or both may have thought it more prudent not to resume writing. For Atticus' life too was in danger because of his relations with Cicero and Brutus. Moreover, it is not unlikely *a priori* that some coolness had arisen. Cicero's role of leadership had been assumed against Atticus' advice, and Cicero on his side was probably one of those 'Optimates' whom we know on contemporary authority to have crititized Atticus for befriending Antony's family and friends in Rome—a peace of provident humanity eminently in character.

Two historians whose lives overlapped Cicero's differed on the point about which we should most like to be informed—his bearing in prospect of death. Asinius Pollio is said by his junior contemporary Seneca the Elder to have given a malignant account of his end; he closed a review of Cicero's career and character with these words: 'and for my part I should not regard even his ending as pitiable if he himself had not thought death so sad a thing.' Whereas Livy (and the generality of historians) represented him as dying bravely, commenting in a similar review that Cicero bore none of his life's misfortunes as a man should *except* his death. Pollio was a censorious writer, with a special animosity (so Seneca says) to Cicero's reputation; on the other hand his review which is quoted by Seneca *in extenso*, is otherwise notably fair. Perhaps his strictures referred mainly to happenings before the actual death-scene. In view of Cicero's past record it would not be surprising if the catastrophe in August temporarily demoralized him. But there is no proof of it.

All four Ciceros were proscribed. According to Plutarch the two elders, who had been together at Tusculum, fled towards the coast, hoping to get a boat to take them to Greece. On the way they decided to separate. Quintus was characteristically short of money, and went back (to Rome? Or to Arpinum?) to collect some, intending to follow later. The brothers embraced for the last time, with tears. Both, to be sure, were men of feeling.[1]

[1] Plutarch's pathetic account may have a good deal to do with modern mis-

A few days later Quintus was betrayed by his servants and killed along with his son (whose previous movements are unspecified). The young man's fate was perhaps the saddest of the three. With at least a large share of his uncle's brains, charm, and ambition, it was hard to die at twenty-three. One would like to believe the story, found in a late source, that he resisted torture rather than reveal his father's whereabouts.

We have several accounts of Cicero's slaughter. Plutarch's is far the most elaborate and colourful, but the details (though some of them no doubt came from Tiro) are hardly reliable. Livy gave the essentials:

Marcus Cicero had retired from Rome shortly before the advent of the Triumvirs in the well-grounded assurance that he could no more be plucked from Antony's vengeance than Brutus and Cassius from Caesar's. He fled at first to his house at Tusculum, and then made his way along by-roads to Formiae with the intention of boarding a ship from Caieta. Several times he put out to sea, but was forced back by contrary winds or his own inability to tolerate the tossing of the vessel on the dark, rolling waters. At last, weariness of flight and of life came over him. He went back towards his house on the higher ground, about a mile from the shore. 'I shall die' he said 'in the country I have so often saved'. Accounts agree that his slaves were brave and faithful, ready to fight it out; but Cicero ordered his litter to be set down, and told them to submit quietly to the harsh ruling of fate. As he leaned forward out of the litter, steadily offering his neck, his head was cut off. That was not enough for the stupid savagery of the soldiers; they cut off his hands too 'because they had written something against Antony.' So the head was brought back to Antony and placed by his orders between the hands on the rostra, where earlier that same year admiring listeners had heard him denouncing Antony with an eloquence never matched by human tongue. Passers-by could hardly bear to raise their eyes for tears or look upon the remains of their butchered countryman.

Cicero's son, his only surviving blood-relation, was safe for the present in Greece. When Brutus arrived in Athens in the autumn of 43, he had volunteered for military service, no doubt cheerfully. As in the earlier war, he was given a cavalry command, in which he distinguished himself highly. A year later Brutus and Cassius met defeat at Philippi, but young Cicero escaped, and was able to return to Italy under an amnesty in 39. With whatever motive, Octavian took him into favour,

conceptions about their relations subsequent to the quarrel in 48, but has no real bearing on the matter. It was only natural that some of the old affection should return at such a moment.

making him Augur, Consul (in 30), and later governor of Asia. In one respect he established a reputation all his own, as the hardest drinker in Rome. He seems to have been the last of his line.

As for the rest of the family circle, Dolabella was already dead, killed in the East by his own orders as he was about to fall into Cassius' hands. Atticus survived his friend for ten years, in high favour with the dynasts. His daughter (the 'merry little thing' of Cicero's letter) married Octavian's right-hand man, Marcus Agrippa, with Antony to make the match. His granddaughter was the first wife of Tiberius, Augustus' stepson and successor; and if the child of that marriage had outlived his father, Atticus' great-grandson would have been Rome's third Emperor. Of Pomponia we hear only a story of a savage punishment inflicted on a freedman who had betrayed her former husband and son. Terentia lived to 103. St. Jerome's statement that she was married a second time to the historian Sallust (an enemy of Cicero's) and a third to Messalla Corvinus, a grandee of the Augustan period, is more interesting than plausible.

Afterword

Virtus is one of those Latin words which make translators pause. In philosophical writing 'virtue' may do well enough, and in other contexts it often means 'courage'. But sometimes the root sense 'manliness' (*vir* being a *man*, as opposed to a mere human being) carries connotations of energy and effectiveness, even greatness. At the climax of his history of Catiline's conspiracy Sallust introduces two contrasted personalities as preeminent above all contemporaries in *virtus*: Caesar and Cato. Both were masters of their circumstances, Caesar bending them to his will, Cato from his moral fortress defying them.

Clearly Cicero was not that sort of man. In his various phases he became what circumstances made him, sometimes paltry, sometimes almost heroic. His ambition was rooted in insufficiency. Carrying all his life a set of traditional ideas which he never consciously questioned, he seldom ignored his code, but was easily swayed and perplexed by side issues and more or less unacknowledged personal inducements. His agile mind moved on the surface of things, victim of their complexity. Always the advocate, he saw from ever-shifting angles, and what he saw he rarely analysed.

Often confused himself, he perplexes us. He failed to realize that self-praise can defeat its end. Alongside the image of the wise and dauntless patriot which he tried to project into posterity has arisen the counter-image of a windbag, a wiseacre, a humbug, a spiteful, vainglorious egotist. And that is not because, as some of his admirers have urged, the survival of his private correspondence has placed him at a disadvantage. His published speeches bewray him to a generation intolerant of his kind of cliché. The flabbiness, pomposity, and essential fatuity of Ciceronian rhetoric at its too frequent worst does him more damage than any epistolary 'secrets'. No other antique personality has inspired such venomous dislike. His modern enemies both hate and despise him—from titanic Mommsen, obsessed by scorn of political inadequacy, romantic worshipper of 'complete and perfect' Caesar, to Kingsley Amis' young schoolmaster who had the bad luck to be reading the Second Philippic in class.[1] The living Cicero was hated by some, but not despised. His gifts, matching the times, were too conspicuous. And many opponents were disarmed; Mommsen himself might have capitulated to a dinner-party at Tusculum.

Is it not time to value Cicero by other standards than his own? Not as statesman, moralist, and author, but as the vivid, versatile, gay, infinitely conversable being who captivated his society and has preserved so much of himself and it in his correspondence. Alive, Cicero enhanced life. So can his letters do, if only for a student here and there, taking time away from belittling despairs to live among Virgil's Togaed People, desperate masters of a larger world.

[1] 'The last forty minutes had been spent in taking, or rather hauling, the Junior Sixth through not nearly enough of *In Marcum Antonium II*. For a man so long and so thoroughly dead it was remarkable how much boredom, and also how precise an image of nasty silliness Cicero could generate. "Antony was worth ten of you, you bastard," Patrick said.' ('Take a Girl like You', Chapter V).

References

Extracts quoted in the text come from the following Latin sources. Unless otherwise stated the author is Cicero.

Att. = *Epistulae ad Atticum*
Fam. = *Epistulae ad Familiares*
Q.Fr. = *Epistulae ad Quintum Fratrem*
Brut. = *Epistulae ad M. Brutum*

page
177 *Att.* 11.9.3; 11.17; Plutarch,
   Vita Ciceronis 37.3–4.
178 *Fam.* 14.20.
179 *Att.* 11.5.4; 11.8.2; 11.9.1–2.
180 *Att.* 11.10.1.
181 *Att.* 11.12.1–2; 11.13.2.
183 *Att.* 1.17.1–14.
186 *Fam.* 9.1.
187 *Fam.* 9.2.2–3; 6.18.5.
188 *Fam.* 6.7.5–6; 4.13.
190 *Fam.* 9.20.3.
191 *Fam.* 9.17.1–3.
192 *Fam.* 9.26.
193 *Fam.* 7.26.1–2.; 7.28.2.
194 *Fam.* 9.2.5; *Att.* 12.4.2.
195 *Att.* 12.21.1; 12.40.1; 13.51.1.
196 *Att.* 13.46.2; *Fam.* 6.18.4; 9.18.
197 *Fam.* 9.7.2; 7.28.3.
198 *Fam.* 4.4.3–4.
199 *Fam.* 13.68.2; 12.17.1; 9.15.3–4.
200 *Fam.* 15.18.
201 *Fam.* 4.14.3.
202 *Att.* 13.28.3; 12.11.
203 *Att.* 12.9.
204 *Fam.* 7.4; 9.23; *Att.* 12.13.1;
   12.14.3–4.
205 *Att.* 12.15; 12.16; 12.20.1.
206 *Att.* 12.12.2; 12.21.5; 12.23.1;
   12.26.2.
207 *Att.* 12.28.2; *Fam.* 9.6.4.
208 *Fam.* 4.4.4–5; *Att.* 12.18.1.
209 Lactantius, *Institutiones Divinae*
   1.15.19–20
210 *Att.* 13.33a; 12.32.1.
211 *Fam.* 4.5.4; 4.5.6.
212 *Fam.* 4.6.
213 *Fam.* 9.11; *Att.* 12.38a.1.
214 *Att.* 12.40.2–3; 12.26.2; 12.46.1.
215 *Att.* 12.45.1.
216 *Att.* 13.9.2; 13.11.1; 13.18;
   13.16.1.
217 *Att.* 13.25.3; 13.34; 12.7.1.
218 *Att.* 13.1.1; 13.49.

219 *Att.* 13.50.3; 13.51.2; 12.40.2;
   13.28.2.
220 *Att.* 13.31.3; 12.50; 12.49.1–2.
221 *Att.* 13.10.1; 13.40.1; 13.47;
   12.38.2; 13.9.1.
222 *Att.* 13.38.1–2; 13.39.1–2; 13.41.
223 *Att.* 13.37.2; 13.42.1.
224 *Fam.* 9.12.2; 7.30.1–2.
225 *Att.* 14.1.2; 13.52.1–2.
227 *Fam.* 6.15.
228 *Fam.* 11.28.2–4.
229 *Att.* 14.21.3.
230 *Att.* 14.12.1; 14.13A.
231 *Att.* 14.13B.
232 *Att.* 14.13.6; 15.1.2.
233 *Att.* 14.13.1; 15.16A; 15.5.2–3.
234 *Att.* 14.9; 14.10.3.
235 *Att.* 14.12.2; 15.15.2; 14.20.3.
236 *Att.* 15.1.4; 14.13.5.
237 *Att.* 14.13.2–3; 14.19.1.
238 *Att.* 14.22.2; 14.7.2; 14.11.2.
239 *Att.* 14.16.3; 15.16; 15.15.4;
   15.17.2.
240 *Fam.* 12.16.1; 16.21.
242 *Att.* 14.13.4; 15.11.
244 *Att.* 16.6.1–2.
245 *Att.* 16.7.7.
246 *Fam.* 12.22.
248 *Fam.* 12.23.2–4.
249 *Att.* 16.8.
250 *Att.* 15.2.3; 15.12.2.
251 *Att.* 16.9; 16.11.6.
252 *Att.* 16.10; 16.13.1–2; 16.14.1–2.
253 *Att.* 16.15.3; 16.15.4.
255 *Att.* 14.10.4; 14.14.1; 14.17.3.
256 *Att.* 14.19.3; 15.19.2; 15.21.1.
257 *Att.* 15.29.2; 16.5.2.
258 *Att.* 16.1.6; 16.3.3; 16.14.4;
   Philippics 3.17–18.
261 *Philippics* 3.33; *Fam.* 10.28.1–2;
   9.24.2–4.
263 *Fam.* 12.4.1; 12.5.2–3.
264 *Fam.* 12.6.2; *Brut.* 1 (2.1).
265 *Brut.* 9 (1.3).1–3; *Philippics*

page

  14.36–8.

267 *Fam.* 16.27.1–2.

268 *Fam.* 10.27; *Brut.* 2 (2.2).1.

269 *Fam.* 10.35; *Brut.* 21 (1.13).1.

270 *Fam.* 10.12.5; 11.12.1–2.

271 *Fam.* 12.25a.1; 11.14.1.

272 *Brut.* 11 (1.4).3; *Fam.* 11. 20.1;
    11.21.1; *Brut.* 18 (1.10).3.

275 *Att.* 9.7C.1.

277 Livy ap. Seneca, *Suasoriae* 6.17.

  c

Index of Persons[1]

[1] Some names occurring only in translated extracts are omitted.